ROLES OF THE NORTHERN GODDESS

———— •◆• ————

While much work has been done on goddesses of the ancient world and the male gods of pre-Christian Scandinavia, the northern goddesses have been largely neglected. *Roles of the Northern Goddess* presents a highly readable study of the worship of these goddesses by both men and women. Drawing on evidence from early literature, popular tradition, legend and archaeology, this book investigates the many roles of the northern goddess. The early hunting-goddess was a powerful figure worshipped by men across northern Europe and Asia. Local goddesses were worshipped in relation to all aspects of the shared work of the household and farm. Moreover, there were links between the goddess and sovereignty, and thus with northern rulers. The goddess emerges from these writings as both benevolent and destructive, a powerful liminal figure closely concerned with birth and death and with the destiny of individuals.

Illustrated with photographs and detailed figures, *Roles of the Northern Goddess* will be an invaluable guide for all those studying religion, mythology and anthropology.

Hilda Ellis Davidson has been a lecturer at Royal Holloway College and Birkbeck College, London, Vice-President of Lucy Cavendish College, Cambridge, and President of the London Folklore Society. Her many publications include *The Anglo-Saxon Sword* (1962), *Gods and Myths of Northern Europe* (1964) and *The Lost Beliefs of Northern Europe* (1991).

ROLES OF THE NORTHERN GODDESS

Hilda Ellis Davidson

ROUTLEDGE

London and New York

First published 1998
by Routledge
11 New Fetter Lane, London EC4P 4EE

Simultaneously published in the USA and Canada
by Routledge
29 West 35th Street, New York, NY 10001

© 1998 Hilda Ellis Davidson

Typeset in Garamond by
Florencetype Ltd, Stoodleigh, Devon

Printed and bound in Great Britain by
Biddles Ltd, Guildford and King's Lynn

British Library Cataloguing in Publication Data
A catalogue record for this book is available from the British Library

Library of Congress Cataloguing in Publication Data
Davidson, Hilda Ellis, 1914–
Roles of the northern goddess/Hilda Ellis Davidson
p.   cm.
Includes bibliographical references and index.
1. Goddesses – Europe, Northern.   2. Europe, Northern – Religion.
I. Title.
BL473.5.D38 1998 97-18309
291.2'114'094–dc21 CIP

ISBN 0–415–13610–5 (hbk)
ISBN 0–415–13611–3 (pbk)

CONTENTS

———— •◆• ————

— Contents —

PLATES

— •◆• —

FIGURES

INTRODUCTION

— ◆ —

Goddesses are everywhere.

(Kinsley 1989: x)

There is general agreement that the concept of a goddess goes back into the remote European past. When the brilliant cave paintings of the hunting peoples of the Ice Age were being produced in Europe in the Upper Palaeolithic period, memorable female shapes were also created. We have striking examples in the so-called Venuses of Lespugue, and Kostenki (Ukraine), which have been dated as early as 25,000 BC and are perhaps even earlier. These belong to a class of small figures about 6 in. (16 cm) high, in ivory, bone, coal or clay, representing a woman with drooping head, pendulous breasts, swelling buttocks and abdomen, and tapering legs narrowing to a point, as if the figure were intended to be stuck upright in the earth. The finest surviving examples are no crude shapes, but give the impression of delicate spring flowers pushing upwards from a bulb and presently to open in fulfilment (Figure 1a). A different type of figure is one from Wallendorf carved in limestone, which does not lend itself to such graceful shapes; this is rounded, squat and solid, but outlined with an economy and sureness of touch which suggests a long tradition of skilled craftsmen (Figure 1b).

Indeed the large number of surviving figures marked by similar stylistic features indicates that they continued to be made over a long period, over an area stretching from the Pyrenees to European Russia, and that they served as important and necessary symbols for the small communities of hunter-gatherers. They have been found in storage pits under house floors and also near the hearth, although a few have been left in sites which could have been meeting places or sanctuaries (Knight 1991: 367).

While some figures are simple and uncomplicated, possible complexities in this female symbolism are illustrated by a figure from Laussel in the Dordogne, again dated as early as 25,000 BC, carved on a limestone block outside a rock shelter. It shows a woman with the usual rounded curves and pendulous breasts, her left hand resting on her swelling abdomen, while in her right she holds a bison horn. Her head is turned towards the horn, but her face is featureless. The horn she holds is marked with thirteen incisions, a number perhaps deliberately chosen to indicate the thirteen days of the waxing moon or the thirteen lunar months (Marshack 1972: 333). This figure was marked with red ochre and cruder female figures were carved on blocks in the vicinity.

Figure 1a Venus figurine in mammoth ivory from Lespugue. Ht 14 cm. Museé de l'Homme, Paris. Lelly Aldworth.

The early assumption about these female figures was that they were examples of fertility magic, intended to promote the increase of plant and animal life and to bring healthy children into the community. Then Erich Neumann, who was much influenced by the teaching of Jung, worked out the concept of the Great Mother, the all-powerful Mother Goddess, as the dominant force in religion before the conception of a supreme male deity developed (Neumann 1955). He pointed out the various aspects of the goddess, and the richness of the symbolism associated with her. Other followers of Jung such as Buffie Johnson (1988) and Anne Baring and Jules

Figure 1b   Venus figurine in limestone from Wallendorf. Ht 11 cm. Naturhistorisches Museum, Vienna. Lelly Aldworth.

Cashford (1991) in their joint work, *The Myth of the Goddess*, have accepted the idea of a supreme female deity, and claimed that many symbols in early art were associated with her cult.

The archaeologist Marija Gimbutas in particular has sought to give much support to this theory by assembling a wealth of evidence from early figurines and decorative patterns. She has concentrated on the worship of the great goddess in what she calls Old Europe, an area that includes Greece, southern Italy, Crete and Malta and extends northwards up to southern Poland and western Ukraine (Gimbutas 1982). Between the seventh and the third millennium BC, ending in the early Neolithic period, she sees the goddess as the accepted symbol of birth and death, fertility and resurrection, ruling as the main supernatural power in a peaceful and matriarchal society, until the Indo-Europeans with their militant male deities and supreme sky god destroyed it. She links the cult of the goddess with the moon, and with a large number of symbols used by early peoples, such as rounded vessels, sets of lines thought to indicate water, circles, spirals, lozenges and various linear patterns. Other early symbols which she associates with the goddess are figures of living creatures: birds, snakes, fish, frogs, bees, hedgehogs and bears. The superb collection of illustrations in her *Language of the Goddess* (Gimbutas 1989) will remain of value even if her interpretations are not found wholly acceptable.

Other scholars reject the claim that the female figures from the early hunting communities necessarily represent a goddess. It has been pointed out that in Africa and India figurines of this kind may be used by women for different purposes, such as to instruct young girls at initiation, as lucky amulets carried by those hoping for children (Ucko 1962: 44ff.), or even for purposes of display and recognition when encountering other tribes (Gamble 1982: 98). Knight (1991: 373) suggests that some could represent women in seclusion during menstruation, linking this with the red ochre that occasionally marks them.

A different line of approach is taken by Alexander Marshack, who thinks that such figures, together with the paintings of animals and occasional male figures in the caves, might be based on early tales and myths (Marshack 1972: 333ff.). While the animal paintings could be associated with shamanic rituals, the female figures might be linked with women's mysteries. This by no means rules out the worship of a goddess, since myths regularly retold would be likely to include tales of what Marshack calls 'a widely venerated female being'. But it might be a mistake to assume that there was only one supreme goddess in these early myths; separate female deities in different localities might have had different significance for their worshippers, as was certainly the case in Crete and Mycenae (Paris 1986: 197). In *The Roots of Civilization*, Marshack (1972) has also collected evidence for very early knowledge of calculation and means of recording time, based on observation of the moon. He argues that in view of the impressive achievements of Palaeolithic art, we should not content ourselves with any oversimplified explanation of the evidence, and this is surely a wise conclusion, since the nature of the earliest beliefs in a goddess among the hunting peoples remains highly problematic.

The conception of a goddess who was Mistress of Animals may go back to very early times, linked with a shamanic religion that involved men as well as women and a belief in a male deity who was also Ruler of the Wild, able to help or hinder hunters. During the Neolithic period, the development of agriculture took place in various parts of Europe, but hunting still formed an essential part of community life. Female figures with rounded maternal outlines continued to be produced, and some were represented as actually giving birth. One of the most striking examples of this (Plate 1) was discovered in a grain bin in one of the shrines in the town of Çatal Hüyük in Turkey, now dated to the sixth millennium BC (see p. 13). In Malta megalithic tombs and temples of the fourth millennium contained figures of women of vast proportions, but with small heads and slender arms and feet, like the small terracotta model of a sleeping woman from the Hypogeum of Hal Saflieni. Such figures, however, do not

Plate 1 Terracotta figure of goddess giving birth, from grain bin in shrine (Level II) at Çatal Hüyük, Turkey. Ht 11.8 cm. Courtesy Museum of Anatolian Civilization, Ankara.

necessarily represent worship of a supreme goddess; the latest work on a great burial complex on the island of Gozo suggests that there was no emphasis on a female deity in the main shrine there (Malone *et al.* 1993: 82). The female figures might be priestesses, or votive offerings for healing or magical purposes (Ridley 1976: 116ff.). Over this vast period of time we must allow for considerable flexibility in interpretation of the divine powers, and it cannot be assumed that the goddess symbolism continued with little or no variation throughout the prehistoric world.

As well as the rounded figures which seem to emphasize motherhood, there are flat shapes representing the female form, and also figures with bird-like heads and masked faces. A number of impressive standing stones, the 'statue menhirs' of Brittany and Portugal, with staring eyes, small breasts and many-stranded necklaces, have been interpreted as female guardians of the land of the dead. In 1957 O. G. S. Crawford named this menacing motif the Eye Goddess, and found examples in decorative art in northern and western Europe and northern Africa. Again, however, there are complications: in one impressive figure cut on stone found in a passage grave at La Trinité-sur-Mer in Brittany (Figure 2), what appears to be a brooding face with two eyes and an enormous mouth may also be seen as a headless female form with breasts and a huge vulva below (Burl 1985: 148). Here the dual conception of the goddess, as the mother giving birth and as the terrifying devouring power who receives the dead, has been conveyed with a sophisticated economy of design. It seems indeed that an immensely rich complex of imagery associated with the goddess existed from very early times, connected with death and the underworld, with the world of growing plants and living creatures, and also with the seasons of the moon (see p. 89).

The moon linked the goddess with measurement of time and with the tides, as well as with women's menstrual periods and the nine months' growth of a child in the womb. It has been suggested that the three faces of the moon, the new moon, full moon and waning moon, could correspond with the three aspects of the goddess in later times. We have the virgin, the mother and the aged woman, matriarch or crone, as one possible series, while another is that of bride, mother and layer-out of the dead (A. de Vries 1974). Possible symbols for the goddess were the rounded vessel, based on the fruitful womb, together with cave and mound and ship. Trees were linked with her too, and many goddesses had sacred groves. Certain animals, particularly the sow, the cow, the mare and the dog, were associated with her well into historic times. The concept of the goddess as mistress of the wild beasts was later extended to include the protection of domestic animals also. Water-birds were important in her cult from the beginning, and it has been thought that the swelling outlines of some female figurines might have been inspired by the idea of the egg within the bird. Swan, hawk, raven and crow were favourite symbols of later northern

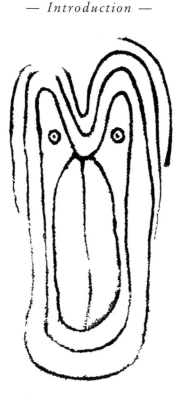

Figure 2 Carving on stone from passage grave at Lullang, Crach, Trinité-sur-Mer, Brittany. Lelly Aldworth.

goddesses. While the link with the moon meant that the goddess was transported into the heavens, she was at the same time associated with the depths of earth and water, so that her haunts might be caverns and clefts in the earth, or rivers, lakes and the sea. Such concepts and symbols survived into historic times, although their significance may alter over long periods; continuity has too often been taken for granted without paying attention to the changing background or to the context in which the evidence has been found.

In course of time, powerful kingdoms and empires grew up in the Middle East and southern Europe; great cities developed, and warring rulers embarked on conquests and invasions. In Egypt, the Middle East and Ancient Greece, the goddess played a major role both for the ruling classes and for the simple people of the countryside and market-place, so that she became a more complex figure. We have evidence from both art and literature concerning the character of the wilful and engaging Inanna of Sumer. We know a good deal about the formidable Athena, guardian of the city state of Athens, and about Isis, the majestic and compassionate goddess whose influence came to extend far beyond Egypt. Much scholarly attention has been given to such major figures, and to various goddesses of the classical world such as Demeter, Artemis and Aphrodite and their Roman counterparts. Here we have no single great goddess, but a series of outstanding female deities worshipped in inspiring cults which once possessed tremendous power for both men and women, both in public rituals and in their own homes.

As the Indo-European peoples established themselves over much of Europe, the northern goddess also took to herself formidable authority, in spite of rivalry from the great sky god. She as well as the male gods dealt out victory to favoured kings and led and inspired armies. She was present on the battlefield and in the skies above when armies met, rejoicing in blood and slaughter. Rulers turned to her for the support of their dynasties, for she was the nurturer of princes and young heroes, and the guardian spirit of aristocratic families. Poets and story-tellers wove complex myths, sometimes beautiful, often bawdy, concerning the dealings of goddesses with their husbands and lovers, and their interference in the human world where they proved benevolent to their favourites and ruthless to those who offended them. Thus the goddess remained a potent force in the male realm of warriors and heroes, while at the same time maintaining her power over those who hunted and cultivated the earth. Meanwhile she held continued sway in the world of women, as she had done from Neolithic times.

There is a rapidly growing interest in the late twentieth century in the importance of women as innovators in many fields at a time when small nomadic communities were extending their activities from hunting and gathering to herding and agriculture. In his collection of surprising facts in *The Mothers* Briffault (1927) was one of the first to stress the major part played by women in originating and promoting new skills in the home. He noted that women's achievements in non-industrial societies in various parts of the world included leatherwork, the making and embroidery of robes, basket-making, spinning and weaving, and the making of pottery, while they played a leading role in the building and decoration of houses and in the running of markets. They were largely responsible for the sowing of seed and raising of crops in the early agricultural communities, and since they grew and gathered herbs they came to be relied on for treatment of illnesses and injuries. They were naturally skilled in midwifery and the rearing of children, while spinning and weaving remained essentially women's work for thousands of years. To this impressive list of skills could be added the care of the home, with hearth and fire as its centre, and the production of butter and cheese in the dairy, as well as the overseeing of the supply of fresh water.

In a discussion on the division of labour between men and women, Judith Brown (1970) pointed out that this was largely determined by the necessity of child care. Women tended to take over work which did not require them to move far from the home centre, which was not dangerous or demanding to perform with small children around, and which could be easily resumed after an interruption. Although some special feminine skills were later taken over by men as communities grew larger, some, like dairy-work, spinning and midwifery, remained the special province of women up to the nineteenth century, in some regions. Again women have always ruled the hearth, which formed the centre of the house; as the people of a remote mountain village in Greece still say, it is the woman who holds the house together (Du Boulay 1974: 131). It was part of the duty of the women of the community to rear the young and to prepare young girls for marriage and childbirth, while it was they too who tended sick and elderly people, and made ready the dead for the final rites of burial or cremation.

Unfortunately our knowledge of organized rituals among women in early times and even in the Middle Ages remains sadly limited. Men were ignorant or uninterested, while Christian writers were likely to disapprove of such matters, and women had little motive for making records even if they possessed the means to do so. Yet this is an important field which has been largely neglected, and the approach to the northern goddess taken in this book will be based on the special skills and mysteries of women, beginning with their care of domestic animals and work in the dairy, and continuing with their contribution to the growth and harvesting of grain, their skills in spinning and weaving and the production of tapestry and embroidery. I shall deal also with their responsibilities in the home: preparing food and brewing, helping with childbirth, bringing up children and training girls for marriage, tending the sick and wounded and taking part in funeral rituals. These are activities that bonded women together, and the early cults of the goddesses were necessarily concerned with them.

It must never be forgotten that many devout worshippers of goddesses were men. The goddess of the hunters was a major power in early times in northern Europe as elsewhere, and Chapter I on the 'Mistress of the Animals' begins with her. Other functions of the goddess in which men were much concerned were those of sovereignty and battle, as will be apparent in the course of this book. In some activities, such as that of harvest or the organization of funerals, men and women divided the work between them, just as the house was divided to suit their separate needs and responsibilities.

Most of our knowledge of pre-Christian beliefs in this area comes from Scandinavia and Iceland, where conversion to Christianity was delayed until about AD 1000, and where a rich Icelandic literature has preserved many myths and early religious traditions. In mythographical studies based on Icelandic written sources, however, the goddesses commonly receive no more than a brief mention at the end of detailed chapters on male gods such as Odin and Thor, or enigmatic male figures such as Balder and Loki. One reason for this is the limited and confused nature of the evidence about female supernatural beings in early northern literature. Although we have a large number of goddess names from Germanic and Celtic tradition, both from surviving literature and from inscriptions on stones from the Roman provinces, there is little direct information about their cults. Nor is it easy to sort out the names and types of female supernatural powers; some names may be earlier titles of the more powerful goddesses; others may belong to local spirits of a minor kind, associated with springs, woods and hills, or to the guardian spirits of powerful families.

When Snorri Sturluson at the end of the twelfth century gave a list of the goddesses in his brilliant account of Norse mythology in the *Prose Edda*, he mentioned as many as sixteen names taken from early Icelandic poetry, and added more elsewhere in his works, but few of these appear in the myths we know, nor have we evidence for their worship. Snorri was writing some time after the acceptance of Christianity in Iceland, and some of his names could be creations of the poets, imaginary wives or daughters of the gods, or names invented for valkyries, the battle goddesses introduced into tales of heroes. The only goddesses who appear frequently in the myths and are known to receive worship in the Viking Age are Freyja, the powerful goddess of fertility, and Frigg, wife of Odin and queen of heaven; there is considerable argument as to whether these have developed out of one original Germanic goddess, Frea, and represent two different aspects of her character (Näsström 1995: 104; Grundy 1996). The goddesses Gefion, Gerd, Fulla and Skaði occasionally figure in myths and may represent important goddesses of early times in the North, but little was remembered about them by the time Snorri was collecting his material. It is also possible, as Britt-Mari Näsström (1995) has shown in her detailed study of Freyja, to see some of them as aspects of one Great Goddess. Snorri himself in *Ynglinga Saga* (10) remarks casually that Freyja alone of the gods still lives. He could mean that many of the rituals and traditions once associated with Freyja in her various aspects continued to have importance for women in their daily life, and I believe that there is a surprising amount of material to be discovered concerning the early pre-Christian goddesses in this field.

There are rich possibilities also in the study of traditional tales and lore about supernatural female beings, as Ann Ross pointed out:

> Powerful female deities, when they ceased to be actively propitiated, became embedded in the folk memory and perpetuated in the tales and especially in the topographical legends of the country.
>
> (A. Ross 1967: 67)

This is true of material from Ireland, Scotland and Wales, and also borne out by further evidence from France, Germany and Scandinavia, where concepts of female supernatural beings were kept alive in popular tradition well into the nineteenth century, and even now are not wholly forgotten.

Particularly fruitful fields are those of legends about hunting from forest and mountain areas, traditions of the spinning rooms where legends and traditional lore were passed on to young girls in each generation, and local legends about women saints in the Middle Ages. Again the supernatural helpers and destroyers in the famous collections of fairy-tales, the *Märchen* collected by the Grimm brothers and the tales retold by Perrault in seventeenth-century France, may have roots deeper than we realize, preserving memories of supernatural female guardians of children who have been half-Christianized into fairy godmothers (see pp. 152–3).

The goddesses from western Europe were clearly regarded with mingled fear and trust; they were seen not only as the Giving Ones, but also as beings who could ruthlessly punish and destroy. Beside the early sources and later popular traditions there is important evidence from iconography, ranging from carved stones to amulets, and from a few place-names.

In this book I am deliberately using material from different cultures and backgrounds when the comparisons appear to throw light upon the nature of earlier goddess cults. The possible dangers of this kind of approach ('sweeping through enormous quantities of data for the pattern which informs it all') have been indicated by Juliette Wood in an article on 'The Concept of the Goddess' (Wood 1996: 10). Here, however, I am not striving to establish any particular theory about origins or significance, but merely seeking practical information as to the part played by the cults of the pre-Christian goddesses in the lives of men and women. It is clearly essential to make clear the nature, date and background of the sources for the evidence, but if this rule is kept, then the experience of one community and culture may help towards our understanding of another where practical matters such as spinning, dairy-work or midwifery are concerned.

In *The Divine Consort*, a series of studies on Indian goddesses, David Wulff (1982: 284) emphasizes the 'extraordinary qualities and inexhaustible riches which the figure of the Goddess possesses', and wonders why so few psychologists of religion have been drawn to study her. Both Freud and Jung recognized her appearance in the phantasies and dreams of their patients, and accounted for it in different ways. If scholars have been somewhat reluctant to explore the symbol of the goddess, however, there has been plenty of enthusiasm at a more popular level. Robert Graves's book, *The White Goddess* (1961), has misled many innocent readers with his eloquent but deceptive statements about a nebulous goddess in early Celtic literature, on which he was no authority (Wood 1996: 10ff.). In addition we have members of modern witch cults claiming to worship a goddess whose cult has survived from pagan times, and the enthusiasm of feminists for the goddess figure as a splendid symbol to inspire those battling for women's rights (Wood 1996). Meanwhile studies like *The Female Dimensions of the Divine* by Joan Engelsman (1979) make it evident that for many thinking people the study of the goddess is more than an academic excursion into forgotten faiths and mythologies, like the doomed lifework of the unhappy Casaubon in George Eliot's *Middlemarch*.

We are faced with the question of why the goddess concept stubbornly refuses to die, but has continued in various forms from the remote past to the present day, arousing strong feelings among scholars as well as passionate popular interest and curiosity. As Christianity was established in northern Europe, traditions associated with goddesses reappeared in legends and beliefs concerning the Virgin Mary, St Anne and many female saints. Again various characteristics of goddesses of northern Europe reflect to a marked degree much earlier ones in the Mediterranean area and the Middle East, and we need to consider the possible reasons for this.

It is essential that the study of the northern goddess should be approached with an open mind, without any preconceived theories into which the all too scanty evidence is forced to fit. Such a study may well prove frustrating and elusive, but at least is unlikely to be dull.

CHAPTER I

MISTRESS OF THE ANIMALS

——— •◆• ———

THE RULER OF THE WILD

The inhabitants of north-western Europe were hunters for a vast period of time before they adopted a more settled way of life and took to herding domestic animals and cultivating the earth. Even after this, hunting continued to be of great importance, particularly in forested and mountainous regions; it was a way of obtaining food for the community, and a challenging and exciting occupation, involving great risks but promising considerable rewards. It would be surprising if the hunters did not seek supernatural help, and many think that the earliest goddess worshipped in the communities of the Palaeolithic Age was a hunting one. Where hunting is still necessary to supplement a way of life, for instance in parts of the Caucasus, it is possible to gain some idea of how such a goddess became established in myth and local legend.

Comparatively little work has been done in Britain on this subject, but Swedish, Finnish, Russian and German scholars have discussed the character of the hunting-goddess in considerable detail. She was regarded as the ruler of the forest and wild places, guarding and protecting the animals that dwell there. She allowed hunters to kill her creatures if they kept her rules and earned her favour, but if they offended her, she was a dangerous enemy, destroying them without mercy. Such a goddess might be in company with a male ruler of the wild, to whom the hunters also turned for assistance. It is hard to discover which came first; some think that the famous naked goddess of Laussel with her bison horn was a deity of this kind, linked with the moon, which must have been of great importance for the hunters. It was of primary importance also to women because of the relationship of the lunar calendar to menstruation and childbearing, and these two aspects appear to come together in the character of the early goddess (Marshack 1972: 335ff.).

At Çatal Hüyük in Anatolia, a town established as early as the seventh millennium BC, the symbolism in one of the shrines indicates that the female deity worshipped there not only was associated with birth and with grain (see p. 53), but also presided over hunting. At Level III, the 'Hunting Shrine' where hunting scenes were painted on the walls, a goddess with leopards appears beside hunters clothed in leopard skins, surrounding a stag or bull (Mellaart 1967: 182). Moreover the skulls of bulls are shown emerging from between the thighs of the goddess in other shrines, suggesting that she is the Mother of the Beasts hunted and sacrificed (Burkert 1983: 79). The Phrygian goddess Kybele ruled over wolves and lions and was associated with mountains, and she is thought to be the goddess depicted as giving birth at Çatal Hüyük (Vermaseren 1977: 9ff.).

Marija Gimbutas saw the Lady of the Beasts as one aspect of the Great Goddess, supreme in an early matriarchal society (Gimbutas 1982: 152, 197ff.), but it must be stressed that the hunting-goddess is found in many parts of the world, far beyond the confines of Old Europe as Gimbutas defined it. As Burkert points out, female dominance is unlikely in Upper Palaeolithic hunting societies (Burkert 1983: 80), while the hunting-goddess, worshipped primarily by men, showed hostility towards women.

The concept of a divine ruler of the wild, male or female, is thought by some to have evolved out of a belief in an animal soul, rather than from animistic beliefs in spirits inhabiting the world of nature, or Mannhardt's 'tree-soul' imagined in animal or human form (Wikman 1961: 12). There may well be a link with the animal guardian spirit of the shaman, since shamanism is an inheritance from the ancient hunting culture, even though not found among all hunting peoples.

A tradition found among some hunters is that the slain animal will be reborn if its bones are preserved and certain rituals carried out (Friedrich 1941: 32). In three villages inhabited by the Minaro in a remote area of the Himalayas, Michael Peissel (1984: 41ff.) found that the people still worshipped male and female deities who were rulers of nature, whose help was needed when they hunted the ibex. There was a goddess Mu-shiring-men to whom a unicorn ibex with a golden horn belonged, whose rules must not be broken when hunting. When they killed an ibex, they etched out the figure of one on a rock, to cancel out their guilt in killing one of her animals, and this ensured that it would be restored to life (Peissel 1984: 41ff.).

The ruler of animals may be pictured in animal form, perhaps because early hunters observed that there was always a leading animal in the herd, just as there was a headman among the hunters (Hultkrantz 1961: 58–9). Among the Siberian tribes, an outstanding animal viewed by the hunter might be taken as the 'master' of his kind, although sometimes this 'master' was pictured as a monstrous creature, or as half-animal and half-human (Lot-Falck 1953: 63–4). In the case of a goddess who guarded certain animals, she might teach the hunters skills and give them directions where to find game. Taboos and rituals imposed by her had to be faithfully observed, and in the Caucasus the goddesses were far stricter over this than the male supernatural rulers of forest or mountain (Chaudhri 1996: 169).

It is usually the economically valuable animals that are said to possess guardians of this kind. In Europe in early times the most important was the bear; a bear cult extended across Europe and Asia to Japan, where Ainu ritual and sacrifice continued into the twentieth century. Deer were also of primary importance in many areas of Europe; the goddess was often said to herd and milk them, and might appear in the form of a white hind.

Hunting is primarily a male occupation, although Briffault (1927: 446ff.) found some communities where women were skilled hunters and responsible for the fishing. There is ample evidence for a goddess worshipped by the male hunters, who made offerings to her and respected and feared her power. In many warrior societies youths were trained as hunters; there is the same need for male co-operation in communal hunts as in the organization of war parties, and the same types of weapon were used (Feest 1980: 17). Thus young men could come directly under the influence of the goddess but, as in the case of the Greek Artemis (see pp. 16–19), she could also preside over the training of young girls.

The memory of a hunting-goddess, mistress of the wild creatures, still survives in the Caucasus, where deer and mountain goats are hunted (Chaudhri 1996). Among the Ossetes the main hunting deity was the male Æfsati, on whose goodwill the success of the hunt depended; he was pictured as old and bearded and sometimes blind or one-eyed, with beautiful daughters who according to legend were sometimes allowed to marry poor huntsmen. Similar male divinities were regarded as patrons of the hunt and rulers of the animals among other Caucasian peoples, but there were also hunting-goddesses.

One of these was the goddess Dali, held in mountainous regions of Georgia to be responsible for the hoofed and horned animals, while birds and fishes, wolves, bears and foxes came under the rule of male gods. In surviving tales and poems about her relationship with the hunters, Dali is generally described as young and beautiful, with wonderful long hair, either black or golden, but she nevertheless inspired terror in those who encountered her. She sometimes took on the form of one of her animals, perhaps a pure white hind or an animal with a golden horn, and would tend and milk her flock. She might accept a hunter as her lover, but this meant that he could have no sexual relations with mortal women hereafter, and the affair might well lead to his death,

Again in a remote part of Japan, where particular groups known as *matagi* continue to hunt bears in the mountains, there are vigorous traditions still surviving concerning the goddess Yamanokami, a powerful deity with no male associates (Blacker 1996). Here as in the Caucasus the goddess is a beautiful and erotic figure, but capable of changing into a monstrous and destructive one, ready to kill those who offend her. There were strict rules concerning the hunters' wives, and all women were excluded from the hunting ground; no articles associated with them might be taken there, nor any woman's name mentioned. Men had to refrain from sexual intercourse before a hunt, and women might find it prudent to stay indoors on Yamanokami's festival. Such surviving traditions about the hunting-goddess help us to understand the earlier concept of a merciless and destructive goddess, with bountiful gifts for those she favoured, but whose continued favour could never be relied upon.

A possible representation of an early European goddess of this type associated with the stag is on a wagon found in a cremation grave of the seventh century BC in Strettweg in Austria (Megaw 1970: 59). Also in the grave were several metal vessels, an axe, a spear and three horse-bits, suggesting that the dead was a warrior or a hunter. The wagon (Plate 2) is a bronze platform on wheels, 240 mm long, holding a group of figures thought to be the work of a Greek craftsman (Sandars 1968: 215). The central figure, towering high above the rest, is a female one, wearing earrings, and carrying a wide, shallow bowl on her head, beneath which she wears a protective pad of a type still in use in countries where women bear burdens in this way. A pair of mounted warriors are placed before and behind her, facing away from her; in between one pair is a woman, and in between the other an ithyphallic man brandishing an axe. At the front of each group is a fine stag with antlers, flanked on either side by a youthful figure which might be of either sex; these have their hands on the stag's antlers. The central figure wears a belt while the rest are naked. The link between a possible goddess and the stag on what appears to be a cult object suggests that this group was concerned with the worship of the Mistress of the Wild associated with the wild deer hunted in the forest.

In Ancient Greece, Artemis was worshipped as a goddess of this kind, separate in nature from the goddess of the grain. Like Yamanokami (Blacker 1996: 178) she ruled the wild countryside, outside the settled communities and cultivated land, and may be seen as a goddess of the boundary area between tamed and untamed, a divinity of the margins (Vernant 1987: 420). She was also the guardian of children and unruly adolescents, until they were ready to return to the city and adult life (Ellinger 1991: 445–6). Young men training to be warriors came under her sway, and she imposed rigid rules against undue savagery and destructive slaughter in warfare as well as hunting, although she cannot be regarded as a war goddess. She had many local names, and the Romans worshipped her as Diana; she was followed by nymphs who aided her in her hunting, and were forbidden to have sexual relations with men. She might appear as either a bear or a hind, and according to Pausanias her temple in Arcadia contained her statue wrapped in a deer pelt. Strabo refers to her sacred island to which the does swam when the time came for them to give birth; she is a typical hunting-goddess in the protection given to young animals.

Although an unmarried goddess, Artemis helped women in childbirth, while her protection extended over young girls from birth until they themselves became mothers (see p. 152). Athenian girls of good family danced as bears, 'playing the She-bear' at the *Brauronia*, the festival at her shrine in Athens; while those who took part in a retreat there in preparation for

Plate 2 Model of cult-wagon in bronze, from Strettweg, Austria, with figure of goddess in centre surrounded by smaller figures, including two stags. Ht 22.6 cm. Courtesy Stiermarkisches Landesmuseum Joanneum, Bild und Tonnarchiv, Graz.

marriage were known as *arktoi* (Borgeaud 1988: 32). Lilli Kahil (1977) has analysed scenes on fragments of bowls in which little girls and some aged about 12 or 13 are taking part in rites which involve the figure of a bear, representations of Apollo and Artemis, and a priest and priestess wearing

bear masks. She believes that these represent the initation rite at the sanctuary of Artemis, and that the older girls, who are running naked, are those
who had reached puberty. In his illuminating study of myths about the
hunter and the huntress, Fontenrose (1981) has shown how the concept of
a hunting-goddess was deeply established among Greek writers. She was
followed by a troop of young women pledged to chastity, who would be
punished, and possibly killed, if they became pregnant. She regularly
accepted hunters as lovers, but such relationships often ended in death. The
best known legend is that of Aktaion, torn to pieces by his own hounds,
when the goddess either turned him into a stag, threw a stag pelt over him,
or shot him with her bow (Fontenrose 1981: 33ff.).

While some men met their deaths as a result of offending Artemis,
she was held responsible for the slaying of a large number of women (see
p. 180). Not only unchaste maidens in her service but also apparently
blameless women were said to be shot by an arrow from her bow, according to references to her in the *Iliad* and the *Odyssey* (Ganz 1993: 97ff.).
Penelope for instance in her unhappiness wishes that holy Artemis would
grant her death instantly and save her from a life of anguish (*Odyssey* 18:
202), while Odysseus asks his dead mother whether Artemis the Archeress
had visited her and killed her 'with her gentle darts' (*Odyssey* 11: 171–3).
Artemis probably came into Greece from Anatolia about the sixth century
BC, and was closely related to Kybele, but may have merged with Greek
hunting-goddesses of similar character.

A Latin spell to Artemis on a copper nail (Grambø 1964: 45) attributes
to the goddess the power to bind her hounds and prevent them from attacking the domestic animals. Her hounds were predatory animals of the wilds,
such as wolves, which may also be called her herds, and this picture of a
goddess restraining or releasing the wild animals at will has been retained
in later folklore of northern Europe (see pp. 24–5). The prayer runs as
follows:

> O Lady Artemis, do not loosen your golden chains. See your hounds
> of plain or forest, white or coloured, let them not with open jaws
> seek out the fields of the plain, let them come empty and let them
> go empty. Make them run off, and let them not come to our farm,
> nor touch our cattle nor harm our donkeys. In the name of God, in
> the name of Solomon, and in the name of the Lady Artemis.
>
> (Grambø's translation)

Hunting dogs are shown on the bowls from the sanctuary of Artemis
already mentioned, and dogs are frequently associated with later hunting-
goddesses, such as the goddess Dali in the Caucasus. Important too is
the weapon which the goddess carries. Artemis has a golden bow, and
Callimachus describes how just after her birth she was given her dogs by
the shepherd-god Pan:

To you the bearded one gave two half-black dogs, three with spot-ted ears, and one spotted all over, who could pull down even lions, when they clutched their throats and dragged them still alive to the camp. He gave several others, seven bitches of Cynosuria, swifter than the wind, none quicker to pursue deer and the unblinking hare, quick also to signal the bed of the deer, and the burrow of the porcupine, and to lead us along the track of the gazelle.

(Borgeaud 1988: 63)

Direct evidence for a hunting-goddess in the Roman Empire is less easy to find, although Diana took over the attributes of Artemis. There are, however, several examples of a male hunting-god, armed for the hunt and perhaps carrying game, yet at the same time displaying protectiveness and even affection towards his quarry. Miranda Green in *Symbol and Image in Celtic Religious Art* (1989: 102) shows a male figure from a sanctuary in a mountainous region of the Donon, carrying a bag which holds the fruits of the forest, pine-cone, acorns and nuts. He wears a wolfskin and carries a hunting knife and a curved chopper, with a lance at his side, and rests his hand on the antlers of a stag which stands close to him, appar-ently unafraid. Arrian in *Cynegetica* (XIV) refers to the Celts seeking the blessing of the gods before going hunting, and refers to a hunting-goddess to whom the sacrifice of a domestic animal was made, together with the first-fruits of the hunt, while Diodorus Siculus (V: 29) alludes to the practice of nailing up part of the first animal taken 'in certain kinds of hunting' (M. J. Green 1992: 62).

Another possible representation of a guardian of the forest is the bearded deity on one of the outer panels of the Gundestrup Cauldron who is hold-ing up two stags by the hind legs (Figure 3). He could be withdrawing his creature from the attacks of the hunter, or indicating his power to provide a gift to a favoured worshipper. The horned figure often called Cernunnos, on the much discussed inner plate of the Cauldron, could also be a hunter-god; he is accompanied by a stag whose horns match his own, together with a boar, but since we still remain undecided as to the date and place of origin of this bowl, interpretations remain precarious (Davidson 1993: 25ff.). From the Roman period we also have one attractive little figure in bronze, from Muri, near Berne, of a goddess seated with fruit on her lap facing a bear (Figure 4). Her name is given in the dedication as Artio (Bear); this occurs again in a rock-cut inscription in a little valley near Bollendorf, where bears may have been hunted (Wightman 1970: 217).

A series of papers edited by Åke Hultkrantz appeared in 1961 under the title *The Supernatural Owners of Nature*; these show clearly that the concept of the Mistress of the Wild is found in many parts of the world. As well as examples from Sweden, Finland and Latvia, there are papers on a goddess of forests in India, and on female spirits of the forest in Africa,

Figure 3 Deity with stags on outer plate of Gundestrup Cauldron. National Museum, Copenhagen. Lelly Aldworth.

while Hultkrantz himself has studied beliefs in such guardians of the wild among the North American Indians. It would be surprising therefore if a goddess of this kind were not present in northern Europe, and the evidence to be discussed in the next section shows that memories of a female supernatural power ruling the wild were amazingly long-lasting.

HUNTING-GODDESSES IN NORTH-WESTERN EUROPE

Our knowledge of the goddesses worshipped by the Anglo-Saxons in the comparatively short period between their settlement in England and their conversion to Christianity is sadly limited. Frig, whose name was given to Friday, has left little trace of her cult in place-names, although *frigedune* in a recently discovered charter of 936 has been accepted as meaning 'Valley of Frig', indicating that Friden in Derbyshire was named after her (Brookes *et al.* 1984: 150–1). There are hints of memories of a goddess associated with the grain harvest in an Anglo-Saxon charm (see pp. 61–2), while Bede alludes to the winter festival of the Mothers, and mentions two possible

Figure 4 Goddess Artio in bronze with inscription from Muri, near Bern, Switzerland. Ht 20 cm. Bernisches Historisches Museum. Eileen Aldworth.

goddesses, Hreda and Eastre (*Opera de Temporibus*, ed. Jones 1943: 211–12); Jacob Grimm (1883: 288ff.) found traces of these two names in Germany. However, none of these figures offers us any indication of a Mistress of the Wild to whom hunters turned for assistance.

Yet a great deal of hunting must have gone on in Anglo-Saxon England, and among the early settlers it would have been essential for survival. There were large tracts of wild countryside, hills, forest and marshland, beyond the cultivated land around the halls and villages, as well as an area of extensive fenland in eastern England which could be crossed only by boat or over ice in winter, a gloomy and dangerous region inspiring beliefs in sinister beings inhabiting it (H. C. Darby 1974: 9). There is moreover one supernatural character in the Anglo-Saxon poem *Beowulf* dwelling in the wild regions whose behaviour might indicate memories of a hunting-goddess. This is the mother of the monster Grendel, who preyed upon the Danes in their royal hall of Heorot.

The home of this supernatural being is beneath a lake, but she ranges over the wild boundary region with her notorious son, who is described as a *mearcstapa*, a strider over the marches (*Beowulf* 103). The mother of Grendel comes to the hall of the Danish king to avenge him, after he has been overcome in a fearsome wrestling match by the Geatish hero Beowulf, and struggled back again to the lake to die. She kills one of the leading Danish noblemen, and then makes off over the moors. Next morning Beowulf with a band of followers sets out to track her to her lair, and the episode where he dives into the waters of the lake and is seized by her and dragged down to her home is one of the most vigorous and dramatic narrative sections of the poem. Although condemned by some early critics as mere folk-tale stuff, unworthy of an epic work, it has come to be recognized as an essential part of *Beowulf*, after the publication in 1936 of Tolkien's paper on 'The Monsters and the Critics'.

The she-monster does far less harm in the hall of Heorot than her son, but proves an opponent more difficult for Beowulf to defeat. She has him on the ground and is on the point of dispatching him with her knife when he manages, with divine help, to seize a huge sword of giant workmanship hanging on the wall, and cuts through her neck. Beowulf then finds Grendel's dead body, and takes back the huge head to Heorot, along with the hilt of the wondrous sword, but makes no attempt to take that of the hag. The last we hear of her is that her poisonous blood stained the waters of the lake and was so potent that it melted the blade of the sword used to slay her.

The terms used to describe Grendel's mother emphasize her close association with both the wilderness and the depths of the water. She is called *brimwylf*, wolf of the lake (1566), *grundwyrgen*, accursed monster of the deep (1518), and *merewif mihtig*, mighty woman of the mere (1519); in each case the word used indicates an expanse of water, either sea or lake. Moreover she is specifically called the ruler or guardian of the depths, *grundhyrde* (2136), which would be appropriate for a being remembered as a Mistress of the Wild. Such a power might rule the creatures of the water as well as the forest and the mountain, as Hultkrantz (1961: 61) makes clear. The mother of Grendel was clearly a powerful and dangerous adversary, and she appears in the poem to be a kind of hag, a monster-woman (*aglæc-wif*, 1259), of dark intent (*galgmod*, 1276). At the same time the word *ides* is used of her on two occasions. This is a poetic word, indicating a lady of high standing; elsewhere in the poem it is used of the queens Wealtheow and Hildeburh (five times in all), and of queens in general (1941). It seems unlikely that this term is applied in a mocking sense; in line 1259 it is used together with 'monster-woman', and in line 1351 she is said to have been seen 'in the likeness of a lady'. In view of the well-established ability of the hunting-goddess to alternate between the form of a beautiful, seductive woman and that of a fearful hag, this deliberate use of *ides* would strengthen the case for taking Grendel's mother for a being of this kind.

Grimm believed that *ides* was used earlier for female supernatural beings, connecting it with ON (Old Norse) *dís* and OHG (Old High German) *itis*, OS (Old Saxon) *ides*; it is used of goddesses in the Second Merseburg

Charm (Grimm 1883: 400ff.), which would support the argument for seeing Beowulf's adversary as a goddess, although De Vries rejects this derivation in his *Wörterbuch* (77). Even so, the *Beowulf* poet consistently associates the word with queens and the power to rule, while Grendel's mother is called *hyrde* (guardian) in line 2136.

There is a direct association with the world of the hunter in the passage describing Beowulf and his company pursuing the hag after her killing of the nobleman Aeschere. They follow the tracks left earlier by the wounded Grendel in his flight, but suddenly begin to behave as if on a hunt, blowing their horns and getting out their bows. One of the water-creatures on the lake is wounded by an arrow and then attacked with boar-spears, dragged on to a rock and killed, although it does not seem to have threatened the party in any way. If Grendel's mother, guardian of the deep, were indeed one of the Rulers of the Wild, then the creatures of the lake would be under her special protection, and the killing of the water-creature could be seen as a deliberate challenge. This would account for her ferocious attack on Beowulf when he dived into the lake.

Again there seems to be a link between Grendel's mother and the stags hunted in the forest. If pursued to the lake, they are said to be unwilling to plunge into its dark waters even when sorely beset by the hounds (1368ff.). This could be because these animals had been marked out for death by their guardian, for it was generally assumed that hunters might successfully kill an animal when the Ruler of the Wild rejected it. The domain of Grendel's mother could have included the stags of the forest, which we know were hunted by the Danes, from the description of the antlers adorning the royal hall of Heorot. The building of this hall in the wild marches, which so angered Grendel, could also be viewed as a direct challenge to the Rulers of the Wild, provoking the attacks on the Danes in the night hours.

Grendel himself is represented as the son of the hag, whose father is not known; this again is consistent with traditions concerning the hunting-goddesses, who might accept hunters and heroes as their lovers for a time and give birth to children. Their sons might be wild animals or possess human form; in the *Kalevala* (XLVI), for instance, Mielikki not only is the mother of the first bear cub, but also has a son called Nyyrikki in the red cap, who is not an animal.

Other influences may have affected the *Beowulf* poet's portrayal of Grendel's mother. The overcoming of a giantess by means of a wonderful sword occurs in a number of tales in Icelandic legendary sagas, as Nora Chadwick (1959) and others have pointed out. But the main characteristics of this fierce supernatural being from beneath a sinister lake strongly suggest memories of a hunting-goddess and Mistress of the Wild, such as might be familiar to an Anglo-Saxon audience.

In Iceland the rocky terrain made hunting on a large scale impossible, in contrast to the forested and mountainous regions of Norway and

Sweden, and there were no powerful wild creatures to hunt, so that it is not surprising to find little trace of a Ruler of the Wild in saga literature, or among the deities in the *Prose Edda*. The most probable candidate for such a role is the goddess Skaði, who was worshipped in Norway (Holtsmark 1970). She is said to have married the god Njord, associated with the sea and with lakes, but was forced to leave him because she longed for the forest while he had to live by the sea. She went hunting with a bow, travelling on skis, and may have had connections with the Saami (Lapps) in northern Norway (Davidson 1990: 31). In Iceland the local land-spirits, who could be of either sex, were said to help those whom they favoured on hunting expeditions; in *Landnámabók* (329, H284; 330–1) we hear of two brothers followed by the spirits when they went hunting or fishing, and this brought them good luck. In general however the Icelandic settlers sought help from the land-spirits for their sheep, goats and pigs.

Some evidence for a Mistress of Animals is found in Ireland, where there are memories of a goddess, Flidais, in early literature (see p. 37). As is usual in the Irish tales she appears in sources of the ninth or tenth century as a queen rather than a supernatural figure, the wife of king Adammir (or alternatively of Ailill Fionn), but she is remembered as the owner of super-natural cattle and the mistress of stags. When her son became king, it was said that cows and deer were milked together because his mother was a 'tamer of deer', and the wild deer were known as her cattle (Ó hÓgáin 1990: 231). Another tradition is that she was unfaithful to her husband and allowed him to be killed, giving her herd of wonderful cattle to her new husband Fergus Mac Roich, king of Ulster.

There are many later examples from northern Europe of popular belief in a mistress of the wild to whom hunters might turn for help. The *Kalevala* gives information about both male and female spirits of the forest. A male spirit, Tapio, presides over the forest creatures, and those hunting the elk may appeal to him to lead the way to the island or mound where an animal may be killed (XIV: 32); his son Nyyrikki, who wears a red cap, may cut notches on the trees to show the hunter the way. But the hunters may also call upon Mielikki, described as 'forest mistress', and beg her to take her golden keys and open Tapio's shed, or to send one of her maidens to do so. This means that she will release certain animals for the hunters to take. When Lemminkäinen made such entreaties, he did not easily obtain an answer from 'the kindly, the pleasant forest mistress', and complained:

> She does not hear at all
> hardly ever wakes
> though I keep begging
> with golden tongue beseeching
>
> (*Kalevala* XIV: 75–8,
> Bosley's translation, 1989)

Clearly Mielikki, like other goddesses of this type, has two contrasting aspects: in this section of the poem she is first called clear-skinned and fair to look on (XIV: 46), but later 'quite black to look on, of appearance grim' (XIV: 109–10). Lemminkäinen makes a further plea to Tapio's daughter Tuulikki to drive the game and bring it within his reach (XIV: 173ff.), but it is to Mielikki that his main appeal is made when he goes out to hunt the elk, addressing her as:

> forest mistress,
> dear, game-giving forest crone
> blue-cloaked thicket dame
> red-socked swamp mistress
> (XIV: 218–21)

In a later section of the poem, Vainamoinen sets out to hunt a bear, and he also relies on Mielikki for help, calling on her to tie up her dog tight (XLVI: 57ff.). Mielikki is said to be the mother of the first bear, whom she rocked in a cradle which hung from a bough, giving him sharp teeth and claws when he promised to refrain from evil use of them (XLVI: 378ff.) Once more dogs are important for the hunter, and in the *Old Kalevala* (Magoun 1969), there is a reference to the unlocking of the dog's mouth so that it can scent and follow the game (VII: 217ff). The *Kalevala* makes it clear that the concept of a hunting-goddess residing with her family in the woods, with attendants to carry out her commands, was still familiar in Finland in the nineteenth century.

Hultkrantz (1961: 7) has shown that the figure of a guardian goddess of this kind survives in later forms of culture in regions where hunting continues to be of importance, and this was certainly the case in both Finland and Scandinavia. Gunnar Granberg's doctoral thesis, 'Skogsrået i yngre Nordisk Folktradition', based on material from the archives of a number of museums and published in 1935, shows clearly how widespread was the belief in the wood-spirit in Scandinavia and surrounding countries. Such evidence was largely ignored by Mannhardt (1868) in his work on spirits of the countryside, and he tried to link such figures with the corn-demon (Granberg 1935: 9). While Granberg's most detailed evidence comes from Sweden and Norway, he compares this with similar beliefs in forest spirits in central Germany, Finland, Russia, Poland, Denmark and Scotland.

The female wood-spirits were sometimes helpful to hunters and charcoal-burners, the people most likely to encounter them, and might make sexual advances to them, but in general they were viewed as dangerous, hostile beings. Their appearance varied from that of a beautiful, seductive woman to an ugly hag, or they might be fair to view from the front, but behind have an empty back like a hollow tree-stump or a wooden trough, or alternatively, as in northern Sweden, a tail (Rooth 1961: 118ff.). While usually young in appearance, they were sometimes seen as old women or in bird or animal form, or might take on the shape of a man's wife or sweetheart. One terrifying characteristic was the ability to increase in size and become as huge as a great tree (Granberg 1935: 90ff.). Sometimes, as in the *Kalevala*, the wood-spirit had a husband and offspring, and in Germany and Denmark she might belong to a group, but in Sweden and Finland she was often a solitary being (Granberg 1935: 74ff.).

The usual term, *skogsrå*, used for such beings in Sweden must be linked with the word *råda*, to rule, possess (Granberg 1935: 105), while she is also known as *skogsfruen*, the Lady of the Woods. The term *sjörå* is found for the spirit who rules the sea or lake, and the Finnish term *haltija* for a female wood-spirit is also derived from a verb meaning to rule (Wikman 1961: 13–14).

Tales of such a mistress of the woods with a hollow back and rump were collected by Erixon (1961) from a remote village in the south of Östergötland. It was important to keep on good terms with her if one wanted good luck, according to one story-teller who claimed to have driven her off with a burning piece of wood after he had been sleeping beside a fire in the forest, but it was risky to have dealings with her. Rooth (1961: 118ff.) gives further evidence for beliefs in such a figure changing in size, and for elks and boars being called her pigs and oxen. Tillhagen (1961: 123ff.) found ninety-nine examples from Sweden of a female mountain spirit, usually seen as a stately lady in rich clothes but sometimes as an old woman in grey, but only twenty-three cases of male spirits and twenty-three of spirits in animal form. The forest spirit, guarding the animals of the woods, was more of a threat to hunters than the mountain one. Tales of the *skogsrå* are further discussed by Lindow (1978) in his collection of legends and folk-tales from Sweden. In one tale a *skogsrå* met two hunters and blew down the barrel of one man's rifle, to bring him good luck in the hunt (Lindow 1978: 105). Granberg (1935: 119) has similar examples of this, although he found that the *skogsrå* might also blow into a gun to prevent it working. These beings often took mortals as lovers, and might lead travellers astray.

In Norway it is more difficult to distinguish the Mistress of the Wild from the supernatural 'under-earth' people or *huldrefolk*, who possessed herds of wonderful cattle and figured in legends of the mountains (see p. 31). The wolf, bear and elk were said to be the domestic animals of these Otherworld people, and there are tales of hunters coming into contact with them (Grambø 1964: 33ff.). One famous hunter of the seventeenth century, Olav Austegarden, was said to have killed some of their animals; on one occasion he heard two girls in the mountains discussing whether to take back their bull, because they had seen the hunter with his spear, but one said the bull would be safe, because the man had not washed. Olav rubbed dew over his face, however, and then killed the 'bull of the hill', as it is called in a verse; this was presumably an elk. In another tale of a fairy bull being killed, there was a ring in each of the animal's ears, and the hunter's family afterwards used one of these as a door knocker. The reference to spears in some of the tales might indicate a tradition going back to the time before guns came into general use.

Similar stories are told of Peer Gynt, the name by which Peder Laurissen was known, another hunter of the seventeenth century famous in folk tradition. In one tale a voice is heard saying:

> Look after your boar;
> Peer Gynt is out
> with his tail [i.e. his gun].

The reply came that the boar was safe, as Peer had not washed, but he used his own urine to rub over his face, and killed his animal (Grambø 1964: 35). In a similar tale from Sweden, the Lady of the Forest told a hunter that those who were unwashed and fasting could not harm her animals, but he put water in his shoe, washed his face in it and drank it.

Sometimes these Otherworld women permitted a hunter to shoot one of their animals. In a story from Nergaard (Grambø 1964: 36), a hunter was in a hut with a hole in the roof, and heard a woman calling down from above and asking for some tobacco. He passed it up through the hole on a stick, and then she asked if he had something in which she could wrap her baby, whereupon he tore off the tail of his shirt and passed that up to her. 'You shall have a big elk to take home with you', she told him, and next day he saw a large elk bull and heard a voice saying: 'Bull, my bull, be careful of that unwashed man'. He then washed his face with dew and shot the elk. We have examples in these tales of the hunters' special language, calling a gun the hunter's tail and the elk a bull. Similar use of 'avoiding language' by hunters has been noted by Anna Chaudhri (1996: 167) in the Caucasus and Carmen Blacker (1996: 182) in Japan.

It is interesting to find a group of similar hunting stories collected about the end of the nineteenth century in the Highlands of Scotland, in which the supernatural woman plays a part closely resembling those associated with the cult of the hunting-goddess from the Caucasus (Davidson and Chaudhri 1993). A number of these tales were collected and translated from the Gaelic by James MacDougall (1910) and John Gregorson Campbell (1900), Scottish ministers who were interested in both local folklore and Celtic studies; some of them, like the Norwegian stories, were told of famous local hunters of the past. Here the supernatural woman who sometimes threatens and sometimes helps hunters is called a hag or *glaistig*, and is a guardian of the deer, whom she herds and milks. She is particularly protective of her hinds; on one occasion she is said to have told the hunter Donald Cameron not to be so heavy on the hinds, but Donald quickly retorted: 'I never killed a hind where I could find a stag', and had no more trouble with the tall *glaistig* whom he met driving her hinds through the forest (MacDougall 1978: 57).

Occasionally the *glaistig* allowed one of her animals to be shot. In one of Campbell's tales (1900: 122) she was angry when one of her hinds kicked her while she was milking it, and exclaimed that she wished Donald MacIan might come upon it. That very day it was shot by Donald, probably the famous bowman who followed Cameron of Locheil. Dempster (1888: 226) recorded a tale of the Hag (Cailleach) of Clieber who made all the deer of the Reay forest bullet-proof, but one of Lord Reay's men saw her milking her hinds, and when one ate a strand of blue wool she struck it saying: 'Lord Reay's bullet will be your death today'. A hind shot later had a hank of blue wool in its stomach. Again when Donald MacIan of Lochaber got the better of the supernatural guardian with the help of his dogs, he was able to shoot a white hind, which he had long pursued unsuccessfully. As his arrow flew he heard the *glaistig* cry out 'Stick in the stomach, arrow' (MacDougall 1978: 67).

In a tale recorded more recently from the Cairngorms, two poachers took refuge in a mountain hut in a blizzard, and were told by an old woman they met there that they must leave a fat hind for her on a certain cairn on the first Monday of every month (Gray 1987: 14). This suggests a tradition of hunters leaving part of their game as an offering to the guardian of the woods, as has been done in the twentieth century in the Caucasus. Granberg (1935: 153) found evidence in Norway for small offerings, such as a coin, salt or buttered bread, left by hunters, charcoal-burners, or those losing a horse or cow in the forest.

As in one of the Norwegian tales quoted above, it was often in a mountain hut, or bothy, that the *glaistig* was encountered. She might appear as a frail old woman, asking leave to warm herself at the hunters' fire, and then increase in size until she became a monstrous being. In one tale she first enters as a small hen (MacDougall 1978: 68); in another she appears as a great black shadow coming round the door, and has one huge tooth as big as a distaff (Campbell 1900: 124). In the Scottish tales she often asks for snuff, but the only safe way to offer this is on the point of a knife (MacDougall 1978: 60). She plays a particularly destructive role along with some companions in a tale told by MacDougall (1978: 75–6) of a party of hunters who were spending the night in a bothy when one expressed the wish that they had their sweethearts there with them. At this point some girls came in whom they thought they recognized, and welcomed with delight, but one of the men was ill at ease. When his apparent girlfriend asked for snuff, he passed it to her on the point of his dirk, and kept well away from her until at the crowing of the cock the girls ran out of the hut. He then found his friends lying on the floor with their throats cut and their veins sucked dry. A similar tale of three brothers was recorded by Dempster (1888: 162), in which the visitants have webbed feet.

Hunting dogs play an important part in the Scottish tales, and often attempt to defend their masters against the supernatural visitants. It seems that these narratives have been influenced by the widespread international tale of 'The Two Brothers', since several contain an episode in which the old woman begs the hunter to bind up his dogs so that they cannot attack her, and gives him one of her long hairs for the purpose. If the hunter is unwise enough to make use of it, it becomes a chain of iron when the hag attacks him and he calls on his dogs to help. However, in the Scottish tales there is no brother to help the hunter, and he usually gets the better of the hag and survives with the help of his faithful dogs. In one tale from Strathdearn he has one old dog and one young one, and after the old woman had fought with them and got the worst of it, she exclaimed: 'If the young dog's tusk had been in the old dog's mouth or the old dog's sense in the young dog's head, I would not have escaped from them' (MacDougall 1978: 69). The motif of the dogs bound by a hair, found in these tales, is present in the earliest printed version of 'The Two Brothers' from Italy (Davidson and Chaudhri 1993: 153ff.)

It seems possible that this group of tales from the Scottish Highlands has been influenced by earlier traditions of a local supernatural being who acted as guardian of the wild deer, and might be benevolent or hostile to hunters. She approved of those who did not kill too many animals, particularly hinds. She is said to protect and milk the deer, and some of the tales suggest that she might welcome a hunter to her bed, like her Swedish or Caucasian counterparts, or the Greek Artemis (see p. 18), but once more such an experience might prove fatal for the hunter. Mention of a White Hind is another interesting feature, since this a shape traditionally adopted by the goddess (see p. 15) and found in tales from the Caucasus (Davidson and Chaudhri 1993: 155–6).

Ranke (1934) traced the development of 'The Two Brothers' tale to various parts of Europe and Asia; it could have come to the Scottish Highlands from Norway in the period following the Viking Age, when there was frequent communication between northern Scotland and Scandinavia. Bruford (1967: 18) found no versions of the motif which he calls 'The Swelling Hag' in southern Scotland or in England. The suggestion by Geddes (1951: 296) that the supernatural women were based on female Lapp deer-herders in Norway in tales brought over by Norwegian settlers is unsatisfactory, since among the Saami it was not the women who acted as herders of the reindeer, while McCay's (1932) earlier theory that the supernatural women were priestesses of a deer-goddess cult has no serious evidence to support it. However, the resemblance between the supernatural women in the Scottish tales and the goddess who rules over the animals of the wild in many areas of Europe and beyond is a striking one.

The decline of the mistress of the forest is perhaps to be seen in popular traditions in Germany and Denmark of the Wild Hunter, sometimes identified with Wodan and sometimes with the Christian Devil, hunting down woodwives (Olrik 1901: 142; Davidson forthcoming). Grimm has an unpleasant tale of a peasant who cheekily echoed the huntsman's cry finding a quarter of a little woodwife hanging by his stable door as a reward for his support (Grimm 1883: 929). It seems that the goddess might also lead the Wild Hunt, the dangerous host of the unquiet dead, riding with their baying hounds through the night. Artemis, Hekate, Diana and Herodias, as well as the German Frau Holle, were all named as leaders of such a troop. But on the whole the picture of the goddess as Mistress of Animals who helps or hinders the hunters at her will is remarkably consistent over a large part of the world, as well as long lasting.

GUARDIAN OF THE DAIRY HERDS

An example from the ancient world of a goddess who ruled the animals of the wild, bringing domestic animals under her protection, is Nimhursag of Mesopotamia. This powerful goddess is thought to have ruled over the stony desert border area in the west, extending to the Iranian mountains, and was named 'lady of the foothills' (Jacobsen 1976: 104ff.). Her husband was sometimes said to be Shulpae, king of the wild animals of the desert. In particular, she was the protectress of donkeys, and may originally have ruled over the wild desert asses, but later she was regarded as the mother of herd animals, of domesticated donkeys, sheep and cattle. Although milk was not much used as a drink among the people, Nimhursag had a dairy in her temple to provide it for the royal children, pictured on a frieze from al-Ubaid, while a holy flock of sheep grazed in the temple meadows. Such a change in the role of the goddess must have taken place in many regions, and can be recognized in northern Europe.

I have discussed elsewhere the importance of milk as part of the diet in the north, and its close association with goddesses from Roman times onwards (Davidson 1996). Such an association can be seen in Ancient Egypt, where the goddess Hathor was depicted as a cow, or wearing a sun-disk flanked by a cow's horns (Rundle Clark 1959: 87; Blecker 1973: 31ff.). In India the cow was linked with the goddess Aditi (Lodrick 1981: 6), while the goddess Sri-Laksmi emerged from the primeval Ocean of Milk (Kinsley 1989: 61). The importance of the cow probably preceded the coming of the Aryans (Ferro-Luzzi 1987: 109), and milk and milk products are still regularly offered to the deities, since milk is seen as a life-giving drink (O'Flaherty 1980: 28).

At the time of the Roman Empire, milk was not drunk much in southern Europe except on the farms, since it quickly went sour in the hot summer, while butter also soon turned rancid and was seldom eaten fresh. In the Mediterranean area, moreover, wine from grapes and oil from the olive were available as a good substitute. Sheep's milk was drunk on farms, and cheese made from it, but this was not women's work.

In northern Europe the position was very different: many milk-based products such as butter, cheese, curds and whey, cream and skimmed milk formed an essential part of the diet from early times (Lysaght 1994: viii). Svale Solheim (1952) has shown the importance of the well-being of the cows and of women's work in the dairy in his detailed study of farm life in Norway during the summer, when the cattle were taken up into the mountains. Milk was obtained from ewes and she-goats as well as from cows, and from deer also according to legend, but in northern Europe the cow was the chief source, and milking and dairy-work were under the control of the women. Thus it was the cow that had the closest links with the goddess.

The tradition of the forest goddess milking her deer, and also that of the wild animals such as wolves or elks being described as her herds (see pp. 26–7), may be the result of transition between the activities of the goddess as ruler of the wild and her later role as protectress of domestic animals. In Norway the supernatural women of the forest had their own herds of cattle, and Solheim has many tales 'told for true' of how one of these splendid animals, well nourished, with large udders and of unusual colours, came into the possession of a family. Sometimes it was a gift in return for help from one of the women on the mountain farm, or obtained by barter, or by throwing steel over the animal's back (Davidson 1996: 100ff.).

Elsewhere in Celtic areas there are tales of marvellous cattle belonging to Otherworld women dwelling under the water, as in the Welsh tale of the Lady of the Lake, who brought a herd of fine animals with her when she became the wife of a farmer but returned with them into the lake when he unwittingly broke the contract made between them (Wood 1992) (see pp. 66–7). In Denmark cattle were said to belong to the merwomen, who might bring them up to graze on the land (Simpson 1988: 235). Thus there are many tales of contacts between women working in the dairy and female beings from the Otherworld, who had their own herds of cows and took an active interest in what went on at the farm.

Work in the dairy was a precarious business, and if things went wrong, there might be insufficient butter and cheese to get through the coming winter. The churning of milk in the old stand-churn, in particular, could often end in failure for no obvious reason, so that the butter would not come, and this was continually attributed to evil magic. In Ireland well into the twentieth century it was still believed that malicious neighbours might steal cream by magical rites on 1 May (Lysaght 1994: 212ff.); it would be surprising if such problems and fears in the dairy did not result in constant appeals to a goddess in pre-Christian times. There is ample evidence for such appeals to the Virgin Mary in Solheim's collection of spells, prayers and rites associated with the well-being of cows, milking, and work in the dairy on the mountain farms. Lily Weiser-All (1947) has studied symbols on wooden dishes used in the dairies in Norway, and found that a number of protective or magical signs had been added which were not part of the ornament, such as concentric circles, whirling discs and circled stars which appear to be connected with the sun. Similar symbols have been found on pipe-clay figures of goddesses (Figure 5) from Roman Britain and Brittany (M. J. Green 1991: 128 ff.) and on buckets from the Oseberg ship-burial, where other ritual objects are linked with the goddess cult (see pp. 110–12).

There were also special rites concerned with milking which linked it with the sun. On Our Lady's Day (Feast of the Annunciation), 25 March, the girls doing the milking were told to go out early, so that on a clear day the rising sun would shine on the vessel holding milk, as this would ensure good luck with the dairy-work throughout the coming summer (Solheim 1952: 7). At the midsummer festival of St John the Baptist they began to milk three times a day, and in the evening tried to ensure that

Figure 5 Figure of goddess in pipe-clay from Rezé, Brittany. Ht 20 cm. Musée de Bretagne. Based on drawing by M. J. Green (1991). Lelly Aldworth.

the rays of the setting sun shone on the pail in which the milk was carried (Solheim 1952: 512)

While herding and stable-work were usually done by men, women were responsible for the milking and cheese and butter-making. It is in this area then that one might look for definite links with goddesses, and these may be found on some of the carved stones from Roman Britain which show female supernatural beings associated with fertility and the well-being of the farm. I have claimed elsewhere that the carving from Corbridge of Rosmerta stirring a vessel closely resembling the old stand-churn (Plate 3) is an example of a goddess working in the dairy (Davidson 1996: 93). This would be a highly appropriate symbol for plenty in northern Europe, although not likely to be pictured on carvings from the Mediterranean area. Other stones show Rosmerta again with her 'tub' (Webster 1986: Plates 6–10), which has caused great puzzlement to scholars; on a stone from Gloucester she is pouring into it something which could be cream (Figure 6).

Figure 6 Rosmerta and Mercury on stone from Shakespeare Inn, Gloucester. 58.5 × 43 cm. Gloucester City Museum. Eileen Aldworth.

Plate 3 The goddess Rosmerta stirring a stand-churn, on stone from Corbridge. Base 20 cm wide. Courtesy Corbridge Museum.

Another figure not easy to interpret is a little wooden goddess found at Winchester in 1971, who holds a key in one hand and a folded cloth in the other (Figure 7). Ross suggested that this was Epona holding the *mappa*, the cloth held up by the Byzantine Emperor to start a chariot race (A. Ross 1975: 335), but this seems unlikely, since Epona is normally depicted with one or more horses (see p. 40). However, both these attributes could be connected with domestic animals. Keys were a symbol of the power of the goddess to control wild creatures (see p. 24), and prayers were made in Norway to the Virgin Mary to 'lock in all the wild animals in the forest' (Solheim 1952: 248). The key was also a favourite symbol when appealing

Figure 7 Wooden figure of goddess from Winchester. Ht 18 cm from photograph by A. Ross (1979). Eileen Aldworth.

to the goddess, and later to the Virgin Mary, for help in childbirth (see p. 148). A cloth too might be used to help in calving and to ensure a good supply of milk from the cows; an example from Ireland is the *brat*, the mantle or girdle of St Brigid, still to be found on farms up to the twentieth century. This could be a ribbon or scarf or simply a piece of material left out to be blessed by the saint on her visit to the farm on the eve of her festival. It might be preserved for years, since its potency was held to increase with the passage of time, and it would be laid on the back of sick animals or on cows when calving.

In Ireland customs involving milk are connected with St Brigid; some may go back to the earlier goddess Brigid, said to be the daughter of the Dagda, who had links with the powerful Brigantia of the British Celts (A. Ross 1967: 360). The goddess was connected with cattle, and said to possess two oxen, Fea and Feimhean, after which two plains in Ireland were named, and also 'Triath king of the swine', from which another plain took its name. These three animals cried out to the goddess if rapine was committed in Ireland, which suggests that she was the guardian of domestic herds (Ó hÓgáin 1990: 60). The feast day of St Brigid was on 1 February, which was the date of Imbolg, one of the four main festivals of the Celtic year; Imbolg is thought to mean parturition, and was probably linked with the birth of young animals. St Brigid too was said to have the power of increasing herds of cattle, sheep and pigs.

The use of St Brigid's 'mantle' (*brat*) has already been mentioned. The piece of cloth left outside to be touched by her during the night before her festival was carefully measured next morning, and if it had stretched, this was a good omen for cattle, crops, and the health of the family. It was used not only to help cows in calving, but also to ensure that nursing mothers had a good supply of milk (Danaher 1972: 33).

In the seventeenth century, there was a great shortage of milk in early spring, when the cows depended on winter fodder and no milk could be taken from them until they could be freed from the demands of their calves. Part of the celebrations of 1 May in England, as Charles Phythian-Adams (1983: 87ff.) has shown, was rejoicing in the new abundance of milk and cream now that the cows were out in the open pastures; in the seventeenth century the young people who had celebrated May Eve in the woods would visit farms and indulge in all kinds of rich milk dishes – syllabubs, curds, junkets and cream cakes – on May Day morning. St Brigid was relied on to relieve the people from this time of scarcity; when there was little milk in January,

> the old people used to say ... 'It won't be scarce very long now, as Brid and her white cow will be coming round soon'. I heard that some of the older women of the Parish would take a blessed candle to the cow's stall on Brigid's Eve and singe the long hair on the upper part of the animals's udder, 'so as to bring a blessing on her milk'.
> (Ó Catháin 1995: 5)

St Brigid was said to have been Abbess of Kildare, although there is little definite information about her (Ó Cathasaigh 1982: 82ff.). In her *Life* written by Cogitosis, a seventh-century member of the Kildare community, it is stated that in her girlhood she churned butter and guarded her father's flocks. The tale of her birth from one of the Irish *Lives* of the saint (Stokes 1890) is of especial interest. Here her mother was a bondmaid, made pregnant by her master Dubtaig, and as she walked over the threshold at sunrise with a pail of milk, her child was born. The milkmaids washed the baby in the milk, and indeed there is evidence in records of a Church Council held at Cashel in 1171 for this being done to new-born children (Lucas 1989: 9). The birth of Brigid on the threshold symbolizes her liminal position between the human and supernatural worlds; she was said to be nourished on the milk of an Otherworld cow, since she could not digest ordinary cows' milk. This was the white animal with red ears held to accompany her on her Eve when she visited the farms, and sometimes a sheaf of corn was left out for it (Danaher 1972: 15). On that evening a figure representing the saint might be made from the churn-dash wrapped in hay or straw, and fresh butter was churned to form part of the meal, while gifts of milk or buttermilk were taken to poor neighbours (Danaher 1972: 27). A dish of porridge or a fruitcake might be left for Brigid on the flat end of the churn-dash with its handle stuck in the ground.

Other goddesses were said to possess a cow. The Hag of Beare, the *Cailleach Bhéarra*, once a powerful goddess in Ireland (see p. 73), had one, and Calc, her fosterchild, would sit on its back when he bathed in the sea, according to a tale of the tenth or eleventh centuries (Ó hÓgáin 1990: 119). The Mórrígan, the Irish battle goddess, appeared to the hero Cú Chulainn as a red-eared white heifer, followed by fifty similar beasts (*Táin Bó Cúalnge*, Book of Leinster, ed. C. O'Rahilly 1984: 194). Flidais, probably a goddess of hunters (see p. 24), had a cow called Maol (hornless) which yielded enough at one milking to nourish 300 families (Ó hÓgáin 1990: 231). St Brigid's cow was also said to be white with pink ears, and this might be based on a breed of cattle which goes back to Roman times in Britain; one isolated herd of these animals has survived at Chillingham in Northumberland. Whitehead (1953: 39) believed that they might have descended from white cattle brought from Italy by the Romans to be used for sacrifice, which could account for the link between this particular type of cattle and the Otherworld in early Celtic tradition in Ireland and Wales.

The idea of a 'fairy cow' with unlimited supplies of milk has long persisted in folk tradition. Charlotte Burne found this legend well known in south Shropshire toward the end of the nineteenth century (Burne 1883: 39) and the vicar of Middleton-in-Chirbury carved scenes from the tale on a pillar in the church in 1879. The tale was that when there was a famine in the region a pure white fairy cow appeared on a hill every morning and evening; anyone might milk her so long as only one vessel was brought to be filled. However, at last a mean old witch brought along a sieve, and milked the cow dry. The Shropshire site where the cow was said to appear was Mitchells Fold, where there is an early stone circle, while two others are recorded not far away. There is an impressive view of hills in all directions, and this would be a convenient central place for people from a number of villages to meet.

The tale is found elsewhere in England, and in some versions the cow died of grief; at Preston in Lancashire its huge bones were said to have been found on Cow Hill (Burne 1883: 41). At South Lopham in Norfolk, however, a mark on a stone showed where it stamped its foot in anger (Westwood 1985: 257–9), while in Warwickshire it became a monstrous Dun Cow, ravaging the countryside until it was slain by Guy of Warwick (Westwood 1985: 220). The tradition is also found all over Ireland, where the cow is 'the Grey of Goibniu', Goibniu being the mythical smith of the gods (Ó hÓgáin 1990: 240–1). One variant of this is that the cow with a miraculous flow of milk came from the sea, and helped a poor family, until one of them struck her with a spancel. Ó hÓgáin suggests that here we have echoes of ancient traditions of a cow goddess, and that since we find the story in England, Ireland and Wales, it is likely to go back to medieval times. Ó Cáitháin (1995: 143) refers to tales in which the bountiful cow is identified with that of St Brigid, also said to yield vast quantities of milk.

In India there is a widespread tale of a bountiful cow which did not need to be milked, since it let its milk fall on the ground, and Gabrielle Ferro-Luzzi (1987) collected over 400 versions of this in the 1980s. The basic form is that of a cow emptying its udder over an ant-hill or cairn, under which was later discovered the image of a god or a sacred lingam, resulting in the building of a temple by a local rajah. While the author found few parallels in the Stith-Thompson Index from western Europe, it is worth noting the legend of St Kenelm, told in a medieval poem of the thirteenth century in the *Southern English Lectionary* (J. A. W. Bennett and Smithers 1966: 103). There is no historical evidence for this story of a boy-king Kenelm who was murdered by his wicked sister, and whose body lay undiscovered until a white cow belonging to a widow was observed to be spending the whole day in a certain valley away from the herd. The cow took no food, but remained 'fair and round', with a milk yield greater than those of the other cows. While other miraculous elements are introduced, like a letter delivered to the Pope by a dove, it was the cow's behaviour which led to the discovery of the body of the boy martyr. This would be in keeping with earlier traditions which extend the protection to animals given by the goddess to children.

The supernatural cow and its bounty is widely established in legends in northern Europe and linked with the goddesses so that one might expect to find it in early mythology. In Snorri Sturluson's account of the northern gods there is indeed a primeval cow called Audhumla, interpreted as 'rich hornless cow' (Turville-Petre 1964: 319, n. 4). She existed before the gods along with the giant Ymir, whom she nourished with her milk. The cow licked the salty iceblocks which existed before the worlds were formed, and a handsome being called Buri emerged. His son Bor was the father of the god Odin and his brother, who slew Ymir and created the earth from his body (*Gylfaginning* 5). We do not know what source Snorri used when he recorded this in the thirteenth century. Bruce Lincoln (1987: 68f.) believes that it comes from an Indo-European myth, but in the Iranian parallel he quotes, the primeval animal was an ox and not a cow. Possible traces of such a myth are found in popular tradition in east Yorkshire, where in the eighteenth century there was a legend of the giant Wade (known to the Anglo-Saxons) depending on the milk of a cow called Bel (Charlton 1779: 40).

As in India, milk was regularly offered to supernatural beings, like the brownies and the 'Maidens' in Scotland who gave help to certain families and helped with the herds of cattle and sheep; on a farm at Lismore, for instance, a Maiden protected the cattle and received cold whey in return, until a new dairymaid one evening left hot whey instead, and the helpful being departed, never to return (MacDougall 1978: 52). What seem to be memories of a supernatural female being linked with the dairy are found in literature of Tudor England. Ben Jonson refers to a 'mistress-faerie' called Mab, who took milk or cream from the dairy, and could 'hurt or help' the churning, in a masque of 1603 (Jonson 1603: vii, 122; 11, 53–6). Milton also mentions Mab in 'L'Allegro'; in *Romeo and Juliet* (I, 4) Shakespeare calls her the fairies' midwife, a link once more between the protective spirit of the dairy herds and childbirth, although earlier references to this elusive figure are lacking.

The association between the goddess and the cow, an animal loved and tended by women, appears to have been well established in northern Europe; there are signs also of her protection being extended to the domestic herds. A special link between the goddess and the plough and her use of oxen to guide it, will be considered later (see pp. 65–7). Of a different nature, however, is the relationship of the goddess with the horse and the dog, animals important on the farm and elsewhere which worked for men rather than women; this will be discussed in the next section.

THE HORSE AND THE DOG

Horses have close links with the goddess, although it was usually men who worked with them and looked after the stables; among the Mongols they even milked the mares, and had a male guardian figure to protect them in contrast to the female one for women who milked the cattle (see p. 126). Unlike the cow, the horse is not normally taken as a symbol of fertility; it features predominantly in the Mediterranean world as a means of heroizing the dead, something which is part of the warrior ideal and a means of exalting the male ruler (Benoit 1954), while among nomadic tribes it is usually depicted as a fighting animal or a mount for warriors (Linduff 1979: 833).

The dog could be the companion of both the men and women of the house, but tended to be connected with hunters and herdsmen, both male pursuits, and to be trained by men. However, dogs were often valued companions of hunting-goddesses like Artemis (pp. 18–19); they are frequently depicted in company with the Mother Goddesses, and sacrificed at the shrines of goddesses of healing (see p. 159). Certainly both horse and dog have strong links with death and the journey to the Otherworld, and this appears to be an important element in their relationship with the goddess.

It is inevitable that the goddess should be associated with warfare, in view of her connection with death and divination, as will be seen in later chapters. There may also have been a closer link between women and warfare in certain periods than is generally recognized. Among the Celts there is evidence for women taking a major part in violent attacks and even leading forces in battle. The exploits of Boudicca as Queen of the Iceni and the appalling damage she inflicted on the Romans in Britain in the first century AD is by no means the only example of this, as Hope (1970) has shown in his study of Scottish women. The description of Boudicca in Dio Cassius (*Roman History* LXII) suggests that such a woman and those who served her would not at all be content with the goddesses of the domestic arts and fertile fields. We are told moreover of savage sacrifices of high-born Romano-British women, whose naked bodies on stakes were exposed in the temple of her goddess Andraste, said to be a goddess of victory, while Boudicca herself conducted divination concerning the fortunes of war by observing the movements of a hare.

Another formidable woman ruler was Cartimandua in northern Britain, who took over the leadership of the Brigantes from her husband (Hope 1970: 222). Her goddess was Brigantia, also said to have been a goddess of victory (Joliffe 1941: 40). Similar figures are found in Irish tradition, and particularly Medb, Queen of Connacht, who leads her people to war in the *Táin*. Faced with such impressive martial figures of high-born Celtic women, we may feel that the cult of the goddess Epona, guardian of the horses ridden by warriors and used to pull war-chariots, might be likely to flourish among them and their women followers.

Epona was clearly a most popular goddess, since stones and inscriptions were set up in her honour over all the parts of Europe occupied by the Roman armies. She is usually shown riding a horse (Figure 8) or accompanied by a horse and foal or by two or more horses; occasionally a saddled mare and foal are shown without the goddess, and Benoit suggested that here she became the invisible rider (Benoit 1950: 50). She is most often shown riding side-saddle, with the horse moving at a leisurely pace towards the right, although sometimes she rides astride (Linduff 1979: 823). Monuments to the goddess are found mainly in central and northern Gaul, Germany and the Danubian Provinces, with a few in Italy, Spain, North Africa and Britain.

While the goddess is depicted in the Roman fashion, and monuments and inscriptions are mainly found at legionary posts, it has been noted that Epona was most popular in the parts of Gaul and Germany where Roman influence was least strong (Linduff 1979: 823). There seems no doubt that here we have a native Celtic goddess associated with horses, who has been adopted with enthusiasm by the Romans because of the great importance of the horse in the Roman army. Epona offered luck and protection to horse and rider, and attracted many in the army who would be unable or

Figure 8 Goddess Epona riding, from Kastel, Germany. Ht 25 cm. Rheinisches Landesmuseum, Bonn. Based on photograph by M. J. Green (1989). Eileen Aldworth.

unwilling to commit themselves to the more exclusive and demanding Mithraic cult. The account given by Linduff of Celtic horsemen brought in to fill the divisions of the *auxilia* and the bodyguard known as the *equites singulares*, as well as the *numeri*, which were crack corps of mounted soldiers, helps us to understand the reasons for Epona's popularity. Such cavalry men, expert in horsemanship and setting great value on their mounts, were most likely to turn to Epona for protection and luck, and to raise cult images in her honour in forts, camps and stables.

However, there is no doubt that Epona is connected with the Mother Goddesses, and that she is concerned with fertility as well as with the protection of a warrior's charger. While sitting on her mare or stationed between two ponies (Plate 4), she may carry a sheaf of corn or large circular emblems of fruit or bread (M. J. Green 1995: 184–5); sometimes she gives corn to her horses. The Gauls apparently made use of mares on their farms, probably because stallions were preferred in warfare, and the French word for mare, *jument*, comes from Latin *iumentum* (draught animal, beast of burden) (Linduff 1979: 832). One of Epona's gifts could thus be the fertility of the land and increase of produce. It is worth noting that in Wales

Plate 4 Bronze figure of the goddess Epona with ponies (male and female), holding yoke and sheaf of corn. From Wiltshire, provenance unknown. Ht 7.5 cm. © British Museum.

and the border counties the mare was the symbol of harvest, and such a ritual as 'Crying the Mare' continued into the nineteenth century when a mare might be sent round the farms as a symbol that the harvest was completed (see pp. 71–2). Another probable role for Epona was to help in horse-breeding; many monuments show her with a mare suckling her foal, or both being fed by the goddess. Epona shown between two horses, popular in the Danubian provinces, is perhaps represented as a trainer of horses, or as the goddess who helped to domesticate them (Linduff 1979: 836).

There is general agreement that Epona helped the dead in their journey to the Otherworld, even if this function of the goddess was perhaps overstressed by Benoit (Linduff 1979: 834ff.). On a funerary plaque at Agassac in southern Gaul she is shown on her horse surrounded by sea-monsters and various celestial symbols; Miranda Green (1995: 186) suggests that this may show her as guardian of the dead on their way to the Otherworld, which could be reached by water. On other funeral monuments she is depicted leading a walking figure, who appears to represent the dead. Her occasional holding of a key has been taken as a symbol of this aspect of her nature, but the key can also refer to birth and to the protection of domestic animals (see pp. 34, 149). Occasionally Epona, like other Mother Goddesses, is represented by a triple image.

Other possible goddesses associated with the horse have been sought in Welsh and Irish literature, and in particular Rhiannon and Macha. In both cases there is a strong link between the supernatural woman and the horse, but other motifs from such traditional tales as 'The Supernatural Wife' and 'The Mother Wrongly Accused' have been introduced, resulting in a mass of complications, as Gruffydd (1953) has shown in his study of Rhiannon.

She plays a part in several tales in the Welsh *Mabinogion*; the tale of 'Pwyll, Prince of Dyfed' begins with her appearance on a 'big fine pale white horse', moving at a 'slow even pace', like the mount of Epona on numerous monuments, although she cannot be overtaken even by the fleetest of steeds (Jones and Jones 1949: 9ff.). Later she is accused of killing her child, and her penance is to stay by a horse-block for seven years, and to offer to carry on her back any guest or stranger arriving at the court. Even more striking is the episode concerning the mare belonging to Teyrnon, a superb animal whose foals were always born on May Eve, but then mysteriously disappeared. Teyrnon finally saw a monstrous arm come through the window and seize on the new-born colt, and he struck it off, whereupon he found a boy child in swaddling clothes on the threshold. He and his wife adopted the baby and gave him the colt born on the same night; this boy was Rhiannon's lost son, the hero Pryderi, who plays a major part in other tales in the collection. A clear link with the Otherworld is the tradition of the birds of Rhiannon, which in the tale of Culhwch and Olwen in the *Mabinogion* are said to waken the dead and send the living to sleep.

Macha appears in an Irish version of the tale of the supernatural wife. She is a beautiful stranger who enters the house of a widower, Crunnchu, and takes over all the duties of the household; she goes round the room clockwise in the ritual manner, and finally comes into his bed, and from that time all prospers for him. After she has become pregnant the husband foolishly boasts of her fleetness of foot when he is at the king's court, declaring that she could outrun the king's horses, and thus breaking the prohibition never to mention her name. The king insists that he makes good his challenge, and when she pleads for a delay because she is on the point of giving birth, it is refused. Undoing her hair, she races against the horses and reaches the post first; then she cries out and dies, giving birth to twins. Her last act is to curse the men of Ulster for their inhumanity, and to decree that in the hour of danger and war they shall be incapacitated by the pains of childbirth for five nights and four days.

Sjoestedt (1982: 41) explains this as 'a collective rite, a symbolic mime in honour of the mother goddess' and suggests that Macha in this tale is a goddess of fertility, presiding over the rites of childbirth, while references to the hour of greatest danger suggest that this Mother Goddess is a protectress in war as well as peace. She points out that a second Macha, daughter of Aed, is a very warlike figure, holding the kingdom when her father dies, and making her opponents build her a royal centre in Ulster, called Emain Macha, the Twins of Macha. Macha's association with both childbirth and warfare fits in well with the character of Epona, who is often shown with twin horses beside her. In the tale of the birth of Cú Chulainn in an eighth-century text, twin foals born the same night are given to the new-born child, and one is the famous Grey of Macha (Ó hÓgáin 1990: 131). A third Macha, the wife of Nemed, was said to die in the plain which her husband had cleared, so that it was called after her; the name Macha means 'pasture' (Ó hÓgáin 1990: 284–5), so that here there is a link with the fertility of the earth.

Macha's part in a horse race, symbol of struggle for kingship, would be in keeping with her role as goddess of sovereignty (Ó hÓgáin 1990: 285). Rhiannon also is associated both with childbirth and the birth of a foal, while she takes the place of a horse as a beast of burden, just as Macha takes her place among the racing horses owned by the king. The name Rhiannon has been derived from British *Rigantona*, 'Great Queen', while that of Teyrnon, who brought up her lost son as his own, may be derived from an earlier form, *Tigernonos*, 'Great King' (Gruffydd 1953: 99ff.).

Thus all three possible goddesses associated with horses have links with sovereignty. The possession of valuable horses was a mark of high status among the Celts, and the king was chosen from among those who rode and owned them. Miranda Green (1995: 187) associates Epona with the protection of territory, and Benoit's emphasis on the mounted figure as a means of heroizing the dead becomes relevant here. Oaks (1986) discusses the relation of cavalry to sovereignty, emphasizing the part played by horse and chariot races as part of the ritual of kingship. She sees Medb, who incidentally could outrun horses on the track (Sjoestedt 1982: 50), as based on an earlier goddess of sovereignty like Macha and Rhiannon, suggesting that while the romanization of Gaul meant that Epona lost many of her aspects connected with rule, she maintained her specialized equestrian nature for the Gaulish cavalry. As a result, we have a rich gallery of portraits of a riding goddess, training and protecting horses and their young, and connected with childbirth and fertility. Oaks (1989: 82) suggests that there may be an echo of this in the tradition of the Virgin riding her donkey on her flight into Egypt with the Christ Child.

On the Germanic side there seems to be no powerful female rider to match Epona. However, the link between the supernatural woman on her horse and death comes out in the figures of the Scandinavian valkyries, sent down by Odin to the battlefields to escort heroic kings and heroes to Valhalla. Once more there is a clear link with the power of kingship, and individual valkyries helped and instructed princes (Davidson 1988: 923). In a funeral poem celebrating the death of King Hakon of Norway in the tenth century, the valkyries are described as dignified figures on horseback, wise in demeanour (*Hákonarmál* 11).

Another link is suggested by the riding figures on the wall-hangings from the Oseberg ship-burial, discussed in Chapter III (see pp. 107–10). The royal funeral procession depicted there is dominated by horses, some of them of impressive size, while as many as fifteen horses had been killed at the funeral and laid in the splendid ship in which two women were buried. There are many women included in the procession depicted on the hangings, some possibly divine figures; although most of these are walking or carried in wagons drawn by horses, there is one dominating woman in a hood who seems to be sitting side-saddle on a red horse (see Figure 19b, p. 111) and it has been suggested that this could be the goddess Freyja (Ingstad *et al.* 1992: 242) (see p. 110). Horses were certainly associated with the fertility pair Freyr and Freyja, and said to be kept in their holy places (Davidson 1993: 104). The greatest insult Olaf Tryggavson could think of delivering to the pagan goddess worshipped by Jarl Hakon was to take her image, stripped of its adornments, from the temple at Trondheim and drag it along at his horse's tail to be burnt along with the image of Freyr (*Flateyjarbok* I, 326: 408) (see pp. 177–8).

Another link between horses and fertility rites in Scandinavia can be found in the horse fights which took place in Norway at certain times in the year, continuing in mountainous areas up to the eighteenth century until finally abandoned because of injuries caused to the animals and the violence which often broke out among the spectators. Svale Solheim published a detailed account of such fights in 1956, showing how they were associated with the end of the summer when the workers in the mountain pastures returned to the farms and the harvest was gathered in. He believes that the horse fights were part of the festival to ensure good crops; it was said in the seventeenth century that if the horses bit one another lustily, this meant a good harvest (Solheim 1956: 40). The word used for such contests was *skeid*, meaning either horse-fighting or horse-racing, but probably originally racing (Solheim 1956: 46). Some animals were specially bred to compete, and it was a great honour to possess a champion (*skeidfol*) who could get the better of all opponents.

There are local tales of famous horses competing who appeared to have come from the Otherworld, said in later times to be fairy horses or horses of the devil. In Fyresdal one such horse appeared from the fells and won fights for several years on end. Another with golden shoes was caught by a man called Leiv Røysland, but on one occasion he struck it, some said playfully, while taking off the bit and reins, and it kicked him to death. It appeared for three years after this, but no one dared recapture it (Solheim 1956: 41–2). Such traditions are interesting to compare with those about the supernatural cattle said to be seen and occasionally acquired in the mountains (p. 31).

The custom of horse-fighting was taken to Iceland, and there are some realistic descriptions in the sagas of fights which resulted in violent killings and feuds. Place-names such as *hestaþing* (horse meeting) and *hestavig* (horse fight) survive at places where these were held. A mare was tied up nearby to encourage the horses to fight, and the owners drove them on with 'horse-staffs', as shown on a stone from Häggeby, Sweden, which may be as early as AD 500 (Figure 9).

Solheim (1956) has found interesting parallels in horse races which took place in the Hebrides, together with a riding procession, at Michaelmas.

Figure 9 Fighting stallions on stone from Häggeby, Sweden. Statens Historika Museum, Stockholm. Lelly Aldworth.

Horses also played a traditional part in celebrations in Norway when girls rode to church on the first Sunday after returning home from the mountain pastures, and in both cases the riding is associated with special food prepared by the women to celebrate the harvest. Horse races were evidently linked with the collecting, guarding and putting in order of the newly harvested crops (Solheim 1956: 147); the Hebridean parallels may be due to customs brought into Scotland from Norway in the Viking age. The Norwegian custom of riding round the farms at Yuletide and watering the horses at certain springs which did not freeze may similarly be linked with the Scottish riding festivals at harvest time (Solheim 1956: 152–3).

Such symbolic circling on horses around a farm or village may also be compared with the journey of the goddess through the fields in her wagon (see pp. 57–8). Of particular interest is the reference in *Ynglinga Saga* (29) to the king riding round the hall of the goddesses in pre-Christian Sweden. In Snorri's account, King Athils, who possessed exceptionally fine horses, was at a sacrifice to the *dísir* (goddesses) and rode his horse around their temple, but the horse stumbled, Athils fell, and was killed when his head hit a stone.

In view of the different ways in which a horse can be used as a symbol, Epona may be seen as a many-sided goddess, with strong appeals to both men and women. The goddess associated with the mare could be linked with childbirth and also with the birth of young animals, as well as with the fertility of the land and harvest feasts where the girls provided a feast for the young men. On the male side the horse was a mount for king and heroes, and horse and chariot racing a sport of kings, perhaps a means of choosing a leader. It was also a way of celebrating the funerals of great men, while the goddess on her steed could be seen as a conductor of the dead to the Otherworld. We have a good example here of how the cult of a goddess may appeal to both sexes through the animal with which she is associated, supplying different needs at different times, as Epona did to the cavalrymen fighting in the Roman army.

The close association between the dog and the goddess, particularly throughout the Roman period in Celtic areas, is more difficult to explain convincingly. The Mother Goddesses are continually depicted with dogs at their sides or on their laps, as if these animals were part of the fertility symbolism and a necessary indication of peace and plenty, perhaps because they were needed to protect house and land. Nehalennia, a Germanic goddess worshipped at the point where travellers crossed the North Sea from the Netherlands, is shown on many carved stones holding loaves and apples like a Mother Goddess, sometimes with a prow of a ship beside her (see p. 112), but also frequently with an attendant dog which sits looking up at her (Plate 5). He was on thirteen of the twenty-one altars recorded by Ada Hondius-Crone (1955: 103), who describes him as a kind of greyhound; he has long legs, large ears and a pointed muzzle (M. J. Green 1995: 179). He could perhaps symbolize protection for travellers, who appealed to Nehalennia for a safe voyage.

Plate 5 The goddess Nehalennia on a stone altar from Domberg. She sits on a throne, with her dog on one side and a basket piled with apples on the other, holding a dish of apples and a single fruit. Ht 96.5 cm. Courtesy Rijksmuseum van Oudheden.

Miranda Green (1986: 175) suggests as reasons for the link between dogs and goddesses in the Mediterranean world their importance in hunting, contribution to healing, and association with the Otherworld. Their value to the hunter comes out clearly in the traditions about Artemis, who received her dogs in recognition of her powers over the animal world (see pp. 18–19). Both the Germans and the Celts were enthusiastic hunters, and the Celts were famous for their hunting dogs; various breeds used in Gaul are mentioned by Duval (1952: 252ff.), making use of the vivid descriptions by Arrian in *Cynegetica*, from the second century AD. Mention is made of large, fierce dogs which hunted in packs, following the deer and the boar, whose baying is described as a mournful, lugubrious sound, and also smaller, swift-footed dogs of various colours, used for hunting the hare. Exceptionally powerful hunting dogs from Britain, capable of attacking powerful animals like the wild boar, seem to have resembled wolves.

The Germans similarly depended on hunting dogs, and the tradition of fearsome baying hounds which took part in the Wild Hunt, survived in Germany, Scandinavia and the British Isles up to recent times (Davidson forthcoming). These sinister dogs appear to have been associated with the malicious hosts of the unquiet dead, and at times the soul of the newly dead on its way to the Otherworld was their quarry, while they might also attack the living who were unfortunate enough to encounter them. Although associated with Wodan and his wolves in Germany, as well as with a male Devil-Huntsman in Christian times, the Wild Hunt could also be led by a woman. The Germanic goddesses in particular, such as Percht and Holle, were sometimes said to ride at the head of the menacing host, while the tradition of the hounds of Hekate shows that the concept was an ancient one in the Mediterranean world. Hekate (Distant One?) was a popular goddess of many roles, with a share in earth, sea and the starry heavens, who could give luck in hunting, victory in battle, and help with crops; she was associated with roads and with the kingdom of the dead (Downing 1985). She was surrounded by dogs, and might even bay like a dog or appear with a dog's head (Paulys 1912: 2776ff.); beside food offerings at cross-roads, she received sacrifices of dogs. She roamed over the earth on moonlit nights with her baying hounds, followed by the restless dead. Here we have the goddess associated with a hostile, dangerous animal, in contrast to Nehalennia's faithful hound.

In the Finnish *Kalevala*, in which many of the lays are concerned with hunting, the dog which follows the scent of the wild creatures is represented as under the control of the goddess of the forest. The sinister mistress of Northland gives birth to the hunting dog, and she is addressed in the *Old Kalevala* (VII: 216ff.) as 'Dog Spirit, distinguished woman', and requested to 'take the lock from the dog's mouth, the bolt from the barker's teeth' and 'let the dog just run, the pup go the right way' (Magoun 1969). The hunter here describes his dogs with affectionate pride:

My dog has a tail
like a splendid backwoods fir; my dog has eyes
like a very big bridle ring; my dog has teeth
like an Estonian scythe

(VII: 41ff.)

Although the dogs were treasured possessions of the male hunter, the association with female supernatural beings is evident.

The link between dogs and healing may have been partly due to the fact that the healing powers of a dog's saliva were well known (M. J. Green 1995: 176–7), and also because a small dog, such as those held by some Mother Goddess figures, could be a great comfort to women and children who were ill or cold, bringing warmth and sympathy such as no modern hot-water bottle could provide. Many of the pilgrims visiting the shrines of the goddesses at river sources in hope of healing are depicted carrying a small dog, presumably as a gift to the goddess (see p. 159). This may have been brought as a sacrifice, and there is ample evidence for the offering of dogs at sacred places from the Bronze Age onwards (M. J. Green 1992: 111ff.) Obviously they provided a cheap and convenient form of animal sacrifice, but they must also have been important as a symbol connected with the Otherworld.

Dogs, as we have seen, can be both protective and destructive animals, guarding the house and the herds, and defending the women and children as well as their masters, like the fierce guard-dog of the smith slain by the youthful Cú Chulainn in the *Táin*, which lay on a mound with his head in his paws waiting for intruders, and is described as 'wild, savage and fierce, rough, surly and battlesome' (Book of Leinster, ed. C. O'Rahilly 1967: 161). Dogs could also be fierce attackers in the hunting field, and the faithful hounds of the goddess Artemis destroyed those who angered her. The two strongly opposed sides of a dog's nature reflect the dual nature of the goddess, both protective and destructive in her dealings with humankind. Moreover the dog as guardian of boundaries is a liminal figure, as the goddess often appears to be.

This may help to explain the link between the dog and the Otherworld. It may be a guide on the road or a pursuing fury, and is especially associated with the point of entry, like the Greek Cerberus, the ravening many-headed dog of Pluto described by Hesiod (*Theogony* 312), who guarded the portals of Hades and had to be placated with cakes if a living hero wished to enter. Similarly we find a sinister dog haunting the approach to the realm of the dead in Old Norse mythology. He guards the entry to the underworld, and barks at Odin when the god rides down to find the secrets of the future in the Eddic poem *Baldrs Draumar*. This may be the hound Garm; in the section of the poem *Völuspá* dealing with the breaking loose of the monsters in the final chaos of Ragnarok, there is a threatening refrain:

Garm keeps barking by Gnipa cavern,
the fetter must break and the wolf run free.

Some identify Garm with the wolf bound by Tyr, destined finally to swallow the sun and devour Odin (Nordal 1978: 86), who is mentioned here in the refrain, but Garm is said to bark (*geyja*), which suggests a hound on guard. However, the importance of the wolf in Norse mythology, closely linked with Odin, and so with death and destruction, may have influenced the picture of the sinister dog. The Scandinavian goddesses do not seem to be associated with dogs, large or small. Freyja's chariot was said to be drawn by cats at Balder's funeral (*Gylfaginning* 49), but Snorri may possibly have been influenced here by the lionesses drawing Kybele. However, Ingstad points out that there seem to be cat faces on the wagon from the Oseberg ship, while also mentioning dogs carved on the sledges, perhaps guardians of the world of the dead (Ingstad *et al.* 1992: 248–9). It may also be noted that dogs as well as horses were included among the animals sacrificed at the Oseberg funeral of a great lady, which provides many symbols associated with the cult of a goddess (see pp. 110–12), while they are found also in other important ship-burials. The goddess herself could be represented as a guardian on the road to the realm of death (see pp. 176–7), and her association with the dog may be partly based on this.

It can be seen how the goddess as Mistress of Animals gradually extended her rule, first to the domestic herds, and particularly to those yielding milk, and second to the horse and the dog, animals which bring the hunting and farming worlds together, and were also seen as a link between the familiar world and the realm of the dead. It is a rich field, and the contact between the goddess and the animal world extends into the realm of agriculture, the ploughing and harvesting of crops, as will be seen in the next chapter.

CHAPTER II

MISTRESS OF THE GRAIN

—— •◆• ——

THE ANCIENT WORLD

The association of grain with a goddess could be as old as the first attempts at sowing seed and collecting plants that were useful for food. Much of the pioneer work in growing crops is believed to have been done by women, tending their little plots from a home base while the men were away hunting or fighting. There is a possible parallel among American Indians on the North Pacific coast, where women used digging sticks to replant useful roots and bulbs and move healthy plants into their family plots, marked out by stakes and passed on from mother to daughter (Steensberg 1986: 59–60). On a larger scale, emmer and two-row barley were grown for food in Jericho about 10,000 years ago, while in the period between 8000 and 2000 BC various grains, rice or root vegetables were cultivated not only in the Near East but also in Africa, north China and South-east Asia, Central and South America, and parts of Europe (Bray 1984: 32ff.). There is an obvious resemblance between the birth of a child and the production of grain from seeds placed in the ground, so that one might expect association with a Mother Goddess, and her cult could be strengthened by women coming together to sow seeds and encourage young plants to grow.

Preparation of the grain after harvesting entailed laborious work. Theya Molleson (1994) examined a collection of bones from a Neolithic site in northern Syria at Abu Hureyra, one group dated just before the development of agriculture, about 11,500 to 10,000 years ago, and another about 200 years later, when emmer, einkorn, oats, barley, chick-peas and lentils were cultivated. All these needed much preparation before they were ready for eating; many women's bones from the second group showed signs of considerable physical stress, which Molleson attributes to hours spent daily grinding grain by hand, and perhaps also to the use of a pestle and mortar to remove the outer husk. Seeds did not keep once dehusked, so the work had to be done daily. Many women had collapsed vertebrae of the back and severe arthritis of the big toe, probably caused by frequent use of the saddle quern, a primitive stone millstone along which the kneeling woman pushed a stone over the grain and jerked it back. The coarsely ground grain had also an appalling effect on the teeth. The invention of the sieve, a tremendous step forward, could have been due to the women, since it is an extension of weaving. Later on the watermill came into use and where this was available the work of grinding passed over to the men, although hand-operated mills were still in use in north-western Europe in the Middle Ages (Duby 1968:16).

As early as the sixth millennium BC at Çatal Hüyük in Anatolia the figure of a goddess was placed in a grain bin in one of the shrines of the great temple complex (see pp. 13–14). This goddess, taken to be an early example of the Mother Goddess Kybele, appears to be giving birth (see Plate 1, p. 5), she sits on a chair with her hands on the lions supporting her on either side, and the child's head is seen protruding between her knees (Vermaseren 1977: 16). The grain bins in the temple may have been used to store the seed-corn for the spring or autumn sowing.

As the growing of grain developed throughout the centuries in the Near East and south-eastern Europe, various powerful goddesses became associated with it. In Egypt Isis was said to have taught the people to grow wheat, barley and flax, and to have presided over bread, beer and green fields (Witt 1971: 16–17). The link between bread and beer, both prepared from grain, is emphasized in a hymn to Hathor, another Egyptian goddess, sometimes identified with Isis; she is addressed as 'Mistress of Bread, who made Beer' (see p. 138).

In Greece the chief goddess of grain was Demeter, said to create and preserve plants, to lie with her lover Iasion in the furrow of a thrice-ploughed fallow field (*Odyssey* V: 125), and to have taught the use of the plough to Tryptolemus for the benefit of humankind. The result of her mating with Iasion was the birth of Plutus, whose name indicates wealth, evidently in the form of grain (Ganz 1993: 64). The myth of the search of the sorrowing goddess for her daughter Kore, the Maiden (Persephone), who had been snatched away into the underworld, appears to be a fundamental one, echoes of which can be traced in western Europe. As Burkert puts it:

> Kore is the grain that must go under the earth so that, from this seeming death, the new fruit can appear. Hunger threatens when Kore disappears, but to the delight of gods and men, she returns, and with her the blessing of grain from Demeter.
>
> (Burkert 1983: 260)

The period of four or six months spent in the underworld does not accord with the rapid sprouting of the grain, and M. P. Nilsson therefore identified Persephone with the seed stored in the granary until the next sowing. Since, however, she returned in the spring, when the earth wakes to new life, Nilsson's theory has not met with general acceptance (Burkert 1983: 261).

Brumfield's illuminating study on the festivals of Demeter shows that the most important of these were associated with the sowing of the seed. This was the most critical time for the farmer in the difficult climate of

Greece, and wheat was usually sown in the autumn; water was essential in the early stages of growth if the grain was to ripen before the summer heat. Barley, probably used mainly for porridge and soup, was the favourite crop for poor soil (Brumfield 1981: 15ff.). Seed barley was kept in holy places and mixed with the general supply, a practice continuing in Greece in the 1970s (Brumfield 1981: 61), while water may still be thrown at the farmer as he takes the seed from the bin as a ritual to ensure the coming of rain, accompanied by the wish: 'As the water flows, so may life flow' (Brumfield 1981: 65). It seems that in pre-Christian times an appeal to the sky god Zeus to bring rain to the earth was made together with one to the goddess to produce new life, a widespread concept found far beyond Greece.

The festival of Demeter which took place before ploughing was the Proerosia, where again Zeus was involved as well as the goddess and Kore, and this included public sacrifice and cult activities organized among the women. Another important festival was the Thesmophoria, held in at least thirty cities in Greece, Asia Minor and Sicily. At this certain selected women sacrificed piglets by throwing them into a chasm sacred to the goddess, and brought up the rotting remains some time later to be laid on the altar and mixed with the seed to be sown. Lucan describes this as an offering to Demeter, and mentions also the baking of wheaten cakes in the shapes of snakes and male genitals. References to this festival are somewhat obscure (Brumfield 1981: 70ff.), probably because it was strictly confined to women and our informants are men. Mothers and daughters were said to take part, and it was probably linked with the autumn sowing. The association of pigs, a symbol of fertility, with the fruitfulness of the earth is a feature also characteristic of the goddess in northern Europe (see pp. 63–4). The women danced and feasted, and were also said to jest, blaspheme and use coarse language, because jesting of this kind had cheered Demeter in her mourning for her lost child. It is said that they had to remain chaste for the duration of the festival, while men were sternly excluded.

Again male and female sexual symbols were made in pastry, and indecent jesting and shameful talk, games and mirth were said to form part of the women's celebrations at Haloa in midwinter at Eleusis, together with feasting, with certain foods such as pomegranates forbidden. Much wood was brought, perhaps for bonfires. This may have been linked with the pruning of the vines and viewed as a time when the fields needed to be awakened to new life. Yet another festival called Chloaia (Verdant), one of Demeter's titles, seems to have taken place in early spring when green shoots came up in the fields and brought hopes of a good harvest. At one place a pregnant sow was said to be sacrificed, and at another two piglets, male and female (Brumfield 1981: 135). There is no evidence for a universal harvest festival, probably because the gathering of the harvest varied locally, and each would be celebrated individually, but Demeter has epithets which suggest connection with harvest and threshing (Brumfield

1981: 142ff.). Offerings of first-fruits to the goddess probably went on throughout the year as various crops ripened.

There has been much speculation as to exactly what happened at the Eleusinian Mysteries, which were associated with Demeter's cult. The display of some mysterious holy symbol was apparently linked with the myth of the wandering, rape and mourning of the goddess; there may have been some representation of a divine marriage and birth of a child, while apparently an ear of wheat was displayed at one point (Brumfield 1981: 209ff.). The return of Kore from the underworld may have been part of the Mysteries, and there was a ritual on the final day which included the pouring of water. This took place at least a month before sowing time, but it would have to have been held before the rains began early in November if travellers from a distance were to attend.

As Brumfield argues, it is not unreasonable to expect the cultivation of the land to be associated with human mortality: a message of hope based on new life springing from the apparently dead seed is surely not too sophisticated an image for early peoples to enshrine in myth. It is clear that the Attic festivals, obscure although details may be, re-enacted to some extent the behaviour of Demeter, so that we have fasting, drinking, mourning, bawdy jesting, and the descent of Kore to spend the winter months in the underworld, with emphasis on the flowers which she plucked and the pomegranate which she ate. Here also is a myth symbolizing the loss of a virgin daughter when she becomes a bride, an element also found in northern songs and traditions (see pp. 127–9). The important times of ritual connected with the goddess of grain are immediately before sowing, midwinter, early spring when the young shoots are sprouting, and finally harvest, when reaping and threshing take place, concluding with the storing of the seed.

The worship of Ceres as goddess of grain in Italy goes back to pre-Roman times, and her name is derived from the Indo-European stem *ker-, 'to grow, cause to grow, nourish' (Spaeth 1996: 33). Later her cult was influenced by that of Demeter, and the myth of her lost daughter, Proserpina, introduced. She was worshipped together with Terra Mater, Mother Earth, and was said to have brought in agriculture and established laws for the division of the land into fields. Her association with ships in the first century AD is based on the bringing of grain into Rome by sea (Spaeth 1996: 25, 48).

The detailed study of Ceres by Babette Spaeth (1996) enables us to see possible developments of the goddess of grain. Ceres was linked probably from early times with childbirth and the care of children, strengthened by the influence of Demeter's cult in Rome. She was much associated with liminality, identified with rites of passage, such as birth, marriage, divorce and death, and also with geographical boundaries, such as the division of fields, enclosure of the city, and the gate of the realm of death (see p. 173). Her myth, shared with Demeter, brought in the two primary roles of women in ancient society, the young, inexperienced virgin and the mature, fertile mother (Spaeth 1996: 60). Her rituals and festivals were entirely run by women, but approved of by the Roman establishment. In Republican times she was closely linked with the plebs, perhaps because they were mostly farmers, but later with women members of the imperial family, the mothers of possible future Emperors.

Another goddess with a powerful influence over Roman people was the eastern deity Kybele, the goddess set between the lions, (see p. 53). She was the ancient Mother Goddess who guarded the wild animals, and later became the goddess of farm and granary, and the protectress of cities, known as the Great Mother or Mother of the Gods as well as the Mountain Goddess. At the time of the Punic Wars, when the people were losing confidence in their old gods, the black meteoric stone which represented Kybele was brought from Phrygia by ship in 205 BC. Consultation of the Sibylline books produced a prophecy that Rome would prove victorious if the Mother of Mount Ida came to her, and King Attalus of Pergamum agreed to send the sacred image.

In spite of impressive legends of the goddess insisting on the journey, the decision to obtain the sacred stone seems to have been a deliberate political one (Graillot 1912: 18ff.). Something dramatic was needed to restore confidence, and the cult of the Great Mother was probably already flourishing in Rome. When Kybele's ship arrived, the young aristocrat P. Cornelius Scipio Nasica was chosen as the noblest man in Rome to receive her, accompanied by Claudia, the sister of Appius Claudius, as the most virtuous matron. More legends were later recounted of how Claudia was able to refloat the vessel of Kybele when it ran aground at Capena, proving that she was indeed a woman of unblemished virtue (Graillot 1912: 55ff.). The sacred black stone was bathed in the river Almo, and then housed in the temple of Victory until Kybele was given her own temple on the Palatine. Her sacred stone was covered in silver with a space left where the face would be. There was a splendid harvest after Kybele's arrival, and before long Hannibal departed from Italy, so that she was hailed as a powerful deity who brought benefits to Rome.

Her priests were mainly Phrygians, who had to castrate themselves in a primitive and savage ritual in imitation of the self-mutilation and death of her lover Attis under a pine tree, as recorded in various legends. There was some disapproval in Rome of this aspect of her cult, but in the Antonine period Attis developed into a kind of solar deity who went down into the underworld and emerged again to new life. The priests of the goddess were known as Galli; they wore their hair long, had elaborate robes resembling women's garments, and covered their faces in make-up. They lived a life of devotion to the goddess, often leading a nomadic existence in the countryside, singing, dancing, flagellating themselves, and begging on her behalf, while in addition they did works of healing, prophesied and interpreted dreams. There were also priestesses, who may originally have been freed slave women, who presumably organized the women's cults; they carried the sacred vessels in processions, and played tambourines and cymbals. Undoubtedly many rich and influential women supported the goddess, from the evidence of inscriptions on altars recording sacrifices in her honour.

The death of Attis was celebrated in various festivals in March, and there were passion plays about him, ending in a nine-day fast. On 22 March a pine tree representing the dead Attis was brought in decorated with ribbons and violets, and this was burned and then buried. There may have been a representation of a divine marriage, with Attis returning from the underworld, or a descent into the land of death, but the exact nature of the rites is uncertain. They ended with the bathing of the image of the goddess in the river Almo on 27 March, said to represent the rain causing the crops to grow. There was also a triumphant procession of the goddess through the city on 10 April, when a heifer was sacrificed and there was a special meal of white cheese and herbs, said to be the food of the people before grain was grown, to stress the ancient nature of Kybele.

Her cult prospered in Rome up to the fourth century AD, and was taken into Gaul and Germany. Like Demeter and Isis she was hailed as the bringer of agriculture to humankind, and was often depicted as *spicifera*, the bearer of grain, and shown holding ears of corn. Her cult appealed strongly to all classes of the people, and was supported by several Emperors, in spite of doubts about the worship of Attis. Kybele was a goddess who aroused particular condemnation from Christian writers, and certain parallels between her March celebrations and the Christian Easter must have been offensive to the Church.

The spread of her cult northwards with the Roman conquest of Gaul and Germany may have caused confusion in accounts of rites of the northern goddesses. For instance the cult of Nerthus in Denmark, as described by Tacitus in *Germania* (40) in the first century AD, bears some resemblance to what we know of Kybele's worship (H. M. Chadwick 1924: 221), since it included the perambulation of the countryside and the bathing of the wagon and even the goddess herself at the end of her tour of the farms. There are occasional references to ceremonies perhaps conducted by the priests of Kybele; Pope Gregory in *Liber in Gloria Confessorum* (77) describes how the Great Mother was taken round the fields and vineyards to bring them prosperity, and how Bishop Simplicius in the late fourth century saw people singing and dancing before her idol. When he made the sign of the cross the statue fell, the oxen stood still, and many were converted. Berger (1988) has claimed convincingly that one widespread legend of the Virgin in northern Europe was based on memories of the goddess of the grain. The Virgin on her way to Egypt with the Christ Child was fleeing from King Herod's soldiers through a field where seed was being sown. She caused it to sprout immediately into standing corn, so that her pursuers could be told truthfully that no woman had passed that way since the sowing of the crop. The popularity of this legend, sometimes told of various women saints, and its frequent appearance in works of art in north-western Europe, shows how the power of the Virgin or woman saint to ripen the grain was a familiar concept.

It may be difficult to distinguish between memories of Kybele's cult in the Roman period in Gaul and those of the Celtic goddesses of fertility; two separate traditions of a Mother Goddess of the grain are likely to have met and mingled in the Roman provinces. In the ancient world the idea of grain and the knowledge of how to cultivate it were seen as a gift of a beneficent goddess, but for this gift a price had to be paid. With Demeter and Ceres we have the myth of the lost daughter, never fully restored to her mother, but spending a season in the underworld in the grip of death. The concept of a forlorn goddess wandering far in search of a lost one is found in the search of Isis for Osiris as well as that of Demeter for Kore. In every case the absence of the goddess brings sterility and death to the people, as harvest is denied to them. Such myths, as Burkert has pointed out, are not simple allegories based on the sowing of the seeds and the growth and reaping of the grain; rather we have the idea of a necessary sacrifice, as life is given in exchange for a wonderful gift (Burkert 1983: 260ff.), two frequent animal victims being the bull and the pig. We have also the concept of the maiden who is taken away from her mother to become a bride, and of the birth of a child associated in some way with the grain.

The help of the goddess in the sowing of the seed is particularly stressed, and she is also called upon to assist in the sprouting of the grain and the gathering of the harvest, while there is an additional call on the god of the sky to send rain; this may be associated with a myth of marriage between the deities of earth and heaven. While the note of mourning is present in the rites of the goddess associated with fruitful earth, there is also robust humour, and light-hearted emphasis on various symbols of sexuality. The myths are not merely simplistic pictures of the dead seed restored to new life as the grain grows to swift maturity and is cut down, but include the hopes and fears associated with the main rites of passage – birth, marriage, and death, the mating of men and women, the bearing and losing of children, and the necessity of sacrifice if the life of the community is to continue. All this needs to be borne in mind, when considering the concept of the goddess of the grain in northern Europe.

THE GODDESS AND THE PLOUGH

The digging implement pulled by a rope which preceded the plough proper is generally known as the ard; this came into use in the fourth or third millennium BC in Egypt, Assyria, India, China and many parts of Europe, including the British Isles. Instead of an asymmetrical share, the ard had a spike that cut a shallow furrow when pulled along; this was tipped with stone or bone before metal was available, and later fitted with a metal cap. It was probably designed to be drawn by oxen or cows, since first used about the time of the domestication of farm animals, although a man or woman could draw it; even in the 1990s a woman may be seen pulling an ard driven by her husband on some poor holding in China or Pakistan. Various types of ard are known, and have been given names such as the bow, crook or spade ard; early examples have been found in bogs, like one from Horslev in Denmark dated about 1500 BC, or shown in rock carvings. In northern Europe the ard continued into the Middle Ages, and is still in use in remote places.

Although it did not turn the earth over and was of little use on heavier soils, the ard could be employed together with a spade, and was convenient for light soils or small mountain fields. Indeed Reynolds in his experiments in Iron Age agriculture found it could be effective even on clay or loam, and was 'a complex and efficient tool' (Reynolds 1979: 51). Its advantages were that it was light and easy to draw, and could quickly be put together and repaired. Examination of marks made in and below the plough-soil indicate that in northern Europe the use of the ard goes back to the third millennium in the late Neolithic period (Fowler 1983: 171).

There are representations of a man ploughing with an ard among carvings of the Bronze Age in Sweden (1600–500 BC). Gelling has pointed out two examples from Finntorp, Tanum, in Bohuslän (Gelling and Davidson 1967: 80); there are suggestions of a religious ceremony in the great sun-disk and two small figures with arms raised beside one of the ards. A third Bronze Age carving at Litsleby in Bohuslän (Figure 10) shows what Glob describes as a crook ard, probably made from a forked bough (Glob 1951: 25ff.). A naked male with a large phallus holds the handle, and in his other hand has a branch or small tree. The ard is drawn by two oxen harnessed to a neck-yoke, and two furrows seem to be marked out, so that the plough-man may be cutting a third. He has a round object which Glob thought might be phallic, but could simply be a seed-bag (Reynolds 1979: 17).

In some areas of the world the cutting of three furrows was a rite marking the beginning of spring. In China the Emperor ploughed three furrows in the royal field, and his chief ministers then worked the plough in turn, and similar rites were practised in India and Ceylon (Armstrong 1943: 251ff.; Bray 1984: 1). Almgren (1927: 301) refers to the ploughing of three furrows in Sweden on the first day of spring in the early twentieth century. He describes how the sods had to be turned up in the direction of the sun, and some of the earth rubbed on the forelocks of the horses, while the ploughman was given bread which had been baked at Yule and stored in the corn-bin. A branch from a fruit-bearing tree was carried by the

Figure 10 Bronze Age rock carving from Litsleby, Bohuslän, representing ploughman with oxen. After P. Gelling (1969). Lelly Aldworth.

ploughman, or fixed in the horses' reins; this custom was known in Småland and Scania up to 1921. This makes it probable that the branch carried in the Bronze Age carving was part of a ritual ploughing rite and not merely to keep off the flies.

There is also evidence for the ritual burial of ards in the British Isles, and they were deposited in peat bogs in Denmark and north Germany (Glob 1951: 42). In 1994 a perfectly preserved ard was recovered from a ditch forming part of a henge monument near Dumfries, which has been dated to the third millennium BC (*The Times* 5 September 1994), while other later examples have come from Scotland and from Irish bogs (Rees 1979: 42). Some of the continental examples were judged unsuitable for use, while others were worn out (Glob 1951: 131ff.). Of particular interest is a find from Vindumhede in Denmark, where hair plaits have been found beside an ard, suggesting a link with a women's cult (Glob 1951: 105). There are two examples of plough finds from a later period mentioned by Struve; in one from Sjaelland an incomplete plough was buried with parts of wagons and bones of cattle, sheep and pigs; in the second, from north Germany, the plough was accompanied by human skulls and animal bones (Struve 1967: 57, 59). The suggestion has been made that an ard and the man using it were buried in one of a series of unfurnished graves at Sutton Hoo in Suffolk, dated to the seventh or eighth century AD, but the evidence for human sacrifice is not conclusive here (Davidson 1992: 332, 339).

In the Celtic and Roman Iron Age in northern Europe the ard was replaced on progressive farms by the plough, a larger, more effective implement with an asymmetrical share and mouldboard, which turned the earth over, although the ard remained widely in use (Duby 1968: 18). The heavier plough might be fitted with a wheel carriage to enable it to be turned round without tipping over (Figure 11). It needed powerful animals to draw it, and was more difficult to assemble and keep in good repair (Steensberg 1986: 143ff.). Oxen continued to be used, as they were slow and strong, and would stop if the share encountered an obstacle, although Reynolds discovered that males were difficult to train, and preferred the more tractable cows (Reynolds 1979: 50).

The ritual use of the plough continued to mark the beginning of spring, the season of growth, up to the twentieth century. Although it was usually men who worked the plough, and no women are shown with it in the Scandinavian Bronze Age rock engravings, the sowing of the seed was associated with the goddess of grain, as in Ancient Greece. This is brought out clearly in one surviving Anglo-Saxon charm, an isolated piece of evidence for a pre-Christian goddess in England (Grendan 1909: 105–237). The spell, a mixture of prose directions and alliterative verse, has a number of Christian rites included in it, such as the saying of 'Our Father' and the insertion into the holes from which turves were taken of four little wooden crosses on which the names of the evangelists were written. The four pieces of turf were placed before the altar with the earthy side turned towards it, just as the earth turned up in the spring plough ceremony described by Almgren (1927) had to face the sun, and four masses were to be sung over them. But the lines spoken when these turves were replaced on the four sides of the land, suggest an older ritual. After bowing humbly nine times, the farmer uttered the following prayer:

> I stand facing east, I pray for favour,
> I pray to the great and mighty Lord,
> I pray to the holy guardian of the heavenly realm,
> I pray to earth and high heaven
> and to the true Saint Mary

and then follows a plea for 'harvests for earthly need', some Christian prayers and canticles, and the blessing of the seed, which had to be obtained from a beggar, given twice as much in exchange. The ploughing implements were collected, and incense, fennel, consecrated soap and salt placed on the wooden beam of the plough with the seed. Next came a fresh appeal:

> Erce, Erce, Erce, Mother of Earth,
> May the almighty, eternal Lord grant to you
> fields growing and flourishing,
> increasing, gaining strength,
> bright harvests of shafts of millet,
> broad harvests of barley,
> shining crops of wheat,
> and all the harvests of earth

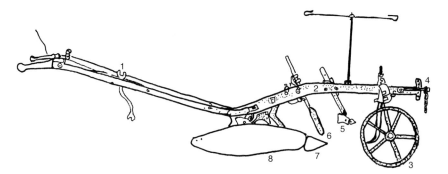

Figure 11 Diagram of plough, showing: (1) guiding handles; (2) beam; (3) wheels; (4) hake, connecting to chains for horses; (5 and 6) coulters, to cut into earth to separate furrow slice; (7) share; (8) mouldboard to turn slice over. Eileen Aldworth.

After a prayer to God and the saints that the fields be protected from witchcraft, the first furrow was cut with the plough, with a further incantation:

> Wholeness to you, earth, mother of men,
> that you may have increase, in god's embrace,
> and be filled with food for the use of men.

Then a loaf 'as broad as a man's palm' was baked from every kind of grain grown on the land, kneaded with milk and holy water, and laid beneath the first furrow. The ritual ends with an appeal to 'the God who created these fields' that every seed might sprout.

Although the spell is given the title 'for bewitched land', its purpose appears to be to ensure good luck at sowing time, resulting in a rich harvest not just for one unprofitable field but for the land as a whole. There has been much discussion as to whether the reference to Erce is a call to an earth goddess, but few have been willing to accept this; if it were really the name or title of a pagan deity, it would be surprising to find it in a spell which has clearly been subject to much Christianization. It might be an example of gibberish, as Grendan (1909: 155, 220) suggested, or perhaps a cry of acclamation. From references to Earth (*folde*), Mother of men, and to Earth bringing forth in god's embrace, together with appeals to St Mary and the god of high heaven, it seems probable that this was originally addressed to a goddess who caused the grain to sprout and grow, with a call to the sky god to send the necessary rain, as in the cult of Demeter (see p. 4).

The idea of the Virgin Mary assisting in the sowing of the seed survived in Carpathia and other areas of Russia up to the nineteenth century. Ralston (1872: 193) gives the following song among those sung at Christmastide:

Afield, afield, out in the open field.
There a golden plough goes ploughing,
And behind that plough is the Lord Himself,
The holy Peter helps him to drive,
And the Mother of God carries the seed-corn,
Carries the seed corn, prays to the Lord God:
'Make, O Lord, the strong wheat to grow,
The strong wheat and the vigorous corn.
The stalks there shall be like reeds.
The ears shall be as blades of grass.
The sheaves shall be like the stars.
The stacks shall be like hills.
The loads shall be gathered together like black clouds.'

Similar examples have been recorded more recently from Ossetia, as in a song from Digoron in western Ossetia, collected by M. Gardanov and published in 1927. Here Elijah, St Nicholas and St George may have replaced earlier pre-Christian deities, while Mary as in the Russian song is the bearer of the seed:

Mother Mary was the bearer of the seed,
while Divine Elijah of the Grain was the sower of the seed.
They made long furrows, broad tilled fields,
How the grain grew for them that year.
The quail danced beneath it;
The cart rolled over it;
This year in our tilled fields that grain will grow.
                    (Gardanov 1927, translated by A. Chaudhri)

Jacob Grimm found German parallels to the loaf to be baked and laid beside the furrow in the Anglo-Saxon charm; there are early references to a loaf as big as the plough-wheel, which might be fastened to the axle while the ploughman drove the plough, moving gently enough 'for a finch to feed her young on the wheel'. This should be made from all the different types of grain grown on the farm (Grimm 1883: III, 1239). Similarly in the Anglo-Saxon spell the turves from the field laid before the altar were to be anointed with oil, honey, yeast and milk from every cow on the land, while samples of wood from every tree and bush growing there (except hardwood trees such as beech and oak), and pieces of every herb (except burdock), were to be laid on the turves. There is a further parallel in the special cake baked at harvest time in the Hebrides from the different grains grown on the farm as well as samples of meal (Solheim, 1956: 91).

In a passage quoted by Grimm (1883: III, 1,240) from an early Latin commentary by Verelius on *Hervarar Saga*, some of the flesh of the Yule boar in Sweden is said to be dried and kept till spring, to be grated in with the seed-corn, while part is given to the plough-horses and part to the ploughmen. Again in Scania a salted pig's head with trotters and tail were kept from the Yule feast, laid on a flat loaf, and shared between the ploughman and his horses at the first spring ploughing (Nilsson 1938: 44). There is a resemblance here to the Greek custom of adding the rotted remains of the piglets sacrificed to Demeter to the seed used for sowing (see p. 54). The boar was associated with the goddess Freyja, and the link with loaf and plough is in keeping with traditions of a goddess of the grain. It has been generally assumed that the choice of the pig as a symbol of the fertility goddess was due to its capacity for breeding, but it is worth noting that Peter Reynolds, in his study of Iron Age agriculture, refers to the pig as 'a potential plough' (Reynolds 1979: 53). The point had been made much earlier by Swift in Book III of *Gulliver's Travels*, although the impractical scientists of Laputa found the use of pigs to replace ploughs too difficult to organize. Wild pigs have very long snouts, and their capacity to turn over the soil when searching for acorns might at least partly account for the association with the goddess of grain both in Greece and northern Europe.

A further ritual use of the plough was that of the marking of a boundary, to protect the area which the plough encircled. In the British Museum there is a tiny bronze figure of a ploughman with his ard and team (Rees 1979: 61ff.), described by Manning (1971) as skilful and detailed work, which was found on the site of a third-century Roman fort at Piercebridge and dated to the second or third century AD. A bronze figure of this kind is likely to have had votive significance; it has been claimed to represent a ritual ploughing, since a cow and bull are yoked to the plough contrary to normal practice. Plutarch in his *Life of Romulus* describes such a ritual used by Romulus when building the walls of Rome. Having marked out the circular line of the walls from the centre of the city, he fitted a brazen ploughshare to his plough, and yoked a bull and cow together to draw it, while those who followed him turned all the clods raised by the plough inwards towards the centre. The walls were built inside the circular furrow cut by the plough, and where a gate was to be made, the plough was lifted over the gap; Plutarch states that the whole wall, apart from the gates, was regarded as sacred. In a further passage taken from Cato, the founder of the city is said to have yoked the bull to the right and the cow to the left, covering their heads with part of a toga (Manning 1971: 134).

As in the case of the spring ploughing of the first furrow, this is a ceremony for men, and proper for the founder or ruler to perform. In Ancient Greece, as Brumfield pointed out, ploughing was linked with male heroes (Brumfield 1981: 169), although it was Demeter and later Ceres who taught it to Triptolemus. However, there are also instances of ritual ploughing of a circular boundary done by women. The most striking example of this from early Norse literature is the ploughing of the Danish goddess Gefion, as told by Snorri Sturluson in two different accounts (*Gylfaginning* 1 in the *Prose Edda* and *Ynglinga Saga* 5), in both of which he quotes as his source a verse composed by the Norwegian court poet Bragi the Old, dated to the ninth century (Turville-Petre 1976: xxiff.). Some scholars have assumed that this came from Bragi's poem *Ragnarsdrápa*, some fragments of which survive, describing pictures on a shield, but this is by no means certain; another possibility is that it is an answer to a riddling question, a type of verse used by poets as an aid in remembering myths (M. C. Ross 1978: 157). A possible translation of Bragi's verse runs as follows:

> Gefion, rejoicing, dragged a deep circle of land, Denmark's increase, away from Gylfi, so that steam rose from the swift-pulling beasts. The oxen with their four heads and eight brow-ornaments (horns?) went forward hauling the plundered island of meadows.
>
> (Davidson 1998)

There are various problems over the exact translation of some of the phrases in the two versions of the poem, discussed in detail by Holtsmark (1944) and M. C. Ross (1978), but the description supports Snorri's account: the goddess Gefion uses four oxen to drag away a fertile piece of land near Uppsala to form the fertile island of Sjaelland. According to Snorri, Gefion was sent north by Odin to King Gylfi in Sweden, who agreed to give her as much land as she could plough with four oxen in a day and a night. She had mated with a giant and borne him four sons, and these she turned into mighty oxen, with which she ploughed out a piece of land where Lake Mälar is now. The oxen pulled the land down the Baltic to Denmark, and Gefion named it Sjaelland and dwelt there with her husband Skjold, founder of the Danish dynasty. As Axel Olrik (1901) pointed out long ago, we know very little of Gefion, and it is possible that she can be identified with Frigg or Freyja, her name being one of those describing the goddess as a giver. Snorri associates her with the land of the dead, stating that unmarried women serve her there (*Gylfaginning* 35); in *Lokasenna* Loki claims that she was given a jewel by a lover, traditions that would fit in very well with what we know of Freyja.

Tales of a gift of as much land as can be walked or ridden round in a limited time are widespread, but instances stipulating ploughing are rarer; Olrik quotes six from Jutland and one from Germany. He thought that the myth as presented in the poem originated in Sjaelland, and was based on a Jutland plough legend; the good farming land on Sjaelland may have inspired the idea that the island had been brought from elsewhere, and the narrow Oresund between Sjaelland and Sweden might have suggested a furrow cut by a giant plough. The route taken from Lake Mälar to Roskilde was one much used by merchant ships in the Viking Age.

There is a possible parallel in an Irish legend concerning the Hag of Dingle, who decided to let her sister, the Hag of Beare, have some extra land. She put a straw rope round an island and dragged it southwards, but the rope broke, and the original island split to form the two smaller islands of Scariff and Deenish (Ó hÓgáin 1990: 67). Here too the piece of land moved was a fertile one.

Gylfi is a mysterious Swedish king used by Snorri as the ingenuous questioner who seeks information about the gods in the first section of the *Prose Edda*. Early Icelandic poets called the sea 'Gylfi's Way' and a ship his horse or his reindeer, and thought of him as a sea-king. He may earlier have been a mythical ruler of the sea, and Olrik suggested that the Gefion myth might reflect rivalry between Viking seamen and the farmers of fruitful Sjaelland. The emphasis in the poem on the number of oxen has puzzled commentators, but one possibility is that heavy wheeled ploughs needing four oxen to draw them would have been unfamiliar to a Norwegian poet like Bragi, although in use in Denmark (Holtsmark 1944: 175).

Gefion is not the only female supernatural figure in the North to drive a plough. In Germany, Austria and Switzerland there is much folklore about various female supernatural beings who helped women at their spinning and assisted young wives, while severely punishing those who were slovenly and did not respect certain rules (see pp. 104–5). While a great deal of the folklore about them is associated with the spinning rooms, it is clear that they also had connections with the world of nature and with agriculture and fertility. Grimm in his *Teutonic Mythology* recorded a number of traditions concerning Holda and Holle from western and central Germany, and Berchta from Upper Germany, Switzerland and Austria, suggesting that these might be memories of earlier goddesses (Grimm 1883: I, 265ff.). In 1913 Waschnitius made a remarkable collection of many such legends and beliefs from different areas, revealing the richness of the material available about these female beings, who were both benevolent and threatening, and played an important part in women's lives (Davidson 1993: 115). They were said to travel in wagons or with ploughs, making journeys to bless the land; Holda for instance was said to go round each year and bring fruitfulness to the fields (Waschnitius 1913: 89). The supernatural being occasionally needed help in getting her plough over a river, and if someone assisted her, she might offer him chips of wood which would turn into gold if he were wise enough to accept them (Grimm 1883: 279).

There are indications of the plough associated not only with the Germanic goddesses but also with the Celtic ones. The fairy wife who came out of the lake in the popular tale from Llyn y Fan Fach in Carmarthenshire in Wales (Wood 1992) brought with her a wonderful herd of cows (see p. 31). When her husband broke the contract made at their marriage, she returned to the lake and summoned her cattle to follow her, calling various animals by name. In the version quoted by Sir John Rhys, she also summoned four grey oxen who were ploughing in a field six miles away. They came to the lake, dragging the plough with them, and this left a well-marked furrow on the land which at the beginning of the twentieth century was said to be still visible. An old woman in 1881 claimed to remember crowds gathering at the lake on the first Sunday in August, hoping to see the water boil up as a sign that the Lady and her oxen would appear (Rhys 1901: I, 10). There was also an Irish tradition recorded in the *Lebor Gabala* of two oxen possessed by the goddess Brigid (see pp. 35–6). A pair of oxen suggests that she too practised ploughing, and seed-corn was certainly associated with St Brigid. It might be wrapped in a cloth or put into a reed basket and hung up beside St Brigid's cross until the time for sowing, when it was added to the rest of the seed. Sometimes the grain from the sheaf which provided the straw for Brigid's crosses was also used in this way (Danaher 1972: 35), while in parts of Ireland people made an effort to start ploughing on St Brigid's Day (Ó Catháin 1995: 4).

There were also various ceremonies from eastern Europe in which women made ritual use of the plough. Ploughing round a village was used as a means to protect a community from epidemics or cattle plagues, and Ralston (1872: 396) gives a detailed account of this in Russia in the nineteenth century. The women came together dressed in white shifts, with loosened hair, and the oldest among them was yoked to a plough, which was drawn three times round the village while the rest followed, making sure that the cattle were safely inside the circle. They sang special songs, some of which Ralston judged unfit to repeat, offering a parallel with behaviour at some of Demeter's festivals (see p. 54). Another protective ploughing ceremony took place at midnight, when the plough was dragged by girls wearing white shifts and with their hair loose, and one carrying an ikon. Bonfires were set alight, and a black cock thrown into the fire by a woman from a second band, wearing black petticoats, after which the women dragged the plough three times round their village. Sometimes there was banging and striking of iron implements together, in order to drive away the evil influence of the plague (Ralston 1872: 396ff.).

The importance of the Plough Monday ceremonies in eastern England was emphasized by Olrik (1901) in his article on the ploughing goddess Gefion, and he pointed out resemblances to the taking round of the plough in parts of Denmark in the nineteenth century. Such ceremonies were usually held around the New Year, before the spring sowing, although a possible alternative was at Shrovetide. At Als in Denmark the plough was taken from farm to farm; there were songs and dancing in which girls took part. The driver of the plough was dressed as a priest and gave a mock sermon, and gifts were collected before leaving for the next stage of the journey (Olrik 1901: 15). The custom of ploughing up the doorposts of those who would not give anything to the ploughboys was practised in Denmark in the late eighteenth century at Shrovetide. This was well known in East Anglia also, and the belief of the plough-gangs there that they had the right to plough up the lawns or doorsteps of any household which did not contribute, and that no law in the world could touch them continued well into the twentieth century (Brockbank 1983: 186).

In the nineteeth century the Plough Festival held on the first Monday after the twelve days of Christmas offered a way for the poorly paid ploughmen to earn a little money for themselves, and frequent changes in the Plough Monday celebrations in the past hundred years show how unwise it would be to assume continuity with pre-Christian beliefs many centuries ago. Even so, the taking round of the plough and its storage in the church, a ceremony revived in the second half of the twentieth century in some Cambridgeshire villages with great success, may be fairly regarded as a resumption of a very ancient custom. Olrik was particularly interested in the young men in white shirts, sometimes carrying ears of corn, known as 'Plough Bullocks', or alternatively as Stots, Jacks or Jags (Hole 1978: 238), and also in a fantastic 'female' figure, a man dressed as a woman, known as the Old Bessy. This old crone, depicted in various ways but usually terrifying or comic, appeared with a man in a calf's skin, or with the Fool, and might ride on the plough itself (Berger 1988: 80). These perambulations of the plough with a woman in charge, who may originally have been a figure from the supernatural world like the German Holda and Perht, suggested to Olrik that Danish customs could have been brought into the Danelaw in the ninth century.

Fragmentary though the evidence may be, there seems no doubt that a goddess figure has been associated with the plough and with the sowing of the seed in spring in northern Europe. Berger has given convincing evidence for the continuation of such a concept in Christian times, with the goddess replaced by the Virgin Mary or some early women saints. The plough remained to some extent the symbol of a female being who could grant fertility; Grimm saw silver ploughs in country churches in Germany in the nineteenth century along with silver ships, another symbol of the fertility goddess. Now that horse-drawn ploughs have been replaced by powerful tractors to turn the earth over, the plough has become the symbol of the old farming way of life, but it remains a symbol also of the renewal of life in the spring and the hope of a rich harvest to come.

GODDESS OR CORN SPIRIT?

In the early twentieth century the myth of Demeter and Persephone was viewed as a simple widespread allegory based on the destruction of corn at harvest time and its rebirth when the new crop grew up in spring. Mannhardt was the first outstanding scholar to fit evidence from British folk traditions and customs into this pattern, along with much material from Germany and surrounding countries, and basing it on a belief in the animated spirit of the corn. Frazer took up this concept with enthusiasm, and in Book V of *The Golden Bough* (1912) he has collected many accounts of harvest customs to confirm Mannhardt's theory.

Such a concept, however, has flaws from the classicist's viewpoint (Richardson 1979: 13ff.). Kore, the lost daughter, the Maiden taken down to the underworld while her mother is left to grieve, represents the spirit of youth as well as growth of corn and plants. There is a distinction between Kore with her Greek name, the close companion of Demeter, and Persephone, whose name is not Greek in origin, and who is queen of the underworld. We no longer feel with Frazer that a simplistic concept of the grain cut down and renewed next spring must have developed automatically into an exalted religious belief in rebirth after death, as the pattern of the grain was interpreted by priests. Further study of the beliefs of so-called 'primitive' peoples has shown that the growth of religion and myth is far more complex and variable. The myth of Persephone has other possibilities beside the 'death' of the grain: Burkert (1983) emphasized sacrifice in return for fruits (see p. 58), while Richardson (1979) pointed out that Demeter is Mother of All, not merely a corn deity, and that she and Kore appear at times as a pair of protective goddesses. Had the Eleusian Mysteries been simply inspired by the growth of grain, it would be hard to account for the significance given to them.

Much of Frazer's evidence is taken from north-western Europe, and it is therefore worth while to examine it in some detail for traces of earlier beliefs in a goddess of grain. His strength depended on his ability to recognize recurring patterns, and the northern harvest customs clearly had some elements in common with Greek traditions about Demeter. What Frazer ignored, however, is the rich complexity of the traditions behind the harvest customs which he laboriously collected from books. He was also unaware of how frequently popular customs change in any given locality, sometimes through alterations in social conditions, and sometimes as the result of a few individuals deliberately reviving old rituals, or giving them a new form. This is evident in work done on popular customs since Frazer's time; however, he has left us a valuable collection of material which deserves fresh consideration.

Mannhardt singles out two possible fates for the Corn Spirit: either it is killed by the reapers, or it lives on in the farmhouse until spring, when it is transferred to the new seed by some symbolic rite (Mannhardt 1884: 29ff.). When the growing corn waves in the wind, a shiver appears to run through it; and this was often described as something running through the field. It might be thought of as a goose, quail, cock, fox, wolf, hare, cow, ox, bull, goat, pig, horse, dog or cat (Frazer 1912: 270ff.) and names such as Oats-Goat or Rye-Wolf were given to the imaginary creatures. Many of Frazer's examples come from Germany and other European countries, and are taken from Mannhardt, but he adds material from the British Isles.

This creature supposed to run through the field when the corn moves in the wind may also be identified with the last sheaf cut at harvest time; sometimes this was made into a rough model of the animal. For instance in Galloway the last bunch of corn was formed into a hare shape with knotted ears, and reapers threw their sickles at it until it was severed below the knot. It might then be taken home and kept until the next harvest (Frazer 1912: 279). Charlotte Burne gives an account of 'Cutting the Gander's Neck' in Shropshire, which went on until about 1856 (Burne 1883: 371). About twenty ears of corn were left standing and knotted in midfield, and the men threw sickles at this until one of them severed it. He was hailed as the winner and carried the sheaf home to the farmer's wife who kept it until the next harvest. The throwing of sickles at the last sheaf may be called 'Cutting the Neck' rather than identified with a particular animal or bird. Charlotte Burne refers to Mrs Bray's account of such a practice in Cornwall, where the corn was tied up with flowers, and the reapers held aloft their sickles and shouted:

> Arnack! Arnack! Arnack!
> We haven, we haven, we haven.
> (Burne 1883: 372)

The reapers then went home with the women and children, shouting and singing. The cry of 'Arnack' here must, as Charlotte Burne realized, be 'A neck'. The custom to 'holla the neck' is referred to in Wright's (1900) *English Dialect Dictionary* (Neck).

There is no doubt that actual killing sometimes took place at the end of harvest and Mannhardt has given many examples. At Gayenne in France a wether was decorated, called 'Wolf of the Field', and then killed in the field itself (Frazer 1912: 275), while Mannhardt has examples of a bull, cow or calf being treated in the same way, part of the meat being sometimes kept to be added to the seed in the spring sowing (Mannhardt 1884: 58ff.). He has one gruesome account from near Grenoble of a goat decorated with flowers and ribbons chased over the field, and finally given to the farmer's wife, who held it while the farmer cut off its head. The meat was used for the harvest supper, but part was pickled and kept till the next harvest, while the skin was made into a cloak for the farmer to wear at harvest time if the weather was bad (Mannhardt 1905: 166). In France and Germany a cat might be decorated with ribbons or ears of corn and killed (perhaps put in the last bundle to be threshed) and then roasted and eaten. In Austria and north Germany a cock might be put in the last sheaf and kept by anyone who could catch it, or it might be killed and eaten at the harvest supper (Frazer 1912: 276ff.). Substitutes for a real creature are also noted: the cutter of the last sheaf might crow in triumph and be called 'The Cock', or a cock might be made of corn, or painted on a board and carried in front of the harvest wagon.

It must be remembered that killing continued in the harvest field even when mechanical harvesters had taken over. Small animals such as rabbits were driven into the last section of the field to be reaped, and then shot or killed with sticks by the men and boys. In such customs identification of the slain animal with a corn spirit seems unconvincing; the interpretation of sacrifice surely fits better, that of a life being given in exchange for the gift of harvest. As for the spirit running through the corn, this is often said to be something told to children ('Don't play in the corn or the Corn Wolf will get you') and was an excellent way of warning them to keep out of the growing crop.

A further example of the concept of sacrifice is the attack sometimes made on a stranger or on the owner of the land, should he enter the field. Mannhardt found examples of intruders bound with corn ropes, wrapped in a sheaf, having hay thrown on their feet, being bitten, or tossed up in the air. Usually the stranger could ransom himself by a gift to the reapers, or the farmer by a promise of drinks for the workers. Reapers in Germany might whet their scythes after tying up the farmer and threaten to use them if he did not stand them beer and brandy, while in Sweden a threshing flail might be put round the stranger's neck and a straw rope round his body (Mannhardt 1884: 32ff.). It appears that it was often the women who made threats and carried out such attacks (Mannhardt 1884: 35).

Linked with what seems to be the concept of a necessary sacrifice, although acted out in jest, is the strong evidence for rivalry among local reapers, threshers and binders, who were forced to work so hard to get in the harvest. Not only was there individual competition among the reapers to cut the last sheaf, or sometimes to avoid cutting it, but also there was the race to get it to the farmhouse or pass it on to another farm, against considerable odds. In Wales the man who cut the last sheaf got a jug of ale, and then might try to throw the sheaf on to another field where men were still reaping, to show that his team had outdone them, or he would carry it to the farmhouse and try to get inside without being drenched with water by the women on the watch for him (Frazer 1912: 144). In Pembrokeshire the successful reaper had to try to get the sheaf there dry, and then hang it from a beam or put it on the kitchen table; if he managed this, he was entitled to unlimited beer and perhaps a shilling as a prize, as well as a place of honour at the harvest supper (Owen 1974: 117). As a penalty for failure he might be shut up in a dark room or the barn and forced to clean all the dirty boots in the house, or beaten on the soles of his feet (Frazer 1912: 267).

Another kind of rivalry is shown in the custom of 'Crying the Mare', which, as Charlotte Burne with her usual astuteness points out, was distinct from 'Cutting the Neck'. This little ritual was performed by the team which was the first to finish reaping. They had the right to send the 'mare' to another farm, and so it went on until the last party of reapers to complete their work had to keep the mare through the winter. According to Charlotte Burne, an actual horse might be used in Shropshire instead of the last sheaf, and at Longmor this was the leading horse of the ploughing team. The horse was adorned with ribbons and led round the farm, and the following dialogue took place:

> I have her.
> What?
> A mare.
> Whose?
> Master A's.
> Where shall we send her?
> To Master B's.
> Who'll ride her?
> (Burne 1883: 373ff.)

Some bold spirit would then volunteer, and the errand might prove a demanding one. When the last sheaf was used, as in Wales, the bearer might be drenched with water, or if he threw it into a field where men were reaping, they might hurl their sickles at him, throw him in the river or bind him in straw. One possible strategy was to pretend he had brought a message and then throw down the 'mare' at the feet of the head reaper or lay it on part of the field still uncut, and make off (Merrick 1904: 195). There was a rule in Pembrokeshire that the mare could be sent only to a farm on the seaward side, a recognition of climatic differences in the time of the ripening of the grain (Owen 1974: 118).

As Burne pointed out, there is plenty of evidence for one custom blending with another in the rituals concerned with animals and rivalry with other farms, but there is little indication of any clear-cut concept of a spirit of the corn to be killed and brought back to life, or preserved through the winter. There was certainly a feeling of continuity; at Llansilan, Denbigh, for instance, as recorded in *Bygones* (31 October 1928), the corn from the last sheaf would be mixed with the seed-corn 'to teach it to grow'. In Transylvania the cock killed when the last sheaf was cut was skinned, and skin and feathers kept to be thrown on the field next spring when they prepared for sowing. This, like the custom of preserving parts of the Yule Boar in Scandinavia (see pp. 63–4), recalls the killing of the piglets at the festival of Demeter and mixing their remains with the seed-corn (see p. 54).

In many other customs associated with the end of the harvest, the last sheaf is represented not as an animal but as a person, and it is in this group of traditions that we may see possible memories of an earlier goddess whose bounty brought grain for her worshippers. Here again we have a vast body of recorded tradition, varying in detail. In many countries in Europe Mannhardt found a tradition of the Corn Mother running through the fields of grain instead of an animal or bird (Frazer 1912: 132ff.). If she were seen there, it was a sign that the crops would grow, but if she became angry with a farmer they would fail; such statements continued to be made in Bavaria in the late nineteenth century (Mannhardt 1884: 300). The figure made from the last sheaf might be called the Corn Mother; it was dressed in women's clothes, and might be set up on the last wagon in the harvest procession and drenched with water, or carried by two lads on a pole, and taken to the harvest supper. Afterwards it might be hung up in the barn to keep the mice away. In Brittany the last sheaf, called the Mother Sheaf and made to represent a woman, had a little puppet of straw, the 'baby', placed inside. If the farmer was a married man, it would be given to his wife, who untied it and gave drink money to the men (Sebillot 1886: 306).

Instead of the dialogue about the mare quoted above, there was a different one in some parts of Pembrokeshire:

> Bore y codais hi,
> Hwyr y dilynais hi,
> Mi ces hi, mi ces hi.
>
> (Early in the morning I got on her track;
> late in the evening I followed her;
> I got her, I got her.)

When asked what he had got, the reapers shouted all together:

> Gwrach, gwrach, gwrach
> (Owen 1974: 116–17)

The word *gwrach* means 'hag' or 'old woman', and the equivalent in Scotland and Ireland is *cailleach*, a word also applied to the last sheaf, together with *carlin*. In Jamieson's *Dictionary of the Scottish Language* (1879–92) he gives *Carlin/Carline* as the name of the last sheaf if cut after Hallowmass: before that it was the Maiden. Elsewhere the English form 'Old Woman' might be used. The rivalry in Wales to be the first to finish reaping is paralleled by accounts from Bernera on the Isle of Lewis (Maclagan 1895: 149ff.). When sickles were still in use, the anxiety to outdo one's neighbours was so strong that the men might work through the night in clear weather. The last ears of corn cut were made into the figure of an old woman in a dress and white cap, wearing an apron with pockets stuffed with bread and cheese like a harvester, to indicate that she helped the reapers. At the harvest feast she was placed at the head of the table, and all drank to her in turn, saying: 'Here's to the one who has helped us with the harvest' and then one of the party led her out to take part in the dance. Finally she was pulled to pieces, and the corn used along with the rest. On Islay, however, she was hung up on the wall until next spring's ploughing, then divided among the men 'to bring luck', and finally given to the horses to eat.

A somewhat different interpretation of the Old Woman is given in J. G. Campbell's description of harvest customs in Tiree (Campbell 1900: 243). Such was the fear of being last that sometimes a ridge might be left unreaped, to avoid the 'famine of the farm', pictured as an old woman who had to be fed until the next harvest. A female figure made from ears of corn was passed round the farms as they completed the harvest, and the last farm had to keep it for a year. These two separate customs were found together at a farm in south Pembrokeshire, where two 'hags' were made. One was kept on the farm, but had to be laid on the farmhouse table or fastened to a hook on the wall, while the other 'hag' was taken to a farm where the harvest was still unfinished, and in both cases the bearer had to avoid being caught (Merrick 1904: 194ff.). However, the first hag brought good luck and promise for the next harvest, and the second bad luck and hunger. The making of two figures representing the Cailleach and the Maiden is also recorded from the Scottish Highlands (Frazer 1912: 164ff.). There are some instances of an Old Man representing winter and famine, reported by Mannhardt from Prussia and Bavaria, but the name was passed on to the woman who bound the last sheaf, suggesting that originally the concept was a female one. The woman who was last among the binders might be tied up in the sheaf and called the Harvest Man, or be nicknamed the Old One until the next harvest (Mannhardt 1884: 19ff.).

The term 'hag' could be applied to a powerful goddess in both Scotland and Ireland. The best known of the Irish Hags is the Hag of Beare (*Cailleach Bhéarra*), associated in particular with the Beare peninsula near Cork (see p. 37), but also the subject of many legends in both Ireland and Scotland. Tales and poems about her go back to early times, and she is represented as having two sister goddesses in Kerry, the Hags of Dingle and Iveragh; it was one of these who, like the Danish Gefion, dragged two islands into their present position (pp. 64–5). Traditions concerning the Hag of Beare form a complex collection of material but there seems no doubt that she represents an ancient goddess with powers over the world of nature (Ó Crulaóich 1988: 154). The Hag was closely linked with the growing of corn and work in the fields; she was said to sow in the late winter and harvest the green shoots before the autumn gales, and to have introduced a new flail with a hollystick handle and a hazelnut striker, for threshing the sheaves one at a time on a clean floor (Ó hÓgáin 1990: 68). Ó hÓgáin suggests that she has become a kind of embodiment of the harvest spirit, but it seems more probable that in pre-Christian times she, like Demeter, was a goddess of growth and fertility who could help or hinder the growth of the grain.

Of especial interest are legends of a female supernatural being competing with a hero on the harvest field, such as the tale of the contest between the Hag of Beare and Big Donagh Mac Manus, collected by Dr Hyde from a man in Connemara and translated by Eleanor Hull (1927: 237ff.). The

Hag came to Galway to farm, with her daughter and her black dog; anyone she hired to help her had to forfeit his wages if he could not keep up with her. The strongest men were forced to give up after a week, and went home to die. In spite of his mother's warnings, Big Donagh was determined to outdo the Hag, and he made love to her daughter, who helped him by giving him the milk from her dog's dish to drink. This made him stronger every day, so that he finally got the better of the Hag in digging up the field. When they started mowing, the daughter put spikes on the ground to blunt her mother's wonderful scythe; the Hag became so angry that she cut her knee and had to leave Donagh to finish the work. Then the time came to reap the oats, and the daughter told Donagh that the Hag had a little beetle in the handle of her reaping hook which made it impossible for anyone to keep up with her, so Donagh snatched it from her, pulled off the handle and killed the beetle. The Hag had to pay him his wages and let him go, after telling him the story of her long life of ninescore years. Soon after this her house was struck by lightning in a great storm, and she died together with her daughter and her dog.

Ó Crullaóich has analysed this tale, which he suggests carries forward 'an extremely ancient formulation of that pattern of opposition between Otherworld Supreme Deity and Semi-Divine/Semi-Human Hero, which O'Rahilly believed existed in Irish mythology' (Ó Crullaóich 1988: 156). Other versions of a reaping match have been recorded from Scotland, some ending tragically for the human contestant. The emphasis on rivalry in the various harvest customs and the compulsive drive to finish before one's neighbour might in the past have been associated with the goddess of the grain, whose favour was necessary if the harvest was to be gathered in and famine averted. Perhaps it was felt also that it was necessary to exert all one's strength to strive against the goddess, who possessed the power to give, but was not always willing to use it.

The last sheaf was also widely known as the Maiden, and the idea of Mother and Daughter working together, or one taking over from the other, is found in the harvest traditions of northern Europe as well as in those of Ancient Greece. In Wright's *English Dialect Dictionary* (1896–1905), Maiden Day is given as the day when the last sheaf is cut, and the name can also be used for the harvest supper. In the Highlands the last sheaf might be called 'The Shorn Maiden', and if the man who cut it were unmarried, it was said that he would get a wife before the next harvest. This caused great competition between the young men, and a handful of corn might be left deliberately uncut by one of them, so that he could go back for the last sheaf after the field had been reaped. As with the Corn Mother and the Hag, the Maiden might be the name given to a straw doll, dressed in ribbons and fixed to the farmhouse wall. In Scotland this might be given to the cattle at Yule 'to make them thrive all the year round' (Jamieson 1879–92: Maiden). At Kilmartin in Argyleshire a tuft of the 'Reaping

Maiden' was given to each of the horses pulling the first load, and the rest hung up in the house until ploughing began, when again a tuft was given to the horses for good luck. The Reaping Maiden was believed to be a protection against fairies and witches (MacPhail 1900: 441). In another account from north-east Scotland, the sheaf was dressed as a woman and kept until Christmas or the New Year, when it was taken to a mare in foal or to the oldest cow in calf, while a few stalks were left behind for the Old Man.

The last sheaf might also be represented as a bride, and Mannhardt gives examples of this from Germany. In Moravia the last ears were cut by a young girl with a wreath of corn on her head, called the Wheat Bride, and she was expected to marry within the year. Sometimes, as in the Vorharz and Saxony, a man and woman represented a bride and groom at the harvest feast, while in Silesia the woman who bound the last sheaf wore a crown of wheat-ears and flowers and was driven to the tavern with her bridegroom as if to a wedding (Mannhardt 1868: 130).

A particularly interesting custom is recorded by Martin Martin in the Hebrides in the eighteenth century associated with St Bride (the Irish Brigid), when the women of each family took a sheaf of oats, dressed it to represent a woman, and laid it in a large basket called Briid's-bed, with a wooden club beside it, calling out three times 'Briid is come, Briid is welcome':

> This they do just before going to bed, and when they rise in the morning they look among the ashes expecting to see the impression of Briid's club there; which if they do, they reckon it a true presage of a good crop and a prosperous year, and the contrary they take as an ill omen.
>
> (Martin 1703: 179)

This strongly suggests a bridal, with the club representing the male god who mates with the goddess; Hope has suggested that this was a pre-Christian ceremony kept up by the women on the farms, later associated with the Christian saint (Hope 1970: 253). Ó Catháin (1995: 53–4) gives similar evidence for a bed by the hearth laid out for Brigid in Ireland. Here marks of her wand are a good sign, but what is hoped for is her footprint in the ashes; this means 'increase in family, in flock and in field during the coming year'.

Hope emphasizes the strong sexual element in harvest customs in Scotland, discreetly glossed over by Frazer. For instance, one possible fate of the intruding stranger in the harvest field may have been to end up as harvest bridegroom rather than as sacrificial victim. A description of the attack made on him by the women in Fife runs as follows:

> He was seized by two or three females and laid on his back. Then one of them held him down and laid herself flat on the person,

and another female tumbled over the two as they lay. This was called Kipping and the man after he was allowed to get up, was expected to give a small sum of money by way of providing some refreshment.

(Hope 1970: 187)

Hope also made the point that the dance which followed the harvest supper often degenerated into what might be described as an orgy once the farmer and his friends had left.

As well as the Hag and the Maiden we have the baby as the third member of the trio. Among the Slavs the woman binding the last sheaf was called the Baba, or Old Woman, but was expected to have a child in the course of the year (Frazer 1912: 145). Mannhardt (1868: 28) refers to a Polish custom where the man cutting the last sheaf is told: 'You have cut the navel-string'. In Prussia the last sheaf might represent a child called the Bastard, and a boy was wrapped in it. The woman who bound it cried out like a woman in labour, and an old woman came to act as midwife, so that here three generations are represented together. Then a cry was raised that the child was born, and the boy in the sheaf cried like a baby, whereupon the grandmother wrapped him in a sack and took him to the barn. The baby given to the Corn Mother in Brittany, passed on to the farmer's wife, has already been noted (see p. 73).

Confused and variable although the evidence of local customs in the nineteenth century may be, it seems clear that three generations of women, the Old Hag, the Daughter or Maiden (who may become the bride) and the Baby, are all associated with the harvesting of the grain. The contrast between old and young woman is sometimes emphasized, as when a woman above the age of childbearing is chosen to make the Corn Mother from the last sheaf, or the prettiest girl is given a wreath made from the finest ears of wheat (Mannhardt 1884: 317). The fertility of the fields is extended also to the women taking part; both marriage and babies were promised to those who distinguished themselves at the reaping or binding, and indeed it was said that women who did not want an increase in the family tried to avoid being singled out (Frazer 1912: 145).

It is clear that women played a considerable part in harvest customs, even though the work of reaping and threshing was largely performed by men. They tried to drench the reaper with water when he brought home the last sheaf, recalling rites performed in Greece in order to cause rain (see p. 54). They had a major part to play in binding the sheaves, and it was usually they who were responsible for the making of the corn dolly from the last ears of corn. They might even help with the death of the animal killed in the field, as when the goat was held by the farmer's wife when her husband beheaded it (see p. 70), while it was usually women who were said to be responsible for attacks on strangers.

77

Above all, the figure of the corn dolly was normally that of a woman, either a Mother or a Maiden; this might be carried on the last wagon bringing in the grain, preside at the harvest supper, or be taken round in the dancing. It was held to have special powers beyond bringing fertility to the fields: it could keep away mice, which harmed the crops, help cows to bear calves and mares their foals, and bring good luck to the poultry and the plough-horses. Alternatively the farmer's wife or the woman chosen to be Queen of the Harvest might be given the place of honour in the procession of wagons, or at the harvest supper and dance. A woman might be impersonated by a man, as in the figure of the Bessy (see p. 68), or the clown dressed as a woman at the 'Hawkie', the wagon bringing in the harvest in East Anglia in the early nineteenth century (Frazer 1912: 146–7).

There seems good reason to claim that in the local harvest customs from north-western Europe there is much scattered evidence for traditions of a goddess of grain formerly honoured in local rituals. There are suggestions of an earlier tradition in a tale told in 1904 by a woman of about 50 from south Pembrokeshire, who had heard it from her mother. When none of the men was willing to take the Hag to a neighbouring farm, a woman offered to do so. She took off her skirt and walked 'in a stately way' in a white petticoat and bodice with a white apron over her head, and no one dared stop or challenge her as she laid down the sheaf: 'Sure, 'tis a ghost,' they said (Merrick 1904: 195–6).

The traditions concerning the Hag, who could either help or hinder the farmer in his endeavours, and the emphasis on the two women, old and young, are of especial interest in this connection. Frazer's reasons for rejecting any signs of goddess worship because gods were not restricted to definite departments of nature, individual names are lacking, and the rites are magical rather than propitiatory (Frazer 1912: 169) are of little relevance in analysing nineteenth-century popular customs; it is possible, as Ralph Merrifield has demonstrated, for ancient ritual to 'survive the religious beliefs that gave birth to it', and to be 'reinterpreted in the light of current beliefs or adapted to relieve new fears' (Merrifield 1987: xiii). Much material that Mannhardt and Frazer surveyed is, in the words of Trevor Owen (1974: 121), 'part of the body of degenerate ritual and ceremony which peasant society maintained for the mere fun of it', influenced to some extent by the use of reaping-hooks and scythes which ultimately gave way to machines. Yet since we know that earlier goddesses were concerned with growth and the fertility of the fields, it is legitimate to look for possible traces of such concepts in these comparatively recent traditions. It is important also to note the part played by women in the bringing in of the harvest, and to remember that this period of demanding labour marked a crucial point in the agricultural year, on which the welfare and perhaps even the survival of small communities depended. Here indeed the favour and support of the goddess were desperately needed.

THE GRAIN GODDESS IN THE NORTH

The varied rituals of seed-time and harvest discussed in the previous section can be linked with iconographical and literary evidence concerning the early goddesses of north-western Europe. The idea of twin female deities, seen as Mother and Daughter, or of a trio consisting of Old Woman, Mother and Young Bride or Maiden, is not an entirely unfamiliar concept. Examples of such a pattern are found in the groups of Mother Goddesses, surviving from Gaul, Britain and parts of Germany under Roman military occupation in the early centuries AD.

We know that both Celtic and Germanic tribes worshipped these female deities, and although the majority of stones which portray them are found in Celtic areas, a number have Germanic names and there are many examples from Upper and Lower Germany. Outside the regions under direct Roman rule, they were less likely to be portrayed in the Roman manner, but in the military frontier regions of Upper and Lower Germany they form a fairly homogeneous group. Here they are usually called *Matronae*, probably from the Celtic form *Matra*, instead of *Matres*, the usual form in Gaul and Britain, while another Celtic form, *Matrae*, is found in southern France (Thevenot 1968: 166). Sometimes in the inscriptions the goddesses are described as the Mothers of a certain territory or tribe, such as the Auganiae in the region round Bonn, or the Treveri round Trier. Occasionally their native names are given, and sometimes these appear to be based on their characters as givers, offering a parallel to the Danish Gefion, or Scandinavian Gefn, as in the case of the *Alagabiae* or *Ollogabiae* (J. de Vries 1957: II, 293).

Attributes of the Mothers link them with the fertility of the earth, and with the growth of grain and fruit. They hold *cornucopiae*, horns of plenty, single fruits or baskets of fruit, including grapes and apples, loaves of bread, and occasionally a basket of corn, as in the case of a group found in Scotland (Keppie and Arnold 1984: 61, plate 19), while ears of corn are held in the right hand of one of the three goddesses from Cirencester (Henig 1993: 39) (Plate 6). They may also hold infants in their arms or beside them, and there are single figures of a Mother Goddess in pipe-clay nursing two infants, as in two examples in the London Museum (M. J. Green 1986: 89) (Figure 12). Single goddesses may be accompanied by small dogs, thought to indicate their link with the Otherworld and the dead (Thevenot 1968: 176–7) (see pp. 47–8).

Roman officials and merchants from various parts of the Empire often set up altars to the Mothers, which makes it difficult to establish what the cult really meant to the native inhabitants of Roman Britain (Henig 1984: 48–9). However, the altars and dedications found in the Cotswolds indicate an undoubted link between these goddesses and the crops, as well as the growth of the family and the well-being of children. Thevenot points

Plate 6 Three Mother Goddesses on a stone from Cirencester. They hold loaves, apples and ears of corn. Courtesy Corinium Museum, Cirencester. Ht 78 cm. ©Cotswold District Council.

out that the monuments in Gaul are usually from habitation sites, near springs or healing wells, while the small pottery figures are found in graves (Thevenot 1968: 177); the little figure of a Mother Goddess was found in a child's grave at Arrington near Cambridge (Figure 13). When we find inscriptions in Roman Britain to the Italian, German, Gallic and British Matres, as on an altar restored by a certain Antonius Lucretianus at Winchester, the donor was probably looking back to various places where he had been previously stationed, and appealing to the local powers for a continuation of good fortune in his new surroundings (S. Barnard 1985:

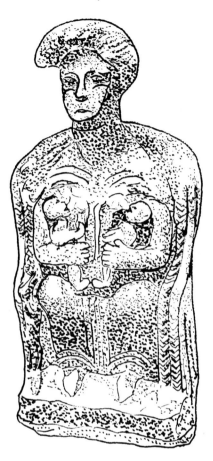

Figure 12 Mother Goddess with two infants in pipe-clay from Toulon-sur-Allier. Musée des Antiquités Nationales, Saint-Germain-en-Laye. Eileen Aldworth.

244). Other dedications made by men in the Roman army are to the Mothers from foreign parts (*ollotatae*), or overseas (*transmarinae*).

Evidently the powers of these goddesses were not limited to making the earth fruitful; they were also seen as the protective guardians of children and concerned with the destiny of individuals (see pp. 130–1). But the farmer must have turned to them when he hoped for a bountiful harvest. The loaves which they hold are of particular interest because loaves played a part in various ploughing and sowing rituals, while baking was one of the skills practised by women and associated with the hearth (see pp. 133–4).

The individual members of the groups consisting of two or three Mothers are seldom identical. Not only do they hold different attributes, but also

Figure 13 Goddess figurine in clay with ram, from child's grave, Arrington. Ht 19 cm. Cambridge University Museum of Archaeology and Anthropology. Eileen Aldworth.

their hairstyles and in a number of cases their faces vary. Two goddesses with benign expressions from Saintes are dressed similarly, with identical neck-rings, but Thevenot (1968: 170) noted a marked age difference in their faces: the figure on the right is clearly younger than that on the left, and her hair falls loose over her shoulders, while her companion looks graver and older. In other groups of three goddesses, similar variations are apparent. Two of the three figures in the well-preserved group from Cirencester (Henig 1993: 39) wear close-fitting caps, and look older than the central figure, the right-hand goddess in particular having an elderly look; the hair of the younger central figure is twisted up but uncovered (Plate 6).

There are also continental examples of a young goddess with flowing hair accompanied by two older ones in caps or head-dresses; J. de Vries (1957: II, 290) noted a group in Ubierland which he thought showed one unmarried and two married women. In the impressive trio inscribed 'To the Matronae Aufaniae' in the Museum at Bonn, dedicated by a Questor of Cologne, a young woman, apparently in her teens, has on either side an impressive larger woman with a huge circular head-dress (Plate 7). There is a similar group, less well preserved, in the Museum at Cologne. Miranda Green points out that this is a familiar pattern in the Germanic provinces,

Plate 7 Altar dedicated to three goddesses named as Matronae Aufaniae, from Bonn. Base 87 cm wide. Courtesy Rheinisches Landesmuseum, Bonn.

and shows a delightful little group in pipe-clay from Bonn as another example (M. J. Green 1989: fig. 86). At Naix she singles out a grim, wrinkled Mother Goddess with two youthful attendants (M. J. Green 1989: 198) and gives additional examples of Mothers of different ages from Gaul. At Nuits

St Georges a central figure holding a napkin or scroll is said to have 'creased cheeks and withered neck, while her companions are younger with round cheeks' (M. J. Green 1989: 192). Again at Alesia one goddess has a high-necked tunic and mural crown (since she is the town's protector), and her two companions are younger women with babies, one with a particularly youthful face (M. J. Green 1989: 193). One goddess is sometimes portrayed larger than the rest, as if she held a superior position.

It seems that the tradition of two or three Mother Goddesses of different ages was known to the inhabitants of both Celtic and Germanic territory in the early centuries AD. We have groups suggesting a mother and daughter, and others which might show three generations, maiden, mother and grandmother. These are the same characters as emerged from the mass of customs, rites and legends connected with the harvesting of the grain in north-western Europe, while the infant frequently held by one or more of the Mothers recalls various references to the birth of a child.

There is particular emphasis once more on three generations of the family in the cult of St Anne, mother of the Virgin Mary. There is no evidence for this in the West in early Christian times, but a church was dedicated to her in Constantinople in the sixth century AD; in the following century a basilica was built over her tomb in Jerusalem. At the basilica of St Maria Antiqua in Rome, left deserted since the tenth century, a fresco of three female saints, each with a child in her arms, was excavated in 1912; their inscribed names identified them as Mary with the infant Jesus, Elizabeth with John the Baptist, and St Anne with her daughter Mary (Bannister 1913: 108). St Anne's cult spread northwards, and her feast on 26 July was kept in England from the tenth century onwards. She became a much-loved saint representing the home and family, who could be appealed to for help in childbirth and in the upbringing of young children (see p. 150). The group representing three generations, Anne, Mary and the Christ Child, was very popular in late medieval art, while paintings of the extended Holy Family present Anne as a matriarch with her three daughters and their lively families of young children. By the late Middle Ages, St Anne had come to represent 'both the notion of the family and the principle of fertility' (Duffy 1992: 182), and seems to have inherited something of the pre-Christian tradition of a matriarchal goddess associated with fertility, as well as the role of the older woman in the group of fertility goddesses.

The idea of a bridal, linked with the harvest both in Ancient Greece and in nineteenth-century harvest customs, can be traced to pre-Christian times in northern Europe. A series of tiny figures on minute pieces of gold foil, from the period between AD 500 and the early Viking Age, appear to represent a divine marriage. These are found in Norway, Sweden and Denmark, and known as *goldgubber*, which might be roughly translated as 'golden oldies'. They were not placed in graves, but left on house sites, and in the foundations of what is thought to be a pre-Christian temple at Trondheim in Norway (Lidén 1969), where nineteen such little pictures had been laid in the postholes which held the timber supports. As many as twenty-six were also found at the trading centre of Helgo in Sweden; these showed considerable variation in the dress and appearance of the little figures, suggesting that the pieces of foil had been deposited there on different occasions. Some have holes, and may have been worn as amulets. The figures are of a man and a woman facing one another, sometimes embracing and sometimes with a leafy branch or an ear of corn between them.

The way in which these little pictures were used is still in dispute. Grieg (1954) suggested that they were worn by a bride at her wedding, and put into the bed on the wedding night. He points out the parallel with the later *Dalarpenningen*, Christian ornaments which might show Christ as the Lamb of God to remind the newly married couple that the Church was the bride of Christ. This could be worn by a bride at her wedding and on the bridal night, while the bridegroom wore a cross (Grieg 1954: 166ff.). The *goldgubber* could have been buried on house sites in order to call down the blessing of the Vanir, deities of household and farm, on a new dwelling. Magnus Olsen (1909) linked such bridal figures with Freyr and Gerd in a poem in the *Edda* on a divine marriage (see p. 86).

If we turn from the iconography of goddesses and saints in western Europe to the evidence from literature, there are possible links with the groups of early Mothers, although the resemblance is not obvious at first glance. The Scandinavian goddesses of fertility, associated with childbearing, marriage and sexual attraction between man and woman, were Frigg and Freyja, and one of the problems of Norse mythology is the nature of the relationship between the two (Grundy 1996). Frigg is represented as the wife of Odin and mother of Balder, whom she strives to save from death; Freyja is the sister of Freyr, said to have taken many of the gods as lovers, including her brother, and to be eagerly sought after by the giants; she too is sometimes paired off with Odin. Both goddesses are associated with childbearing and are invoked by women in labour (see pp. 146–7); both are also associated with apples, just as the Mothers were. It seems likely that Idun, who guarded the golden apples which ensured perpetual youth to the gods, may be identified with Freyja, since she like Freyja is carried off on one occasion by the giants and has to be rescued by Loki. Moreover the maiden Gerd, who may also represent Freyja, is offered golden apples when wooed by Freyr in the poem *Skírnismál*. There is little in the surviving literature to link these goddesses directly with the grain harvest, but this may well be due to the fact that the myths have reached us by way of Iceland and western Norway, where little grain could be grown.

Before the Viking Age a patriarchal system of religion had developed in the North, and Snorri Sturluson, from whom much of our information is derived, portrays the male gods in the dominant positions which they occupy in pre-Christian poetry. Brit-Mari Näsström (1995: 195) sees a parallel here with the powerful goddesses of Ancient Greece, Here, Athena and Artemis, portrayed in the myths as the wife and daughters of Zeus, although they were once independent deities. She points out that in *Gylfaginning* both Frigg and Freyja are listed among the *asynjur*, the unmarried goddesses. Both are associated with fertility, and while Frigg is presented as the divine mother, queen of heaven, Freyja is apparently of a younger generation, the daughter of Njord and Skaði, and is said to hold the title 'Bride of the Vanir' (*Skáldskaparmál* 37).

Here then we have possible traces of the older woman and the bride, and there are even suggestions of a third generation, since Freyja was said to have a daughter Hnoss, of great beauty, whose name could be used for treasure in poetry (*Gylfaginning* 35); later a second daughter, Gersemi (also meaning 'treasure'), is mentioned. In addition she has a youthful attendant, Fulla, who is called a maid and said to go about with her hair loose. She is likely to be the same as Volla, who in the Second Merseburg Charm is called the sister of Friia. These are vague, uncertain figures, emerging from odd references to goddesses which Snorri has noted in the poets, but they suggest the possibility that at one time three generations were represented among the goddesses of fertility and harvest in Scandinavia.

There is good reason to see not only Gerd but also Gefion, the ploughing goddess, as yet another form of Freyja (see p. 65). Both these goddesses are connected with the fruitful earth, and Gerd in *Skírnismál* has something in common with Persephone, since it is made clear that if she remains below in the dark kingdom of the underworld there will be nothing to hope for but sterility and famine. She does not become the bride of the underworld ruler, however; her bridal is to be in the upper world when she consents to meet Freyr at Barri. Magnus Olsen interpreted this poem as concerned with the myth of a divine marriage to bring fertility to the earth, and suggested that Barri, the meeting place of the bridal pair, was derived from *barr*, barley. Some, notably Sahlgren, have objected to his interpretation, but on the whole it has met with acceptance, and makes good sense out of the poem. The main objections seem to come from too literal an interpretation. To protest that because the meeting place is said to be in a grove (*lund*), therefore the lovers could not possibly come together in a barley field (Talbot 1982: 34) is to ignore the use of poetic symbolism; the barley stalks here could represent the sacred grove of a goddess, and we are reminded of Demeter who mated with her lover Iasion in a ploughed field (see p. 53). But, as with all the evidence linking the northern goddess with the fertility of the soil, we are on uncertain ground; by the time our sources came to be written down in Christian times, ideas about the pre-Christian goddesses of Scandinavia had become shadowy and confused.

The memory of a sacred field has survived in *Víga-Glúms Saga*, where a field called *Vitazgjafi*, which appears to mean 'Sure Giver', plays an important part in the story. This field was said to be beside the shrine of Freyr set up by Ingjald, son of Helgi the Lean, south of the Thvera River in northern Iceland, in one of the richer agricultural areas of the island. It seems that the owner of the farm who maintained the shrine had the right to take the produce of the field, and this right passed on to his descendants, who might reap it in turn. Anne Holtsmark, who first pointed out the importance of this tradition, gives other examples of fields shared in this way (Holtsmark 1933: 111). The hero of *Víga-Glúms Saga* kills a man in the field who has cheated his mother out of her share of the crop, and the slaying angers the god Freyr, because the holy field is polluted with blood. There is no indication here as to whether Freyja was concerned with the cultivation of the field, but it would be reasonable to expect that both the male god and the goddess were originally recognized in the agricultural rites, as was the case in Greece.

One of Freyja's names given by Snorri was *Sýr*, 'Sow', and this links up with the golden boar which was the emblem of the Vanir; we know that the sow played a part in the rites of Demeter and that piglets were sacrificed at the time of sowing (see p. 54). St Olaf's stepfather, who was a minor king in Ringerike, was nicknamed Sigurd *Sýr*; he was renowned for his passion for farming, and said to be continually busy on his estate, seeing to the crops and livestock. When Olaf came to visit him to seek his help in gaining the kingdom of Norway, Sigurd was said to be working hard in the fields, with many men: 'Some were cutting corn, some binding it, some bringing it home on wagons, some laying it in stacks and barns' (*Óláfs Saga helga* 33). Snorri makes it clear that Olaf, with his warlike ambitions, and Sigurd's wife Asta, Olaf's mother, despised the king for this.

After Sigurd's death, Olaf asked his young stepbrothers, Sigurd's sons, what they wanted most. Guthorm chose farming land: 'I should like this whole headland to be sown every summer', he declared, indicating land on which ten farms stood. The second son, Halfdan, declared that he wanted cows, enough to crowd all round the water's edge. 'Just like your father', commented St Olaf. But the youngest son, Harald, who was floating chips of wood and pretending they were warships, answered that he would have so many followers that they would eat up all his brother's cows. 'You are bringing up a king', Olaf told his mother, and his young stepbrother was indeed to become the famous warrior king, Harald *Hardraði*.

A humorous short story, *Hreiðárs þáttr* (Faulkes 1967), in which an apparent simpleton is able to get the better of kings and survive in a tough world, contains an interesting episode in which he encounters this same Harald *Hardraði* when he was king; Harald was known to be a man whom it was dangerous to offend, and he was already prejudiced against Hreidar. The young man had made a little pig out of silver, and offered it as a gift;

both the king and his men much admired the workmanship, and Harald then praised Hreidar as a bold man who had won his favour. But when he examined the gift more closely, he realized that it was not a boar but a young sow (*gyltr*), and that Hreidar was insulting him. His reaction was explosive: he flung it down, exclaiming: 'May the trolls take you. Up, men, and kill him!' However, Hreidar seized the sow and got away; he told his friend King Magnus what had happened, and the king's comment was that Harald had taken vengeance for far lesser insults than this, and that Hreidar was a brave man. The nature of the insult here, which puzzles Faulkes (1967: 92), was surely not that Harald's father, Sigurd *Sýr*, was mean, but that he had been a worshipper of the fertility goddess instead of a warrior king serving Odin. The strong feelings attributed to Harald at the sight of the sow, symbol of the goddess, helps us to understand why so little has survived in Norse literature concerning Freyja as goddess of the grain. A second tale confirming Harald's anger when reminded of his stepfather's nickname is found in *Morkinskinna*.

Other links between grain and a goddess have survived from Ireland. Here as in Scandinavia a patriarchal culture weakened the power of the old goddesses, but St Brigid, taking over some of the traditions of the earlier goddess, has preserved links with the grain. Her festival on 1 February was the time to prepare for the spring sowing, and the seed-corn might be left outside to obtain her blessing. Every manifestation of this saint, as Danaher puts it, is 'closely bound up in some way with food production' (Danaher 1972: 13), and her links with dairy-work have already been indicated (see pp. 36–7). She was also associated with baking, since bread or fruitcake was put out for her on her festival.

The festival in early August, Lughnasa, came to be associated with the first potatoes of the season, but before the potato became a stable food in the seventeenth and eighteenth centuries, this marked the beginning of the corn harvest, a fact remembered in a few legends. In Ireland there are no carved figures of Mother Goddesses in Roman style, but Máire MacNeill sees an equivalent of the Gaulish Matronae in the traditions of the Mother Goddess and her sisters in south Kerry and west Cork (MacNeill 1962: 413). At Cullen in County Cork, Lughnasa was celebrated on 'Latiaran Sunday', the Sunday on or before 25 July, the day of St Latiaran, their patron saint. She was remembered only in popular local tradition, and said to be the youngest but most important of three sisters; the two elder were called Lasair (Flame) and Inghean Bhuidhe (the Yellow-haired Girl), but the meaning of Latiaran is not known. Lasair and Inghean Bhuidhe had sacred wells, but Lasair's had been earthed over by order of the MacCarthys when they were chieftains, after a plough had been placed on top; this was said to have brought bad luck to the district. Latiaran's day was at the beginning of harvest, and Inghean Bhuidhe's on 6 May, at the beginning of summer, so that Lasair's might have marked the beginning of spring (MacNeill 1962: 270–1), which would explain her association with a plough. There may have been some confusion here with half-remembered traditions of early Christian settlements or hermitages, but the concept of three sisters of different ages is noteworthy; MacNeill suggests that here Christian legends could have 'attracted to themselves the legends and attributes floating in folk consciousness from old times as the properties of the beneficent female powers' (MacNeill 1962: 274). She comments also on the importance of the cult of St Anne in Ireland; her festival (26 July) was close to Lughnasa.

The link with bread or porridge made from the first-fruits of the crop at harvest time is something which must always have been the responsibility of the women, and Danaher (1972) quotes a description from an Irish tale which is relevant for the understanding of harvest customs. The corn had to be made into bread or porridge before evening, but the complex system of reaping, threshing, winnowing, drying, grinding and sieving could be bypassed by a process known as 'burning in the straw'. The ear end of the last sheaf was set on fire, so that the chaff burned away and the corn was hardened; the grain was then washed clean of ashes and ground in the quern. This was still done in the seventeenth century, since an Act to forbid it on grounds of wastefulness was passed in Dublin in 1634. In the story referred to by Danaher, the corn was prepared in this way for an unexpected visitor, and we are told: 'He ate it, and thought he had never eaten nor even tasted better food, it was so wholesome and tasty, so rich and full of energy' (Danaher 1972: 168). This primitive way of preparing the grain for food takes us back to women's laborious work in the early days, but reminds us also of the pleasures and sanctity which could be associated with the first tasting of the new crop at the time of harvest.

Looking back over the rich but confusing evidence for the goddess as mistress of grain, it seems as if in northern Europe there was no single particular deity responsible for the cultivation of the fields and the growth of the crop. The goddesses to whom the people turned were the same as those concerned with the welfare of farm animals and the produce of the dairy, and it was these who also helped women in childbirth and gave protection to children and young girls, as will be seen in Chapter IV. There is a persistent impression that more than one female being was involved, and the group of female powers seem to represent the different phases in a woman's life. This might be viewed as the goddess herself in her several aspects, or as a group consisting of the three generations, the Grandmother, the fertile Mother, and the young Maiden. It was clearly a widespread pattern, sometimes compared with the three phases of the moon (see p. 6). There was also a consistent link with a male god, perhaps the god of the sky sending the rain, which was essential for fertility and harvest. The drenching with water of individuals or objects has been widely recorded as part of the harvest ceremonies, as was the case in Ancient Greece.

The number three occurs again in the crucial stages in the cultivation of the grain: the sowing of the seed, the sprouting of the young grain in spring, and the harvesting in late summer, were all associated with goddess figures and celebrated in the early customs of the farming peoples of northern Europe. After the coming of Christianity, they might be linked with the Virgin Mary, while festivals of important women saints, like St Brigid and St Anne, were on dates corresponding to these important points in the farmer's year. Another firmly established element in the ritual is that of continuity, symbolized by the retention of part of the last sheaf or a loaf baked from it, or the remains of an animal slain at harvest time, so that it might be brought into contact with the seed used for next year's crop. The link between the goddess and the plough, particularly strong in Germanic tradition, can be explained by the necessity to prepare the earth for the sowing of the seed, even though the plough was usually worked by men.

In northern Europe the recurring threat of the winter dark, so over-powering in countries like Norway and Iceland, must have left its imprint on mythology. There is a threat behind the harvest customs, sometimes symbolized by the old hag who must be supported through the winter, or a gloomy figure of starvation lurking in the background. The relentless battle between hero and hag appears to be another ancient theme to inspire memorable legends, and the goddess may appear as a cruel, destructive deity. The idea of sacrifice is a natural one; to obtain the harvest bounty, men and women must be ready to give in return. They certainly gave demanding effort, time and labour, battling with difficult soils and unpredictable weather.

Both marriage and childbirth were associated with harvest rites. From the time of Demeter onwards, hopes for a plentiful harvest inspired a wealth of sexual innuendo among the women; their outspoken jesting and behaviour formed a background to the sowing of the seed and the triumphant gathering in of the grain. This is something pointedly ignored by Frazer in spite of his classical background. Far more important than the death of a nebulous Corn Spirit seems to be the link between the sowing, growth and harvesting of the grain and the rites of passage for women: puberty, marriage, bearing children, and old age, reflected in the range of goddess figures. It is as though in the myths and customs connected with the grain we are seeing the growth process from a woman's standpoint.

The figure of a goddess, Blessed Virgin or woman saint perambulating through the fields in her wagon or appearing with her plough, together with Mothers holding the symbols of fruit, loaves and healthy children, gives us a direct link with the women workers who helped in the harvest and made use of the grain for the needs of household and community. The grain goddess was a divided personality to her worshippers, a major power to be welcomed, placated and feared, and one from whom there was no escape, since the unrelenting cycle of the agricultural year kept her perpetually in mind.

CHAPTER III

MISTRESS OF DISTAFF
AND LOOM

—— •◆• ——

WEAVING IN THE ANCIENT WORLD

The making of garments from some kind of woven material has formed an essential part of women's activities since what has been called 'the string revolution' took place in the Upper Palaeolithic period in Europe (Barber 1994: 42ff.). This was the discovery of the technique of twisting together small filaments of natural fibres to make strong lengths of string or cord, such as could be used for tying things together, making nets, snares, tethers and much else of practical use, as well as garments and headgear. It was a discovery that might be compared to that of the wheel in importance, greatly extending the range of activities open to both men and women, and pointing the way to further innovations.

Although very little early work survives, there is a bone Venus figurine from Lespugue in France who wears an apron of twisted strings suspended from a hip band at the back, dated to about 20,000 BC (Figure 14). Elizabeth Barber, whose work on early textiles has opened up a rich new field of study, pointed out that the maker of this bone figure has shown not only the twists in each string, but also the ends fraying out into untwisted fibres at the bottom, so that the garment depicted could not have been made from thongs of sinew or hide (Barber 1994: 44–5). A complete skirt made from wool fibres survives from Bronze Age Denmark, dated to the fourteenth century BC; this was worn by a young woman buried in a tree coffin at Egtved, excavated in 1921 (Broholm and Hald 1940: 29ff.). Her bones had disappeared, but the hair, parts of the body and the clothes had survived along with wooden objects, due to acidic groundwater in the grave. The skirt is in the Royal Museum at Copenhagen.

This garment was wrapped twice round the body and worn low on the hips, reaching to above the knees. The thick cords forming it were woven through a narrow waist-band, and caught together at the bottom by a twined spacing cord ending in an ornamental row of knots, which would swing out as the wearer turned or danced. Pieces of other string skirts from coffins of this period in Denmark show that metal fittings were sometimes placed on the ends of the cords; these would have gleamed in the light and clicked as the wearer moved. Such skirts could hardly have been intended either to provide warmth or to preserve modesty, as Barber (1994: 59) points out; when the skirt from Egtved was first discovered, shocked

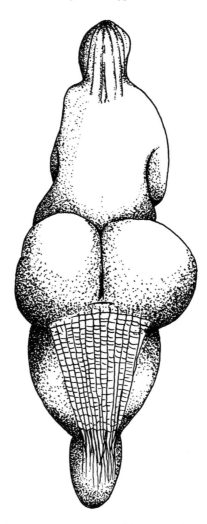

Figure 14 Apron on Lespugue goddess. Based on drawing by
E. J. W. Barber (1994). Lelly Aldworth.

scholars argued that it must have been worn over a linen shift, but it seems
that this was not so. Barber believes that it was intended to convey information about the wearer, perhaps that she had reached childbearing age,
or was a married woman, and she gives some convincing parallels. Mordvin
girls in the region to the east of Moscow would put on a black string apron
at the time of betrothal, worn at the back like that of the Lespugue Venus,
and continue to wear this as the symbol of a married woman well into the
twentieth century. Aprons of string fibres with a front and back, made with

a waist-belt, formed part of folk costumes which still survive in the Balkans, and the front apron was often decorated with woven lozenges, a recognized fertility symbol. The string skirt had a long life in south-east Europe, since examples can still be obtained in Macedonia ending in a weighted fringe like the skirt of the Bronze Age girl; these are said to be exhilarating garments to wear (Barber 1994: 63–5).

Such brief, revealing skirts or aprons might be regarded as a form of girdle. Barber quotes a passage from the *Iliad* (Book XIV) where Here sets out to seduce Zeus and puts on her girdle 'fashioned with a hundred tassels'. Then she asks Aphrodite, goddess of sexual love and fertility, to lend her her girdle, pretending that she needs it to bring together an estranged husband and wife. The obliging Aphrodite 'took from her bosom the curiously embroidered girdle on which all her magic depended, Love and Desire and the sweet bewitching words that turn a wise man into a fool', adding, as she indicated the curious stitches: 'All my power resides in this, and I have no fear that you will come back from your mission unsuccessful' (E. V. Rieu's translation 1950). Clad in this magic girdle, Here indeed proves irresistible to Zeus and successfully distracts him from the threat to Troy. In addition to the string skirts, examples of a special girdle about 12 feet long called a *zostra* have survived from Greece, made in red wool with a deep fringe, in a kind of knotless netting. Such girdles were family treasures, handed down from mother to daughter, and would be used in cases of difficult childbirth, placed on the abdomen of the woman in labour (Barber 1994: 65–6). The word *zostra* comes, like the Greek *zone*, from the Indo-European word for 'belt'. It is worth noting that the *brat*, called the mantle or girdle of St Brigid, was used in childbirth in Ireland in a similar way (see p. 36).

Thus we have examples of a woven garment associated with the goddess of fertility from very early times. They were said to be worn by the goddesses themselves, and Homer's tale of Here and Aphrodite indicates that they could be borrowed for special occasions, like the *zostra*. Small bronze figures of women from Bronze Age Denmark wear extremely brief string skirts or belts of a similar type to those in the graves. Of particular interest is the little kneeling figure from Fårdal, thought to be a goddess, who wears a neck-ring, bracelet and mini-skirt (Figure 15). Her right hand is raised, and the fingers curved so that a cord could pass through, while her left hand holds the nipple of her right breast between two fingers. She wears her hair in a pig-tail down her back, and has huge eyes inlaid with gold (Rosenburg 1929: 1ff.). The figure is on a kind of stand, with holes for rivets, and it has been suggested that she knelt on a wagon or a sledge, or in a processional boat, and was driving the serpent found with her (Sandars 1968: 204). A dancer or acrobat in a similar belt and neck-ring is the survivor of a group of three found at Grevens Vaeng, in Denmark.

Figure 15 Kneeling figure in bronze, Fårdal, Denmark. Ht 6.5 cm. National Museum, Copenhagen. Lelly Aldworth.

The goddesses of Greece were said to weave, and to encourage women in the craft. In the *Odyssey*, which is much concerned with weaving, both Calypso and Circe, women of supernatural powers, are described working at the loom; in Book V Calypso sings as she moves her golden shuttle to and fro, while Circe in Book X also sings as she works at her everlasting loom, while she weaves 'one of those delicate, graceful and dazzling fabrics that goddesses love to make' (Rieu 1945: 164). Even the huntress Artemis may engage in such work, since Helen is described in Book IV as resembling Artemis with her golden distaff. It has been claimed by Elmer Suhr (1969) that Aphrodite was also represented as a spinner, and that the position of the upper arms of the Venus de Milo suggests that she was holding a distaff and spindle.

But the goddess undoubtedly associated with weaving was Athene; we are told in Book VII of the *Odyssey* that the skill of Phaeacian women at the loom was due to the fact that Athene had made them expert in the finer crafts and given them intelligence. Nilsson's (1938) claim that Athene originated as a Mycenaean palace goddess before she became one of the most popular deities of classical Greece have been generally accepted; from the beginning she was associated with domestic arts, and therefore with spinning and weaving (Kinsley 1989: 139). She was a single goddess, without husband or lovers, although encouraging marriage and represented as the nurturer and educator of children. She was primarily concerned with the welfare of the state, and therefore with weapons and martial arts as well as the maintenance of social order, and was the protector and helper of leaders and heroes like Odysseus. In contrast to Artemis, who ruled over the wild places, her domain was the city, where she supported and maintained culture; cities, according to Aristides, were the gift of Athene (Farnell 1896: I, 301).

Athene has some connections with agriculture, giving the olive tree to Athens and teaching mortals to cultivate it, while sacred grain was ground for her by the girl selected as her Millmaid; she was said by Aristides to teach farmers the use of the plough, and like some of the western goddesses (see pp. 66–7) she was known as 'yoker of oxen' (Farnell 1896: I, 291). The making of cloth, however, was her most renowned skill. While Aphrodite may possibly have been portrayed holding a spindle, Athene certainly possessed one and also worked at the loom. She punished the rash girl Arachne, who claimed that she could outdo the goddess in weaving, by turning her into a spider. In Book II of the *Odyssey* it was said to be Athene who had given Penelope her aptitude for weaving; she taught young girls both weaving and embroidery, and according to the *Theogony* of Hesiod, she wove clothes for Pandora when she was created by the gods, and taught her the art of weaving. This was her special gift to women, while she instructed men in ship-building, the making of chariots and ploughs, pottery and metallurgy.

Her statue in the northern sanctuary of the Acropolis was carved of olive wood and draped with a woollen robe, for which the women of the city were responsible, weaving a new robe for her every year, to be presented at the Panathenaia, the summer festival in July celebrating her birth (Neils 1992: 10ff.). This is thought to have been in the form of a *peplos* to be wrapped round the body, pinned at the shoulders and worn with a belt, a piece of woven cloth measuring about 4 feet by 6 feet (Barber 1994: 282). It was a style of dress no longer worn in Athens in the fifth century BC, but retained as the traditional covering for Athene's statue. The main colours of the cloth were saffron yellow and sea purple, and the weaving, decorated with gold embroidery, was said to depict the battle of gods and giants, in which Athene and Zeus destroyed the Titans and achieved victory for the gods of Olympus. The weaving was done by women in the service of Athene, helped by two young girls, the *arrephoroi*, said to be between 7 and 10 years of age, chosen from aristocratic Athenian families to serve the goddess and be responsible for setting up the warp. The work began nine months before the festival, since the robe with its pictorial designs would take a considerable time to complete, while a nine months' period may have been felt appropriate to precede the festival celebrating the birth of the goddess. Young children can be very successful at weaving, on account of their small nimble fingers and keen eyesight, and such a choice is quite credible (Barber 1992: 113). The matrons who made the robe were called the *ergastinai* (workers); they did the weaving and the embroidery which elaborated the woven pictures on the *peplos*, while other young women helped in preparing the wool. Elizabeth Barber has shown how figures and designs might be added in a series of panels, either across the cloth or down the front of the garment, by workers on a warp-weighted loom such as was used in Greece (Barber 1992: 113ff.).

There was a splendid procession through the city to bring the new robe to the temple, and this was one of the rare occasions when women came out into the streets. This is thought to be depicted on the great frieze of the Parthenon, where a folded cloth can be seen which could be the *peplos*. The youthful figure holding it has been thought by some to be a girl, and women and girls are shown taking part in the procession (Robertson 1975: 9–11). The practice of presenting a robe to Athene must have been known earlier, since one is brought to her temple in Troy in Book VI of the *Iliad*; this is an individual offering made by Hector's mother Hecabe, who lays it on the knees of the goddess with a prayer for the salvation of the city. The major Athenian festival presumably developed out of such a custom.

It is now thought that a second woven *peplos* was presented to Athene at the Greater Panathenaia, held every four years, and celebrated with a series of contests in gymnastics, torch races and other sports, as well as music and recitations from Homer. Special amphorae filled with olive oil were presented to the winners. It seems likely that the larger *peplos* offered to the goddess on this occasion was woven by men, professional weavers working on large looms; it would not be used to adorn Athene's image, but hung up in the temple for the next four years (Barber 1992: 113ff.). It was large enough to be displayed like a sail on the mast of a ship drawn on a float, a custom said to have been introduced after the Athenian victory over the Persian fleet at Salamis. The true tapestry technique may have been used on this, and it may have shown recent events such as the Salamis victory as well as Athene's defeat of the Titans.

It seems that there was a strongly established tradition for queens and high-born women to work on scenes from myths and heroic legends, or important events of their own time, in weaving and embroidery. In Book III of the *Iliad*, Helen is said to be weaving 'a great purple web of double width' representing some of the battles between Greeks and Trojans when she was interrupted by the news that Paris and Menelaus were to fight a duel. Euripides in *Iphigenia in Tauros* and *Ion* refers to such woven pictures of mythical symbols or events; these might be taken from the temple store-houses to be set up at a feast (Barber 1994: 153). Social conditions in Athens made it impossible for aristocratic women to take part in trade in textiles, as they could in other parts of Greece, so that for them the weaving which occupied so much of their days was primarily important as a means of recording scenes from myth or history to display in their halls, or perhaps in temples. They also wove fine robes for their own use and for gifts, like the one which Helen, after her return from Troy, presented to Telemachus for his future bride (*Odyssey*, XV).

This is a point of some importance, since it shows that the women must have had considerable interest in the myths and legends, and discussed together how to portray them in their weaving and embroidery. The picture that Homer gives of Penelope's life in the *Odyssey* shows how much of their time was taken up with spinning and working at the loom; the golden spindles of which we read, and which have been found in graves of the Bronze Age, appear to have been put to constant practical use in the halls of the aristocracy (Barber 1994: 209ff.). Meanwhile women of lesser rank, including the many women captives brought home after wars, worked constantly to prepare the wool and to spin and weave it for use in the royal household or for trade. It is scarcely surprising that the goddess was closely associated with these skills which formed so essential a part of women's lives, whatever their rank in society.

While in Ancient Greece women used mainly wool for their robes, in Egypt clothes were made from linen, a more suitable material for the hot dry climate. Various plant fibres were used in early times, especially hemp and nettles, but the possibilities of flax, probably first cultivated for its oil-bearing seeds, were soon discovered, and it was used for weaving in Anatolia and Israel from the seventh millennium BC (Barber 1991: 12). In Egypt the men raised and harvested the flax, and dried the stems in the sun; these were then spread out to catch the dew, in order to rot the fleshy parts away from the usable fibres, a process known as retting. The men used some of these to make ropes and string, but the best of the flax went to the women workers to be made into linen. There were weaving rooms on noblemen's estates and at the rich temples, where many women worked together. Humbler women cleaned and separated the fibres and spliced them to make crude yarn, probably using saliva to stick them together, and rolling them into balls damped in wetting bowls to make them easier to work. Another group twisted the yarn to give it strength when wound on the spindle, to be passed on to the weavers. The workers would include slaves taken in war, organized by women overseers, but some skilled weavers may well have been women of a higher class. Elizabeth Barber (1994: 190) quotes part of a lament by the women weavers at a time of political unrest:

> Wearers of fine linen are beaten ...
> Ladies suffer like maidservants,
> Singers are at the looms in the weaving rooms,
> What they sing to the goddess are dirges.
> (Lichtheim 1975: 153)

Linen was used for sheets, blankets and towels as well as garments, and also for bandages for the dead. It was a symbol of wealth, so that large quantities were provided for the tombs of the rich. The quality of the finest Egyptian linen was extremely high, 'finer than the finest handkerchief you can buy nowadays' (Barber 1994: 194).

The goddess to whom dirges were sung in the weaving rooms in bad times was presumably Isis. She was regarded as patron of crafts and also of scientific knowledge, while as a goddess who encouraged family life she was said to instruct women in spinning and weaving, and to have introduced these skills into the community (Witt 1971: 41). She and her sister Nephthys were described as weaving garments for Osiris (Heyob 1975: 48). Women are sometimes depicted on funerary steles not only carrying the attributes of Isis but also wearing her style of costume, a tunic and a mantle with a fringe and knot (Heyob 1975: 60).

The enormous amount of work in spinning and weaving done by women over thousands of years in the ancient world has left few traces behind. As Elizabeth Barber points out: 'Only to the extent that the women's cloth recorded religious or historical information ... did the women then reap prestige for their work' (Barber 1994: 285). However, this is an important factor in linking weaving with the cults of the goddesses. Beside the great powers, there were supernatural female figures concerned with the weaving of the web of fate. At first there was perhaps one such power, but later the three *Moirai* (Roman *Parcae*) might be pictured as three old women in white robes, or two in coloured robes and one in black. Clotho held a distaff, Lachesis a spindle, and Atropos, the black-clad figure, scissors for cutting the thread. They sang as they worked, foretelling the destiny to come (Greene 1944: 16). They were responsible for the length of life allotted to the new-born child, and it seems as though Atropos cut an appropriate length of thread for each at birth. Sometimes they were represented as more exalted figures in robes spangled with stars, on thrones among the celestial spheres, whose decisions could outweigh the will of the gods. These majestic beings did not weave, but the metaphor of spinning the thread from which the web of life was woven was consistently maintained, a powerful concept, while spinning and weaving remained a familiar part of a woman's life (see pp. 113–15).

WEAVING IN NORTHERN EUROPE

Weaving was known in the North even before the Bronze Age. In Britain there are finds of spindle whorls and what are thought to be loom weights from the Neolithic period, while evidence for cloth in the Bronze Age has come from graves, stray finds and habitation sites; it might be wrapped around bodies or human bones, weapons or hoards (Henshall 1950: 133ff.). A great deal has also been learnt from the clothes preserved in tree coffins from Denmark (see pp. 91–3). Henshall reported the quality of weaving in the Bronze Age to be good, and noted that in some cases a fine thread was used. Wool, flax, hemp and nettle were in early use for weaving in northern Europe (Geijer 1979: 1ff.). Flax was probably first cultivated in Scandinavia in prehistoric times for linseed, and linen was produced from it in east Sweden and Finland in the Middle Ages. Hemp was grown almost everywhere for its fibre and oil-yielding fruit, while some examples of early linen are now thought to have been spun from nettles, though not the common stinging variety.

The upright warp-weighted loom was evidently used in the North from early times. In Switzerland there is evidence for skilled weaving in the Neolithic period, with traces of woven patterns and of linen and hemp thread. There is a picture of a warp-weighted loom on a pot of the early Iron Age from Odenburg in Austria, and it was widely used over Iron Age Europe. By the time of the Roman Empire fine regular cloth was being woven in Scandinavia, and many loom weights of stone or fired clay have survived. Since women worked on looms of this type and spun yarn for their weaving for a period of over 9,000 years, distaff and loom must have become familiar and powerful symbols.

The warp-weighted loom survived up to the twentieth century in remote parts of Scandinavia and Finland, as has been demonstrated by Marta Hoffman in her detailed study published in 1964. Examples can be seen in museums in Scandinavia, Iceland and the Faroes (Figure 16). The Saami (Lapps) continued to use it to weave a kind of blanket known as *grener*, and even practised weaving out of doors during their summer migrations with the reindeer. They kept a few sheep, often sadly neglected, to provide the wool; Marta Hoffmann saw two women working together on such a loom, one walking to and fro to work the warp while the other was seated (Hoffmann 1964: 81ff.). In Iceland the warp-weighted loom was called the Icelandic Loom, and was in use until the eighteenth century or later. The production of the rough woollen cloth known as

Figure 16 Loom from Olderdalen, North Troms, Norway. Based on photograph in Hoffman (1964). Eileen Aldworth.

wadmal, woven by women in their homes, was of great economic importance there during the Viking Age as a major export to England, Norway
and continental Europe, because it was cheap and hard-wearing. It was
used by Icelanders as a monetary base, valued in terms of silver (Gelsinger
1981: 34ff., 127, 253).

As in Greece, weaving was primarily women's work, done in the home
or perhaps in small weaving huts, until about the twelfth century AD when
the horizontal loom worked by a treadle came in, probably when the
woollen industry was reorganized in the Low Countries. Weaving on this
was done by men and organized by the guilds, and much longer woven
pieces of cloth could be produced; the weavers sat at their work instead
of standing as the women were accustomed to do (Geijer 1979: 34). The
spinning wheel came into use about 1300 AD, but in northern Europe
many women continued to rely on the spindle and the 'rock' or distaff
throughout the Middle Ages. When the manufacture of cloth was on a

more professional basis, women and girls gathered in the 'spinning rooms' in Germany and Denmark to work at the preparation of wool and linen thread; these women's gatherings were a fruitful source of folklore and traditions about female supernatural beings (see pp. 104–5). They were centres of feminine activity; in some areas men did not dare to enter, as in Salzburg in the nineteenth century (Wolfram 1933: 145).

Thus, in northern Europe as in Ancient Greece, spinning and weaving formed an important element in women's lives. When in the *Edda* poem *Rigspula* (15) the god Rig visits a typical well-to-do farmer's wife, she is described as sitting spinning:

> There sat a woman, unwound from her distaff,
> With arms extended, prepared for weaving.

The position of the raised arms by those using the distaff was a familiar sight in the Middle Ages. In Iceland women married to the leading landowners supervised their women servants, but also took part in the work of producing wadmal. In *Laxdœla Saga* (49), Gudrun refers to her morning's work in a famous passage when her husband comes home after killing the hero Kjartan as a result of her promptings, and she declares she has produced enough yarn for 12 ells (*alnar*) of cloth. Wadmal was woven in standardized commercial lengths for export, and 12 ells is a large amount, since the Icelandic ell of cloth was 18 in. (46 cm) or half a yard square (Gelsinger 1981: 35, 128). Therefore 12 ells would represent a piece 1 yard wide and 6 yards long. Gudrun was unlikely to have possessed a spinning wheel, and could hardly have spun as much yarn as this in one morning, even with maids to help her, but a possible deeper significance behind her words will be discussed later in this chapter (see pp. 121–2).

Most of the spinning done in Iceland was with wool. Women wore linen, but neither flax nor its substitutes could have been grown there in large quantities, and most of the linen must have been imported. In *Eyrbyggja Saga* some linen sheets from England were clearly regarded as a great treasure, and played an important part in a grim tale of the return of the dead (Davidson 1981: 156ff.).

It is clear that, as in Greece, women of high social standing worked at spinning and weaving on the loom, and also at tablet weaving, to produce narrow bands used for borders on clothes or to provide a starting border for the warp when beginning a piece of weaving on the loom (Geijer 1979: 31). For this type of work a series of small plates or tablets was used, usually square and with a hole in each corner through which the warp thread was drawn. The plates could be rotated by a single hand movement, and the woven part fastened to the weaver's belt (Figure 17). This is a very ancient method of weaving, which could be practised out of doors and in odd moments; it was used by a seeress in Ireland to foretell the results of a battle (see p. 117) Some tablet weaving was of a very high quality, with

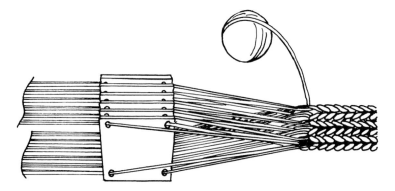

Figure 17 Tablet weaving. Based on diagram by E. J. W. Barber (1991). Eileen Aldworth.

use of silk or gold and silver threads; some particularly elaborate examples from graves of the Viking Age at Birka in Sweden are thought to have been imports from Byzantium (Geijer 1983: 221–2). However, in one of the *Edda* poems, *Goðrúnarkviða hin forna* (28), one of the offers made to Gudrun if she marries Atli is that 'Hunnish women who weave with tablets' (*hlaða spjöldum*) will work with gold for her pleasure, suggesting that these exotic braids may have been made by skilled weavers from eastern Europe employed or working as slaves in the courts of kings. In any case the women of both Anglo-Saxon England and Scandinavia were familiar with tablet weaving, and one of the kennings or poetic terms for a woman used by Icelandic poets in the Viking Age given in Vigfusson's (1874) *Dictionary* is the Gna (goddess) of the tablets (*spjalda*). *Spjald* means a square piece or tablet of wood, like those used for book covers, and can hardly be taken as a square piece of weaving, as is suggested in the *Dictionary*.

Women produced not only clothes and bed-linen for the household, but also hangings for the wall, and this, as in Ancient Greece, was a task which might occupy queens and priestesses. There are references in *Goðrúnarkviða hin forna* (stanzas 14ff.) to the making of such hangings, sometimes woven with figures and symbols, and sometimes embroidered on a woven background. True 'all-over' tapestry, of the kind produced in medieval France, did not become common in the North until the later Middle Ages.

According to the poem, Gudrun stayed in Denmark with Thora, Hakon's daughter, for a time before she was persuaded to marry King Atli. Thora strove to cheer Sigurd's widow by embroidering 'southern halls and Danish swans' in gold thread. They worked together on a tapestry which showed a military scene with 'reddened shields, champions ready for battle, a sword-troop, a helmed troop, the king's followers', evidently depicting episodes from the exploits of the hero Sigmund, father of Gudrun's husband Sigurd. There is mention of a picture in which Sigmund's ship made its way along the coast, and a battle took place on board against Sigar and Siggeir. Although no sea battle is described in *Völsunga Saga*, Siggeir appears there as the husband of Sigmund's sister Signy, and fighting certainly took place when he made a treacherous attack on King Volsung and his sons after inviting them to his kingdom. Only the young Sigmund survived to take terrible vengeance on Siggeir.

Here, as in the accounts of tapestries made by noble ladies in Greece (see p. 97), recent heroic exploits are depicted in weaving and embroidery. Although there are no specific references here to myths, the 'swans' embroidered by Thora suggest tales of swan-maidens, while the tale of the hero Sigmund was closely associated with the heroic cult of Odin. There are other references to hangings showing the slaying of the dragon Fafnir by Sigmund's son Sigurd when he gained the great treasure of the Nibelungs. Such a scene was said to be worked in embroidery adorned with gold thread by Brynhild as she sat in her bower (*Völsunga Saga* 24), while descriptions in verse of two scenes on wall-hangings in which Sigurd first slays the dragon with his sword and then roasts his heart are found in a poem of the eleventh century by Thorfinn, a skald at St Olaf's court (*Flateyjarbók* III, 9: 244). It seems that such woven or embroidered hangings were often used as subjects for verse since, in *Orkneyinga Saga* (85) when the hangings were being put up for Christmas, Earl Rognvald of Orkney challenged a visiting Icelandic poet to make up a verse on an aged warrior depicted on them, and produced his own verse in reply. The picture evidently showed a battle scene in which swords were used and Viking seamen took part. The fact that heroic or mythological scenes on hangings were often described by poets suggests that the women who produced them not only helped to spread knowledge of the myths, but also may have influenced their form and interpretation.

One of the earliest references to wall-hangings is found in the Anglo-Saxon poem *Beowulf* where, in the passage describing how the great hall of Heorot was made ready for a splendid feast to celebrate Beowulf's victory over Grendel (991ff.), tapestry (*web*), gleaming with gold, is said to shine on the walls: 'many marvels to behold for anyone gazing on such things'. This again implies figures or scenes represented on the hangings, which in this magnificent hall might well be decorated with gold embroidery. After the death of the leader Bryhtnoth at the battle of Maldon in Essex in 991, his widow Ælflæd presented a hanging to Ely Cathedral, 'portrayed as a memorial to his uprightness' (*depictam in memoriam probitatis*) (Digby 1965: 48) which may conceivably have shown his heroic death in battle as described in the Anglo-Saxon poem on the Battle of Maldon. Another example of a tapestry as a family memorial is that given by the Frankish Queen Bertha to the church of St Denis in Paris, said to depict the glorious deeds of her ancestors (Bertrand 1966: 46).

Such examples in Christian times suggest that wall-hangings as well as carved stones could serve as memorials for the dead and glorification of the heroic past, and that it would be women who produced them. Their importance is indicated by the Bayeux Tapestry worked for William the Conqueror, with its detailed series of embroidered pictures depicting Harald's encounter with William in Normandy and William's invasion of England. Here we have an exceptional work, presumably created as a deliberate piece of propaganda for the new ruler, but in spite of abundant speculation there is still no definite evidence as to who designed it and was responsible for the embroidery (S. A. Brown 1988). But at least we can be confident that women, and probably those of the highest rank, were concerned in its creation and took a lively interest in the representation. Valuable hangings, regarded as major works of art, were unlikely to be kept continually on view in church or hall, but would be brought out, like the gold-adorned hangings in Heorot, at great festivals or to celebrate important occasions.

Snorri has little to tell us about the goddess particularly concerned with textiles, but it would seem that either Freyja or Frigg was the divine patroness of spinning and weaving women. One of Freyja's names given by Snorri is Hörn, found in place-names in eastern Sweden (J. de Vries 1957: II, 331). It is assumed to come from *hörr*, flax, and this part of Sweden was one of the areas in northern Europe where flax was successfully grown. However, spinning was also linked with Frigg in Sweden, since the constellation known as Orion's Belt was called *Friggerock*, 'distaff of Frigg', over a large area (J. de Vries 1957: II, 304). In other parts of Sweden it was called Mary's distaff.

In Blekinge there was a custom of not allowing spinning on Thursdays, as that was when Frigg's spinning was done. Thursday was generally regarded as Thor's day in the Viking Age in Scandinavia, but it was a day sacred to a goddess in the Baltic countries. Laima, a powerful goddess in Latvia, was associated with spinning and weaving as well as with childbirth and agriculture, and on Thursday evenings certain work was forbidden, particularly spinning, knitting and breaking up wood (Biezais 1955: 323). According to Ralston, the female spirits known as Rusalkas in Russia had the Thursday before Whit Sunday as their special day on which women should not sew or wash linen (see p. 137) or men weave fences (Ralston 1872: 141–2). Throughout Germany the records of Waschnitius (1913) include many traditions of a special day sacred to a supernatural female being on which spinning was forbidden; this varied in different areas and included various evenings before Christian festivals, but was sometimes a Thursday.

This group of beings remembered under names such as Berchta and Holle in Germany and adjoining countries was clearly associated with the world of nature, agriculture and fertility (see p. 66), but they also encouraged spinning and were said to spin themselves; the sound of thunder in the German area of Lucerne was said to be Perht reeling her flax (Waschnitius 1913: 34). One of their main functions was to ensure that the girls in the spinning rooms, from which much of the folklore about these beings seems to have emanated, performed their work well. Grimm (1883–8) noted that Berchta or Perht (the name has many different forms) was remembered in popular tradition in Upper Germany, Swabia, Alsace, Bavaria, Switzerland and Austria as a rather fierce figure who kept a watch on spinners and spoiled work left unfinished by the last day of the year; she might also bring empty reels to the women with orders to spin them full in a short time. In the Tyrol Perht might break the distaffs of lazy girls (Waschnitius 1913: 33), while Frau Holle similarly punished bad spinners by dirtying their distaffs and tangling the thread. In Thuringia she might appear as a grey-haired old woman with long teeth, who left a present on the distaff when a piece of work had been satisfactorily completed; this tradition can be traced back to about 1770 (Waschnitius 1913: 111). Frau Berta in the south Tyrol was said to visit villages and to give thread and yarn to the women, while in return they offered her food (Waschnitius 1913: 44). These female beings were also said to punish naughty children and reward well-behaved ones by sending good luck.

The festivals of these beings varied, but seem all to be in midwinter, near Christmas. On Berchta's special day, according to Grimm (1883: I, 273) certain food had to be eaten, such as dumplings and fish in Thuringia, and she was said to open the stomachs of those not keeping to the approved diet and fill them with chopped straw. Frau Holle and her followers might whip anyone who disobeyed her rules by working on days when spinning was forbidden (Waschnitius 1913: 66). In Christian times these days became linked with the Church festivals, and spinning was also forbidden on Saturday evenings; there were tales of a dead woman returning from Hell with a burnt hand, as punishment for breaking such a taboo (Waschnitius 1913: 132). Here the earlier traditions about a goddess have been replaced by the condemnation of the Christian Church.

Clearly over a large part of northern Europe there were certain days around Christmastide when it was held to be unlucky to spin even after the traditions of a supernatural figure working on that day were forgotten. No doubt such traditions survived for a long while because they ensured welcome breaks from the long hours of labour. Moreover the idea that supernatural beings had power at night, and that night work was dangerous for mortals, was very widespread; in wintertime much spinning was done in the evening after dark (Waschnitius 1913: 164).

Memories of a supernatural being who taught spinning and weaving and helped young girls may be found in fairy-tales of the nineteenth century. Grimm has the tale of Mother Holle in his collection of Household Tales, in which a girl with a cruel stepmother loses her spindle and in terror jumps down a well. She finds herself in Mother Holle's beautiful garden, and stays happily with her, working at spinning and other tasks, until she is able to return home covered in gold as a reward for faithful service.

Another interesting tale is the Scottish one of Habetrot from Selkirk in Scotland (Briggs 1970: 303). Here an ugly old woman befriends a feckless girl who hates spinning, but who as a result of her mother's boasting is faced with an enormous pile of flax to be spun into yarn. The old woman with her fellow-spinners lives under the roots of a tree, and can be seen only by someone looking through a hole in a stone. Habetrot does the spinning for the girl, and when the laird admires her skill and marries her, Habetrot saves her from a dismal future of endless work at the spinning wheel. She tells her husband that spinning will spoil the girl's beauty, giving her deformed lips, a flat thumb and a splay foot so that she will resemble Habetrot and her companions, and he swears that his wife shall never touch a spinning wheel again. This woman from the Otherworld proved more generous than Perht and Holle and the rest were reputed to be, helping a girl who never worked diligently at her spinning and bringing her a prosperous and happy marriage.

These figures whose presence lingered on among women's traditions until the twentieth century have undoubtedly many characteristics of the fertility goddess, whose favours were especially sought by women and girls, and whose wrath might be invoked against those who neglected the work of spinning as well as the duties of home and the rearing of children. The spinning room was one obvious place where women came together and where amusing and cautionary tales could be passed down to each new generation in turn. It becomes clear from the material in Waschnitius' rich collection that the cultivation of the earth and spinning are closely connected. Flax must be grown and tended and prepared for spinning, and Grimm has a description of a woman in white who comes at noontide to women weeding the flax, and instructs them how to grow and spin it (Grimm 1883: III, 1,162). He describes her as a fearsome presence, who might wring the necks of women who would not answer her: 'The people dread her and are glad she has not shown herself this long while past'. It is in such traditions, preserved in many parts of Germany and Austria, that the goddess as the instructress of spinning and weaving can be discerned in both her benign and her threatening aspect.

THE OSEBERG WALL-HANGINGS

The Oseberg ship-burial from the early Viking Age in Norway provides strong evidence for a link between the cult of the goddess and the craft of weaving and embroidery in northern Europe. The mound which contained the ship was raised in the first half of the ninth century in southern Norway, in the area ruled by the kings of Vestfold, and here two women were buried, laid on beds in a wooden grave chamber erected on the deck. Due to acid conditions in the soil, wooden gravegoods as well as textiles were preserved, and the contents of the fine carved vessel were impressive in their richness and variety, in spite of serious damage inflicted when the mound was entered not long after the burial. There is no mention in Snorri's histories of any royal grave at Oseberg, and the mound was not excavated until 1903. When signs of well-preserved wood were found, Gabriel Gustafson took over the work on 3 August of that year, and devoted all his energies to it for the rest of his life, for the preservation, repair and recording of the wonderful objects that the mound contained proved a demanding labour. Among the gravegoods were as many as four looms and a number of instruments for spinning and weaving (Grieg 1928: I, 173ff.), as well as a quantity of woven and embroidered wall-hangings.

Two of the four small looms were unfortunately too fragmented to be reconstructed, and only one of the four survived in good condition, 'well preserved and perfectly made' (Geijer 1979: 29). This could not have been intended for weaving ordinary fabrics, but may have been used for *sprang*, a plaiting technique done with fingers and sticks (Geijer 1979: 222), or for producing figured fabrics, or possibly a circular warp (Hoffman 1964: 330). This loom had a base and was 119 cm high, and the frame of another in beechwood, about 116.5 cm high, has survived, although damaged by those who broke into the mound. There was also a set of weaving tablets holding an unfinished piece of braid, conceivably the work of one of the ladies in the grave chamber, while other weaving tablets were found elsewhere.

The looms appear originally to have been placed in the grave chamber, although some pieces were found in other parts of the ship. In addition there were various wooden articles used in making textiles, including reels for winding skeins of wool and a 'swift' for making it into balls, consisting of crossbars rotating horizonally on a foot (Hoffmann 1964: 290ff.) (see pp. 115–16). There were also clubs for beating flax and others for washing linen, as well as shears for clipping sheep. A number of these objects had been placed in a chest in the grave chamber and were clearly regarded as important.

The most momentous find, however, was that of bundles of cloth rolled together, much of which consisted of wall-hangings, of the kind described in the literature (see pp. 102–4). Anne Ingstad, who has discussed the hangings in detail, suggested that they might have been used to adorn the burial chamber, which was in the form of a little gabled house of wood, roughly constructed. If so they were presumably taken down and rolled up together with bedclothes and other pieces of fabric by those who broke into the grave (Ingstad *et al.* 1992: 212). They consisted of long narrow woven strips not more than 23 cm wide, on some of which many figures were portrayed, riding, walking, or driving in wagons, as well as battle scenes. Sections of the hangings have been painstakingly restored, although the greater part of the work seems irretrievably lost (Hougen 1940). The figures on the hangings were partly woven, with the outlines embroidered in contrasting colours, and many details worked in embroidery. Those who designed and executed them were skilled and experienced artists and weavers; Ingstad claims that no finer work could be produced, even with modern techniques, and thinks that the weaving might have been done on one of the small looms in the ship (Ingstad *et al.* 1992: 189). We have a valuable account published in 1956 by Sofie Krafft, describing her introduction to the hangings fifty years earlier, the beginning of many years of dedicated work recording them under the supervision of Gabriel Gustafson.

The hangings are long and narrow, so if put up in a hall they would be above the heads of those sitting at tables, but below the area darkened by smoke (Hougen 1940: 92), and might also have been used at feasts held on ships in harbour. According to the Icelandic sagas such hangings were regarded as family treasures, brought out at festivals and on important occasions.

When in *Laxdœla Saga* (29) Olaf the Peacock built a magnificent hall at Hjardarholt, he seems to have departed from custom by having 'scenes from renowned tales painted on the wood of the walls and ceiling; they were so executed that it was felt to look more splendid without wall-hangings'. What the subjects of these paintings were is indicated in an early skaldic poem, *Húsdrápa*, by Ulf Uggason, composed about 985 (Turville-Petre 1976: 68). Strophes from this are recorded in the *Prose Edda*, and the scenes they describe are mythological ones: Freyr, Odin and Heimdall riding to Balder's funeral, a giantess launching Balder's funeral ship, Loki and Heimdall fighting over Freyja's necklace, and Thor encountering the Midgard serpent and striking down the giant Hymir. It is to be presumed that scenes of a similar kind were depicted on wall-hangings. In the *Húsdrápa* a procession of gods is described attending the funeral of the dead Balder, whose body was burned on his ship, and we have another description of this by Snorri in *Gylfaginning* (49), which reads as if it were based on a pictorial representation of the scene:

> This burning was attended by beings of many different kinds. First it must be told of Odin that Frigg was with him, and the valkyries, and his ravens, while Freyr drove in a wagon with the boar named Gullinbursti or Slidrugtanni; Heimdall rode the horse called Gulltopp, and Freyja drove her cats. Many frost giants and mountain giants came there also.

The best preserved section of the Oseberg hangings shows just such a concourse of 'beings of many kinds'. There are impressive riders on horseback, like Odin and Heimdall in the poem, and one of them is attended by two black birds. There are many walking figures, some of them apparently supernatural ones, and others driving in wagons, and there is one scene depicting several figures standing beside the prow of a ship (Ingstad *et al.* 1992: 179).

Gustafson, who took a keen interest in the pictures on the hangings, thought they might have depicted the funeral of the queen buried at Oseberg with her companion, pointing out that there are two women driving in the procession in a wagon which closely resembles the carved wagon in the ship (Figure 18). Anne Ingstad also points out striking resemblances, such as that between the lamps with long handles carried by more than one woman pictured on the hangings and two lamps in a chest in the grave chamber. Krafft (1956: 17ff.) thought that the wagons depicted with cloth wrappings over the contents might have held valuable offerings to be placed in the grave, while Ingstad suggests that they contained images of the gods and of Freyja, although there is nothing to support this in the literature.

The difficulty is that this elaborate work could hardly have been produced in the period which elapsed between the death of the occupant of the grave chamber and her burial in the mound. It is possible that they portray some earlier funeral of a great lady or high priestess, or that it is a mythological funeral scene which is represented. It must also be remembered that there were other scenes on the tapestries, particularly those representing battles, which cannot be immediately associated with the Oseberg funeral.

Figure 18 Wagon in procession on Oseberg wall-hanging. Based on painting by M. Storm (Hougen 1940). Lelly Aldworth.

Certainly there are strong suggestions both of mythological inspiration and of religious ritual on the hangings, as Terry Gunnell (1994: 60ff.) has pointed out. As well as the processions there are dancing female figures, and a row of women with their arms raised as if in adoration. There is what seems to be a sacrificial tree with hanging corpses, and individual figures which could be either supernatural characters or men and women representing them. There is an armed male figure in an animal skin, perhaps a berserk, and a horned figure with crossed spears, resembling those depicted on Anglo-Saxon and Swedish helmets (Davidson 1965). There are also groups of women bearing shields who have been taken for valkyries, and women with swine heads, who might represent the goddess Freyja (Figure 19a), as well as some with bird heads, recalling her in her falcon form, while Ingstad thinks that one woman on horseback (Figure 19b) might represent Freyja herself (Ingstad *et al.* 1992: 240). Gunnell suggests that such figures, which are shown together with human ones, could be men and women acting the parts of gods and goddesses in a ritual ceremony.

To suggest that the provision of a number of looms and implements for spinning and weaving were put into the grave merely 'to keep the women occupied' on their long journey (Jesch 1991: 33) seems an inadequate explanation. Moreover, as Ingstad points out, the ship was not prepared for a voyage; there was an anchor and a number of heavy stones to keep it in the mound, while some of the oars were left unfinished (Ingstad *et al.* 1992: 253).

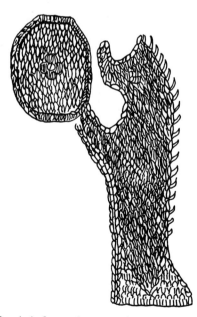

Figure 19a Swine-headed figure from Oseberg wall-hanging. After M. Storm (Hougen 1940). Lelly Aldworth.

Figure 19b Woman on horseback from Oseberg wall-hanging. Based on drawing in Ingstad *et al.* (1992). Lelly Aldworth.

I have elsewhere suggested that the queen or great lady buried at Oseberg was a priestess of either Freyja or Frigg (Davidson 1988: 117–18). This is implied by various items in the richly appointed ship, such as a chest of corn, and apples and nuts in rich containers, all recognized symbols of fertility. The great bed, which could be another symbol of the fertility goddess, associated with a divine marriage ritual, was savagely hacked to pieces by the people who broke into the mound and removed the body of the chief occupant of the grave, while other objects were deliberately damaged

(Brøgger 1945). This suggests a strong hostility to certain symbols in the grave, rather than casual vandalism by robbers hoping to find valuable gravegoods; the intruders could have been Christians who objected to the remains of a priestess of the goddess surviving in their neighbourhood. Again the beautiful little processional wagon with its elaborate carvings may have been used like the wagon of Nerthus to take the representative of the fertility goddess from farm to farm to bring good seasons (see p. 57). The ship itself, suitable for leisurely voyages along the coast rather than sea journeys, but large enough to need fifteen pairs of oars, would have been very suitable for visits to the widely scattered settlements in southern and western Norway, where the many fiords render road journeys difficult. Moreover the symbol of a ship is one closely associated with earlier northern goddesses such as Nehalennia (see p. 47), and was one of the symbols of the Vanir pair, Freyr and Freyja.

Anne Ingstad has argued strongly for the presence of a high priestess of the goddess in the burial chamber, and pointed out how many of the objects placed in the grave might be acknowledged symbols of her cult. The strong emphasis on spinning and weaving is one important factor here. The woman in the great bed could have been a queen as well as priestess, and Ingstad argues that she may have been Alfhild, the wife of King Gudrod the Magnificent, called also Hunting King, and mother of Olaf Geirstaðaralf, the Vestfold ruler who was said to have been venerated in his burial mound after death (Davidson 1988: 121–2). Ingstad goes on to suggest that the second woman in the grave was no mere slave sacrificed at the funeral, as many have assumed, along with the horses, dogs and oxen found in the forepart of the ship (see p. 166), but another woman from the shrine of the goddess; her high status is implied by the fact that she had her own bed in the grave chamber, smaller than the other, but splendidly appointed, and wore shoes of fine workmanship.

An additional piece of evidence for a link between weavers and a ship used for ritual journeys has survived by chance in a Belgian chronicle, the *Gesta abbatum Trudonensium*. This is an account of strange happenings at St Trond in the year 1133. It tells how a man from near Aachen got permission to build a ship, which he put on wheels and had drawn by weavers. They took it to Aachen, Maesdricht (where it was given a mast and sail), Tongres, Borgloon and finally to Trond. Here the abbot warned the townspeople against it, and the weavers had to guard it day and night, but none the less it was welcomed with riotous delight by the townspeople; in the evening half-naked women are said to have rushed to the ship and danced around it. At midnight the dance ended and a great shouting took place, but sadly no words are recorded. This went on for twelve nights, and when more sober citizens wanted to burn the ship, there was such an outcry that it departed unharmed to Louvain, although there the gates of the town were closed against it.

Gelling quotes this strange episode in a discussion of the ship symbols of the Bronze Age rock-carvings in Sweden, suggesting that here we have 'a sudden re-emergence of an age-old celebration' (Gelling and Davidson 1967: 52). Certainly the welcome of the ship is reminiscent of that given to the wagon of Nerthus as described by Tacitus in the first century AD. But why were the weavers responsible for its safety, and for bringing it to the towns? The chronicler states that the man who built it wanted to humiliate them and forced them to draw it, but this sounds unconvincing, although it is quite likely that Christian weavers would be unwilling to join in so disreputable a celebration. The supplying of a mast and sail at one of the towns on the way provides an interesting parallel to the woven sail brought to the temple of Athene by her worshippers (see p. 96). It seems not unreasonable to suggest that here we have an example of popular enthusiasm for the annual welcome of the goddess remembered from earlier times, and that the weavers still supported a ceremony once connected with the deity who had been the patron of their craft. It is usually assumed that it was men drawing the ship, but women also took a leading part in the ceremony once it was inside the town, and the wild rites which took place can be compared with women's gatherings and violent behaviour associated with the birth of children (see pp. 143–4).

The association of the goddess with spinning and weaving is undoubtedly a many-sided one, and the rich evidence from the Oseberg ship offers us new possibilities. We have seen how weaving and embroidery gave women an opportunity to keep alive myths and heroic legends of the past, and how one important function of the goddess of spinning was to train and protect growing girls and help them towards marriage. One further point to be considered is that among the many aspects of the northern goddess Frigg, known to be associated with spinning and weaving (see p. 104), was her knowledge of the future, of the destinies of mortals and perhaps of gods also: 'I deem that Frigg knows the destinies of all', declares Freyja in *Lokasenna* (29), 'though she does not herself declare it' (see p. 121). This is a further important aspect associated with the imagery of spinning and weaving, to be discussed in the following section.

WEAVING AND DESTINY

We know that a Greek goddess might be depicted holding a distaff (see pp. 94–5), and on a round disc brooch from Byzantium, dated from about the sixth century AD, the Virgin Mary is similarly represented with a distaff in her hand (Figure 20). There was a tradition that she was occupied in spinning at the moment of the Annunciation, when the Archangel Gabriel appeared with his momentous news (Ellmers 1974: 233ff.); this was a favourite subject for Byzantine art, depicted on a number of ivories. It is

Figure 20 Disc brooch from Byzantium representing the Annunciation. Based on photograph given by Ellmers (1974). Lelly Aldworth.

not found in the account in St Luke's Gospel, but is derived from the apocryphal book of the second century known as the *Protevangelium of James*, probably by a non-Jewish writer, which deals with the birth and upbringing of the Virgin Mary, her betrothal to Joseph, and the birth of Christ (Hennecke 1963: 368ff.).

According to this work, Mary at 12 years of age left the Temple where she had been brought up for the house of her chosen husband Joseph. When it was decided that a veil for the holy place should be made, the priests sought out seven 'pure virgins of the tribe of David' to weave it, and chose Mary as one of them. They drew lots to decide who should work the various colours, and to Mary fell the task of weaving the 'pure purple' and 'scarlet'. These were symbolic colours, since purple was reserved for the Emperor, while scarlet represented both royalty and martyrdom. She had already spun the scarlet when she heard a voice addressing her as she went to draw water. Trembling she entered the house again, and began to draw out the purple thread. It was at this point that the Archangel Gabriel appeared to her, telling her to have no fear.

On the disc brooch Mary is shown facing forward, seated on a kind of throne, holding a distaff in her right hand while the other hand is raised in a gesture of adoration (Ellmers 1974: 233). Thus we have echoes brought into Christian tradition of the spinning goddess who could influence the fate of the new-born and the destiny of the world, a concept which as we have seen was established in Ancient Greece (see pp. 98–9). Although the *Protevangelium* was rejected in western Europe, savagely attacked by St Jerome and finally condemned by the Pope, the spinning tradition nevertheless persisted there also. Erich Neumann refers to a twelfth-century fresco of the Annunciation in the church of Sorpe in Spain, where a Virgin of Byzantine type stands with a distaff in one hand and raises the thread with the other as the angel approaches her. He mentions also a later painting, of about 1400 from Germany by the Upper Rhenish Master, where Mary sits spinning and the thread passes across the brow of the divine Child, who is lit up in her womb (Neumann 1955: 233). Here the spinning of the thread as a symbol of life and of destiny is clearly emphasized, deliberately linked with the birth of the divine child.

A link with the spinning goddess of the north, however, appears to exist even earlier than this, from the evidence of a small group of gold bracteates dated to the sixth century AD, known as the Furstenberg type (Mackeprang 1952: 103). Four of these have been found in Germany and one in Funen in Denmark, and they appear to have been influenced by such Byzantine models as the disc brooch already mentioned, and perhaps also by representations of a Byzantine Empress wearing a diadem. The extensive studies of Karl Hauck (1985) on northern Germanic bracteates, however, have shown that these were not worn as Christian symbols, but rather as amulets representing aspects of pre-Christian mythology and symbolism, based in most cases on designs from Roman medallions. These are adapted in various ways by northern craftsmen, who sometimes created strange and fantastic symbols and figures. Whereas Ellmers (1974) argues that the female figures on the Furstenberg bracteates were Christian copies of Byzantine originals, this has been rejected by Hauck (1985) and Enright (1990). They have put forward strong arguments for interpreting the woman on the bracteates as a Germanic goddess associated with weaving.

The position is rendered complex by the fact that in only two cases, those of the bracteates from Oberwerschen-B and Denmark, are weaving accesories (a spindle and balls of thread on reels) immediately recognizable. The objects in the hands of the other figures were at first interpreted as hierarchical objects, such as a cross-staff and globe perhaps appropriate for an Empress to hold. Michael Enright (1990) has reopened the debate with a detailed examination of the five separate bracteates, however, and claims that some of these puzzling attributes might also be associated with weaving. Hauck had already pointed out that the object identified as a cross-staff has a cross-bar at both ends, hardly possible for a Christian

Figure 21 Female figure on bracteate from south-west Germany. Based on drawing by Enright (1990). Lelly Aldworth.

symbol, and suggested that it might be a sceptre of some kind. Enright thinks that it represents a weaver's beam, the cylindrical shaft fixed to the top of the warp-weighted loom to which the warp was attached. It usually had a rod fitted through a hole at both ends so that tension could be increased when needed, and thus would resemble a cross-staff with a cross at either end if placed upright. Marta Hoffman (1964) refers to domestic weaving in Lappland done out of doors in good weather (see p. 99): a beam of this kind was set up on two uprights to hold the warp, which was held taut by weights at the bottom. The beam was easily portable, and could be used on journeys away from home during the summer (Hoffman 1964: 62).

A second object which might be associated with weaving is that held in the left hand of the figure from southern Germany (Figure 21); this, Enright (1990) suggests, could be the object known as a 'swift', used for winding a skein of thread on four arms revolving from a central stand (Hoffman 1964: 289ff.). One of these was found in Norway in the Oseberg ship-burial of the ninth century (see p. 107).

Enright (1990) gives several reasons for accepting the female figure on the bracteates as a pre-Christian weaving goddess rather than a figure of the Virgin. Two of the bracteates were found in sites which appear to be associated with pagan cults, and the one from Gudme (a name meaning 'home of the gods') came from what is thought to have been a major cult centre on Funen. The bracteate from Oberwerschen was under the chin of a woman who was apparently a person of some importance, and probably not a Christian. She had with her a spindle whorl, a silver needle by her hand, scissors and a knife. The woman from Grossfahne had three bracteates representing the same female figure, and was buried with a weaving sword, so that the link with weaving is well established. Moreover the figure on the bracteates, while powerful and impressive, seems with her large head and prominent breasts unlikely to represent the Virgin.

With regard to the weaver's beam which he thinks may be the object held in the hand of the female figure, Enright quotes the story from the *Táin Bó Cúalnge* (Book of Leinster: C. O'Rahilly 1967: 143), which may go back to an earlier written source of the ninth century (Lysaght 1986: 203). The seeress Feidelm, a supernatural figure from the Otherworld, is met by Queen Medb, desirous to know what the result of the approaching battle will be. Feidelm was weaving as she rode in her chariot, making a fringe on a small portable loom, perhaps of the 'tablet' type where the end of the warp was fastened to the weaver's waist, used for making coloured braids (see pp. 101–2). She held 'a weaver's beam of white bronze in her right hand with seven strips of red gold on its points(?)' (C. O'Rahilly's translation). In reply to the queen's question: 'How do you see our army?', the reply is: 'I see red on them. I see crimson'.

Here again, as in the legend of Mary working on part of the temple veil, colours form part of the fate foretold. The weaver's beam of white bronze, in this case small enough to be carried in the hand, would have held the top of the narrow warp, and may be compared with the golden spindles said to be used by both goddesses and women of royal status in Ancient Greece (see p. 97), and found in rich graves from the Early Bronze Age onwards (Barber 1994: 208ff.). Feidelm claims to be promoting Medb's interest by gathering forces for the battle, but she reports that the final result of the fighting will be disastrous for Ulster: 'Feidelm the prophetess conceals it not'.

A Norse variation on the theme of weaving as a way to foretell and perhaps also to determine the future is found in a poem quoted in *Brennu-Njáls Saga* (157) and known as the *Darraðarljóð*, Lay of the Spear. Sveinsson (1954) in his edition of the saga dated it to the early eleventh century, not long after the Battle of Clontarf in 1014 with which it is associated. The description in the saga is of a company of twelve valkyries weaving on a warp-weighted loom, a nightmare parody of the familiar loom used in the North. Human entrails form the warp, crossed by a crimson weft, and the weights holding down the warp are human skulls. The heddles are javelins, and real swords instead of weaving swords are used in the weaving.

The song is said to have been heard in Caithness by a man called *Dorruðr* (taken by some to be the wandering god Odin himself, directing the activities of the valkyries), who was out early in the morning of the day on which the battle of Clontarf was fought in Ireland. No names of leaders occur in the poem, and Nora Chadwick thought it possible that it was composed to celebrate some other battle, but later associated with the desperate struggle between the Irish king Brian and Sigurd, Jarl of Orkney, both killed at Clontarf (Kershaw 1922: 117). The valkyries were said to weave inside a *dyngja*, a word used for a ladies' bower in Icelandic, and perhaps originally a weaving room. When their weaving was done they tore the woven cloth from the loom, each taking a piece, and then rode off, presumably through the air, to Clontarf. The grisly 'cloth' apparently determined the course of the battle and marked out those to be slain.

There are many problems over the interpretation of the language of this poem, discussed in detail by Anne Holtsmark (1939), and not least is the significance of the word *Darraðar* in the title; it is usually translated 'of the spear', but the saga writer took it as a personal name. A further possibility is to link it with the small banner or pennant fastened on a spear and used in battle, as suggested by Holtsmark and supported by Dronke (1969: 49). This would help to explain the connection between weaving and battle in the poem, and also the fact that the valkyries were said to tear the cloth into small pieces, which could form such pennants. Holtsmark in addition draws attention to the resemblance between the word used for entrails (*görn*) and that for warp (*garn*), and the obvious one between the weaving 'sword' and the sword used in warfare (Holtsmark 1939: 95).

There is a persistent tradition, going back to the Anglo-Saxon chronicle for 878, of a famous banner possessed by a Danish leader, sometimes said to represent a raven, which flapped its wings to foretell victory and drooped in anticipation of defeat. Many methods of divination before battle are recorded in both Germanic and Celtic sources (Davidson 1988: 149ff.) and in this case the effect of the wind on the banner foretold the result of a battle. In *Orkneyinga Saga* (11) it is said to have belonged to Jarl Sigurd of Orkney, and to have been woven by his mother, who was skilled in magic. The Jarl consulted her when a rival challenged him to battle, and she gave him a banner which she had made, foretelling that it would bring victory to the leader before whom it was carried, but death to whoever bore it. Sure enough, the Jarl lost three standard bearers in the battle, but he was victorious. According to *Brennu-Njáls Saga* (157) he used the same banner at Clontarf, and after the bearer had been killed, one of his men refused to bear the banner, with the retort: 'Carry your devil yourself'. Thereupon Jarl Sigurd took up the banner, and was slain.

Sigurd's mother brings us into the homely world of women's weaving by her words to her son in *Orkneyinga Saga*, when he tells her that he is likely to be outnumbered in the coming fight by seven to one: 'I should have reared you for a long while in my wool-basket if I had known that you must live for ever; it is fate which decides life, not the position in which a man finds himself.' Here again we have the link made between weaving and fate, birth and death, although the emphasis is now laid on the destined moment of death in battle rather than the length of time a man may live. It seems probable that the pennants which high-born women made for their sons and husbands were thought to play an important part in bringing good fortune in battle, and perhaps also in foretelling the fate of warriors.

These small banners, tied to a spear and borne before a leader to show his men where he was in the battle, have been discussed by Peter Paulsen, with examples from Alamannic and other Germanic areas from the seventh and eighth centuries (Paulsen 1967: 115ff.) They might be of woollen or linen material, and Paulsen suggested that a fragment of woven fabric (probably linen) from the Anglo-Saxon cemetery at Finglesham, a twill with a tablet-woven border found along with bronze and iron fragments, might be the remains of a pennant of this kind rather than a needle case, as was originally suggested (S. E. Chadwick 1958: 17, 35ff.). This was found in a woman's grave, which is of interest because it also held a weaving sword with a pattern-welded blade, and Sonia Chadwick Hawkes gives five more examples from rich Anglo-Saxon graves as well as three whose provenance was not recorded. While an old sword might conceivably be adapted for use as a weaving implement, she thinks it possible that these weaving swords made of iron may have been symbols of the rank and social status of the women who owned them, just as the pattern-welded swords used in battle were valued treasures of distinguished warriors (S. E. Chadwick 1958: 35). This offers a parallel once more to the gold spindles of Ancient Greece.

It was suggested by Holtsmark (1939: 95) that the poem on the weaving valkyries was perhaps influenced by the tradition of weaving by the Norns, female deities of fate in Norse mythology, often confused with valkyries in later literature. While, as she points out, no valkyrie names indicate weaving, there is at least one passage in *Helgakviða Hundingsbana* in the *Poetic Edda* which represents the Norns setting up a huge loom whose threads stretch across the sky, at the time of the birth of a prince and hero:

> It was night in the dwelling. The Norns came,
> those who shaped the life of the prince.
> They foretold him to be most famed of warriors
> who would be reckoned best of rulers.
> They twisted firmly the threads of fate . . .
> They set in place the strands of gold,
> held fast in the midst of the hall of the moon.
> East and west they hid the ends;

the prince's lands would lie between;
while Neri's kinswoman knotted a cord (*brá einni festi*)
fast to the north, and forbade it to break.

Clearly these Norns, like the valkyries, are setting up their loom; this time
it is not restricted within a house in Scotland, but stretches across the heavens. The beam which holds the threads of the warp stretches from east
to west, across the realm which Helgi is to rule, and it is held up by a
cord which will not break. There is no question of 'casting a chain' as in
Bellows's translation of the passage (1923: 292); *bragða* can mean to braid,
knot or bind, and *festr* a cord or rope, and these are evidently weaving
terms describing how the warp is set up and made secure. Since it is attached
to the beam stretched from east to west across the heavens, the cord which
fastens it at the top must be in the north. There is no need to be perplexed,
as Finnur Jónsson (1932) appears to be in his Danish edition of the *Edda*
(*Völsungakviða* 4–5), because there is no mention of the south; it is not
relevant here.

Holtsmark (1939: 95) thought it possible that in *Darraðarljóð* references
to fate as something woven might be due to Christian influence, as in similar expressions in Anglo-Saxon Christian poetry, such as 'woven by the
decree of fate' in *St Guthlac* (1325). In the poem *Völuspá* there is a reference to the Norns 'cutting on wood', which could be based on the old
Norwegian custom of recording dates and numbers of days or years by
notches cut in the wood above a farmhouse window, and Holtsmark suggested that this might be an alternative northern image for marking the
length of an individual life (Holtsmark 1951: 81ff.). We do not know much
about the Norns, since in the literature we have mainly references to their
decrees concerning the fates of kingdoms and individuals. In *Völuspá*,
thought to be composed at the beginning of the eleventh century, there
are references to three wise maidens who come from the Well of Urd to
control the destinies of men and women; they seem to be deliberately contrasted with the gods who made decisions to affect the world (Davidson
1988: 163). It is not clear whether these maidens are the same as the three
sinister giantesses who appear earlier in the poem, and are apparently
responsible for the conflicts leading to the ultimate destruction of the
gods, but it seems possible that here we have two pictures of the Norns,
ominous or benign according as they bring evil or favourable fortune.
Concerning the 'maidens of great wisdom' we are told:

> They established laws,
> they meted out life
> to the sons of men,
> and declared their destinies.
>
> (20)

In this poem, however, there is no mention of spinning or weaving.

It seems unlikely that the connection between weaving and fate was a direct borrowing from the spinners of Greek and Roman mythology, though the fact that the Norns are sometimes three in number might be influenced by classical tradition. There may originally have been a single goddess of Fate; in the Viking Age memories were retained of a being called Urd, whose name is given in *Völuspá* as one of the group of three; the names of the remaining two, Verðandi and Skuld, are thought to be late additions (J. de Vries 1956: 272, n. 6). The name Urd corresponds to the word used for fate in Anglo-Saxon literature. Timmer (1940: 226) believed this might once have been the name of a goddess, although it changed its usual significance in Christian times; he points out that in the Corpus Glossaries *wyrda*, the plural form, is given as an equivalent for *Parcae*. In Norse tradition Urd sits beside a spring, the Well of Urd, where Odin himself visits her for counsel, and it is implied that he sacrificed one eye to obtain the knowledge he desired. Here there could be memories of a power to whom even the gods must turn if they desired to learn the secrets of the future.

Although there are no detailed descriptions of a spinning or weaving goddess concerned with the fate of those born into the world, it is indicated in *Lokasenna* (29) that the leading goddess Frigg, said to preside over spinning and weaving, possessed knowledge of destiny. 'I deem that Frigg knows the destinies of all', Freyja says to Loki, 'though she does not herself declare it'. There are further hints in conversations between Frigg and Odin that she has special knowledge of what is to be (Näsström 1995: 113).

I feel that the importance of the spinning imagery concerning the destiny of heroes is confirmed by a memorable passage already referred to (see p. 101) in one of the great Icelandic family sagas of the thirteenth century, *Laxdæla Saga*. This is a saga written very much from the viewpoint of the heroine Gudrun, and concerned with women's problems in marriage, so that some have thought that it may have been composed by a woman. The two main characters are Gudrun and Kjartan, two outstanding individuals of strong character; they were greatly attracted to each other, and were expected to marry, but Kjartan went abroad, refusing to take Gudrun with him. Gudrun resented this, and when Bolli, Kjartan's fosterbrother, led her to believe that Kjartan was involved with a Norwegian princess, she married Bolli instead. When Kjartan returned home, he in turn was filled with resentment, and hastily married another woman. The relationship between Gudrun and Kjartan worsened, and finally to avenge what she took as an insult from Kjartan, Gudrun persuaded Bolli, much against his will, to kill his fosterbrother. This is the crisis point of the saga, reached in Chapter 49.

Gudrun heard that the slaying had been done before Bolli returned home. When they met, she asked him the time of day; he replied that it was nearly noon. 'Morning-tasks are mismatched!' exclaimed Gudrun (Auerbach's translation for *misjöfn verða morginverkin*); 'I have spun yarn for twelve ells of cloth, while you have killed Kjartan'. Her words are puzzling, and some have preferred the reading in another manuscript: *mikil verða hermdarverk*: 'Great effects arise from an act of anger!', while an emendation of *hermdarverk* to *vaðaverk*, a punning word which could mean either a violent deed or work on homespun cloth, has been suggested (Damsholt 1984: 84).

However, it seems to have gone unnoticed by most commentators that Gudrun's spinning could not possibly have beeen done in one morning. The preparation of yarn for spinning takes up more time than the weaving of the prepared yarn, and the amount necessary for a piece of wadmal 1 yard wide and 6 yards long would take more than a morning's work to produce, even if several women were sharing it (see p. 101). Her words are clearly bitter ones, and aroused more bitterness from Bolli, who accused her of grieving more over Kjartan's death than she would have done had he himself been slain. If Gudrun's reference to the amount she has spun was not meant to be taken literally, her words may be interpreted in various ways.

She may have mentioned an impossibly large production of yarn, as Loren Auerbach suggests, to emphasize the enormity of killing such a hero as Kjartan, and this would also fit the alternative reading. Another possibility is that such a piece of cloth would be a suitable size for a shroud, and this might account for Bolli's anger. Only Kjartan's wife would have the right to weave his shroud, but Gudrun might have been hoping that she would need a shroud for her husband Bolli, if he should be the one killed in the battle. Or could it be that in describing herself as spinning while the fight went on, she is alluding to the concept of valkyries weaving before a battle? Gudrun, because of her sex, was restricted to women's work with the distaff while Bolli used the sword; yet it was she who was undoubtedly responsible for Kjartan's death, as she and Bolli both knew, and had brought it about against his will. Now through enormous effort on her part her spinning was completed and the thread of Kjartan's life cut. At this crucial point in the saga, superbly handled by the unknown author, it is surely significant that spinning should be chosen as a symbol for deep emotion and for the ruthless working out of Fate, emphasized throughout *Laxdœla Saga*.

In the Viking Age, a time of great activity in warfare, spinning and weaving as symbols of destiny are associated with the results of battle, and since weaving was performed by women, the task was assigned to the valkyries. The making of woven banners by women to bring good fortune in battle would give additional strength to this symbol, and it would be further strengthened by the association of weaving with a powerful goddess able to determine the fates of warriors and kings.

The constant part which weaving played in the lives of women over many thousands of years, and the nature of the process by which yarn or thread is produced by the use of the spindle and distaff followed by the weaving of new cloth in a certain pattern, made it an effective symbol for creation of new order out of chaos, and of the destiny which governs human life. As Bruce Long (1985: 367) has pointed out in his article on 'Webs and nets', weaving can represent creation and growth; such symbols as nets and webs, rope and fabric have been constantly used for the unfolding of human lives and the development of the worlds. Women worshippers of the goddess linked it inevitably with the birth of children into the world to an unknown future, and their fortunes as they grew up. I owe to Elizabeth Barber the observation that one obvious link between spinning and childbirth is that the cord which joins the mother to her baby must be severed so that the new thread of life can begin, to be cut again at death. The hopes and dangers of motherhood were from the earliest times closely linked with the goddess, and this is an additional reason why spinning and weaving came under her special patronage.

CHAPTER IV

MISTRESS OF THE HOUSEHOLD

——— .◆. ———

GUARDIANS OF THE HOME

The home in early times, whether house or tent, was shared between men and women, and there is ample evidence from northern Europe and Asia of the formal division of the dwelling between the sexes, with protective household deities belonging to each section. In a series of detailed studies of the northern peoples in Europe and Asia, extending from Scandinavia to Japan, Gustav Ränk (1949a) has collected a vast amount of material to establish this. He has shown how there were divisions between the front and back of the dwelling and also between the two opposite sides, the position of the hearth being of paramount importance (Ränk 1949a: 47ff.). The fireplace in early times was usually in the centre, but the stove which replaced it over much of northern and eastern Europe was often to the right of the entrance, with the main table for meals on the left (Figure 22).

The special area for the women was around the entrance and behind the fireplace, where most of the sleeping accommodation was situated, while that for the men was around the table and at the back of the dwelling. Here hunting implements and clothes were kept, and meat and fish stored before the men prepared them for cooking (Ränk 1949a: 37). There might be a ritual door through which they went out to hunt, and by which they returned with their game, with a cult area outside where figures of gods or sacred symbols were placed. Women would probably be banned from this, but would have their own sacred place behind the fireplace (see p. 127) or near the threshold of the front door.

There were obvious practical advantages in such divisions for a mixed community. Both men and women would want to keep small children away from tools and hunting gear, while womenfolk resented men in their kitchen, and needed to preserve areas of privacy. But behind this was a strong awareness of ever present threats to the hunters, the women working in the dairy, and the children born into the family.

There was clearly no complete segregation between the sexes; the male head of the family slept in the main bed in the sleeping area, and men and women usually ate together at the table, though perhaps separating at wedding feasts and special festivals. In some areas, such as Denmark (Rockwell 1982: 44) and parts of rural France (Segalen 1983: 161ff.), the men would sit down to eat while the women remained standing until they

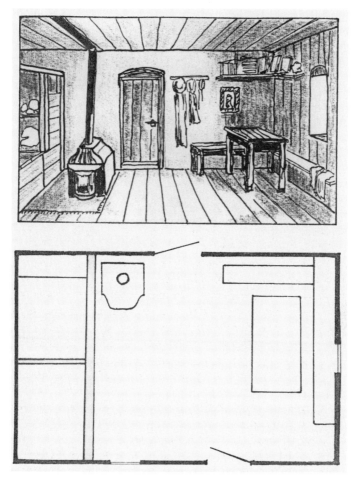

Figure 22 Sketch and plan of house in Russia. Based on drawing by Blomkvist (Ränk 1949a). Eileen Aldworth.

had finished, but this does not necessarily indicate segregation of the sexes, nor the inferior position of women. As Segalen points out, women were responsible for the preparing and distributing of the food, and this enabled them to do it without constant interruption.

A barrier between the areas of the house allotted to men and women in the house was maintained for a long while in remote parts of northern Europe. For instance among the Saami, a 'woman's stone' on the far side of the hearth survived into the twentieth century and was conveniently used as a stand for the coffee-pot. This must originally have marked the place beyond which women could not pass; to cross from the fire to the table on the other side of the dwelling it was necessary for them to come round the front of the house, past the main door. Alternatively this barrier might be marked by a pole (Ränk 1949b: 186) and infringement of the rule was held to cause bad luck. It is worth noting that a large dining table and a double bed have remained essential possessions for a newly married couple in modern Greece, in spite of the inconvenience of such heavy furniture in small town houses (Hirschon 1981: 81ff.).

The times in women's lives when they posed a particular danger to the occupations of the men, and had to be kept away from tools, weapons and anything to do with hunting or fishing, were those of menstruation, pregnancy and childbirth. Sometimes special tents or buildings were provided for them at such times; Sarakka, the Saami goddess of childbirth, had a special tent which is depicted on shamans' drums, and a birth tent was in use among various north Eurasian peoples (Ränk 1955: 23). If the women remained in the main house or tent, their movements were restricted (Ränk 1949a: 131). In some cases young married women were expected to eat behind a screen until after the birth of the first child (Ränk 1949a: 53), and during menstruation periods they might have to stay in the door area, wearing special clothes and eating away from the others (Ränk 1955: 40). These were occasions when women appealed to the goddesses for help, and their figures or symbols were kept in the women's section of the home. The same divinities assisted in the special activities of the women of the household, such as milking and dairy-work, spinning and weaving.

A good example from outside Europe is found in the *yurt* of the Mongols, as described by Friar William of Rubruck, a Franciscan friar from France, who visited the Great Khan of the Tartars during a hazardous journey lasting from 1253 to 1255, which he describes in vivid detail. He tells how in the *yurt* the women sat on the left side of the master of the house, together with strangers, and the men on the right, where they hung up their bows. An image made of felt, resembling a puppet, was put by the master's head where he sat on his bed in the centre facing the door, and another on the wall on the women's side, above the head of the mistress. These appear to be male household gods protecting husband and wife, since they are called the 'brothers' of the master and mistress; a third, 'a little lean one', was fixed higher up between them, and said to be the guardian of the whole house. There is also mention of another image, possibly female, which looked towards the women and girls, fixed near the foot of the mistress's bed. On the women's side of the entrance there was an image with a cow's udder, protecting the women who milked the cows, while on the men's side one with a mare's udder, for the men who milked the mares. At feasts, part of their drink was sprinkled on these images (Ruysbruck 1928: III, 82).

Ränk emphasizes the fact that the goddesses or house-spirits worshipped by the women and presiding over the women's side of the house would be brought into it by the brides who came into the family. Images or figurines were normally passed down from mother to daughter, although he found that among the Tungus in Siberia they were inherited by the daughter from the father (Ränk 1949a: 124). Thus a group of guardian spirits gradually became the common property of a larger kin group (Ränk 1955: 46). The women's household deities could be stuffed rag dolls or wooden images. Among the Altai Turks such figures were made by the mother of the bride or some elder female relative before the girl left home, and the cloth was supplied by her mother's brother. If her new home were not far away, she might leave them with her mother, but it was essential that she had them with her in childbirth; otherwise she might die or her child be born blind. This threat of blindness may be explained by the importance of the dolls' eyes, usually coloured glass beads: the child to be born was expected to have eyes of the same colour (Ränk 1955: 64ff.). Such female guardian figures remained separate from the men's protective deities used at public ceremonies, which were kept at the back of the house or outside the back door, as among the Saami (Ränk 1949b: 125); those of the women would probably be by the stove or near the front entrance.

An example of a goddess linked with certain parts of the house is the Latvian goddess Laima, said to reside in the bath-house, the cowstall and the eating-room, and also to be found in certain plants, as well as on the mountain and in water (Biezais 1955). The link with the bath-house was an obvious one, since this was where births took place and rituals were held before and after the child was born (see pp. 147–8). Work with the cows took women outside the house, and so also did their herb-garden, used for both cooking and medicinal purposes, which explains why Laima was said to dwell in the willow tree, in wormwood and mugwort, and in the raspberry bush (see p. 154).

Over much of northern Europe the pattern for marriage was for the young girl to leave her family home for that of her husband, and this was clearly of major importance in women's lives. The painful nature of the break, and the unhappy time which the young wife might endure in a strange household with unsympathetic parents-in-law, is vividly conveyed in sections 22, 23 and 24 of the Finnish *Kalevala*. The young bride laments at leaving her home, where she was pampered and well fed, for an uncertain future, outlined in the ominous words of the old woman who describes the sufferings of young wives:

> At home a maid has it made!
> In her father's house she is
> like a king in his castle
> with only a sword missing.
> But a poor daughter-in-law!
> In her husband's house she is
> like a Russian prisoner
> with only a guard missing!
> (Bosley 1989: 22, 313–20)

Even more convincing are the instructions given in section 23 as to how the bride is to behave in her new home, listing the laborious tasks she will be expected to perform, while often given poor and inadequate food in contrast to the plentiful meals at home. She must bear this without complaint, she is told, and if asked if her mother-in-law gives her butter to eat: 'always say it is given / brought in a dipper, though you / get it but once in summer / and that from two winters back' (Bosley 1989: 23, 443). The advice to the bridegroom in section 24 as to how to treat his wife helps to complete the gloomy picture of the young bride's subordinate place in the household. Lönnrot took much of this material, such as the speech of the old woman describing the trials of a young wife, from different songs, presumably composed by women (Fromm 1967: 16).

A link between the goddess and the young bride moving away from home into her husband's household is clearly demonstrated in William Sax's (1991) *Mountain Goddess: Gender and Politics in a Himalayan Pilgrimage*. In his fieldwork in Uttarakhand in the former Himalayan kingdom of Gadhwal, the author was assured by the men that once a woman married she was totally cut off from her family and former home, but found the reality very different (Sax 1991: 77–81). Many anthropologists have accepted the men's view, yet not only do the women's songs contradict it, but also the cult of the goddess Nandadevi disproves it completely.

Regular pilgrimages are held in honour of this goddess when her image is brought down from her mountain temple, where she is revered as the wife of Shiva, for a visit to her *mait* or native village, to be welcomed and spoiled. Young wives make similar visits to their parents' homes at the time of the festival. In the women's songs describing the visits of the goddess, much emphasis is laid on the welcome Nandadevi receives from her family in contrast to her harsh life as a wife of an austere yogi in the cold mountains, where, she tells her mother, 'Ice burns my flesh, in the air we breathe poison'. She complains that she wears scratchy clothes of wool, and her 'poor stomach aches from second-rate grain'. At her mother's home life is very different: she has 'butter from seven different places, and breads that are fried with the leaves of the forest' with abundance of milk and rice (Sax 1991: 91), butter once more being regarded as something of primary importance in the diet. Not only do the songs express her reluctance to leave her *mait* after marriage, but also during the pilgrimage it is claimed that when coming down from the mountain, her palanquin drags the men carrying it swiftly towards the village, while on the journey back it is so heavy that they have great difficulty in getting up the slope (Sax 1991: 58–9).

Again in Bengal the return of young brides to their home villages is associated with the festival of a goddess, the powerful Durga (Kinsley 1989: 22ff.). Again there are songs of welcome and farewell which contrast the difficult life of the young wife with her warm treatment in her parents' home, and many women weep when the image of the goddess departs to rejoin her husband. The contrast with Durga as a many-armed goddess triumphing over demons is particularly striking.

We have very little information as to how things went in matrilineal societies, where the bridegroom moved to the home of the bride. Here presumably the young couple had their own house or living quarters not far from that of the parents, as Battaglia (1990) has suggested happened among the Picts, when he argues the case for the continuation of a matrilineal system among the Celtic people of the British Isles in the Iron Age. The number of rich women's graves in certain areas of the North, for instance in Denmark apart from Jutland (Hedeager 1992: 155), has been put forward as evidence for a different marriage system in which women possessed greater independence. Indeed this could happen under a patrilocal system, as in modern Greece, where the father provides living accommodation for each married daughter (Hirschon 1981: 72). There was clearly variety in the position of the young wife in the household, but her situation as emphasized in the *Kalevala* must have been a familiar one in north-western Europe, as in northern India in the late twentieth century.

There is little on this subject in the surviving Scandinavian myths, but one fragment of verse preserved in Snorri's *Prose Edda* (*Gylfaginning* 22), and also known to the Danish historian Saxo Grammaticus in the twelfth century (Davidson 1980: 37), bears some resemblance to the songs about the goddess Nandadevi and her complaints about the discomforts of life with her husband Shiva on the mountain. Skaði was said to be married to Njord, god of the sea, while she herself came from the mountains. It was said that after marriage they spent nine nights in turn in their two abodes, and neither was content. Njord complains of the hilly country haunted by wolves:

> Hateful are the hills. I was not long there,
> only nine nights.
> The howling of wolves seems ill to me
> after the swans' singing.

But Skaði was equally dissatisfied with the seashore:

> I could not sleep on the sea-beds
> for the screaming of birds.
> On its far flight each morning
> the sea-mew wakened me.

According to Snorri, Skaði deserted her husband to return to the mountains, where she hunted on skis, and she is said in *Grímnismál* (11) to dwell in Thrymheim, her father's former home. The episode remains unexplained, but here we have a myth based on the contrast between two regions and different ways of life, and a goddess who supports the woman's viewpoint, expressing the bride's reluctance to give up her home and move to a strange, unwelcoming place.

The guardian goddess appears to have been firmly established in northern Europe, as a figure attached to the family and the family dwelling. In Roman Britain a figure resembling a Mother Goddess is sometimes shown in company with little hooded men, who seem also to be protective figures attached to houses and farms, like the brownies of later legends. A stone in the Corinium Museum at Cirencester shows three hooded figures facing a seated goddess, who has what seems to be a large loaf or cake on her lap (Figure 23). There is another group on a stone from Daglingworth, where the seated figure has fruit and eggs (Toynbee 1959: 3ff.); one of the little hooded figures appears to be offering her a basket or a bunch of grapes.

There seems no doubt that these hooded men were concerned with the well-being and fertility of the farm, like land-spirits in Iceland (Davidson 1989a). The brownies of later popular tradition in England, Wales and Scotland are widely remembered as benevolent house-spirits,

Figure 23 Seated goddess with hooded men on carved stone from Cirencester. Ht 27 cm. Corinium Museum. Eileen Aldworth.

though independent and wilful, who helped the men with their work on the farm, protected the cattle and assisted in the dairy, asking only a share of creamy milk for their efforts. They also helped the women of the house with housework and dairy-work, sometimes came to their aid in childbirth, and made sure that the midwife arrived in time for a birth. They even helped housewives to find their keys when these went missing (Leather 1912: 48). It is interesting to find them associated with a goddess figure in the Cotswolds in the Roman period.

There are also strong traditions surviving in Scotland of a female house-spirit attached to certain families. These supernatural beings were particulary concerned with the well-being of the women and children of the family. The Fairy Wife of Clan MacLeod, on the island of Skye, was said to have wrapped the baby son of the Laird in a silken banner, still preserved in Dunvegen Castle, when his nurse had left him alone, and the words and tune of a lullaby she was claimed to have sung to him are recorded (MacGregor 1937: 20ff.). The household spirit attached to the family of the Campbells of Glen Faochan looked after the servants and punished them if they neglected their work, and after the estate was sold was said to have been heard lamenting among the trees (MacDougall 1978: 47). Another Maiden attached to the estate of Balievolan was said to have taken 'great interest in the family and everything belonging to them' (MacDougall 1978: 49). She looked after their cattle, and was concerned with the fortunes of all the families on the land, sometimes continuing to help individuals who moved to the mainland. Such supernatural women might be given the name *glaistig* or *gruagach*, which was used for the supernatural guardians of the forest deer (see pp. 27–8), but are different in nature, co-operating with the brownies in protecting and helping the household. Thus the home was guarded by a female supernatural protector and perhaps by other lesser beings, who could be appealed to in times of danger and difficulty by the women of the household. In Christian times their place might be taken by the Virgin Mary or women saints.

Such guardian figures may have developed in different ways. New brides might bring new guardians into the household, or the cult of a local goddess might be adopted by the family. Ränk (1955: 67) suggests two possible origins of the 'Mother' figures who served as female guardians among the Saami and other northern peoples: he thinks they might originate from tribal spirits in the paternal line rather than from earlier goddesses from a period of matriarchy as some have assumed, or possibly from malignant spirits bringing disease and calamity, who needed to be placated (see p. 189). But whatever their origin, these household deities were unquestionably of great importance in the lives of the women of the household, who turned to them for the luck on which so much depended, seeking their help and favour for their own special responsibilities in the home, to ensure the survival and prosperity of their families.

FIRE AND WATER

The hearth which formed the centre of the home, and without which life would scarcely have been possible in the cold northern lands, must inevitably have been dominated by a goddess. The Romans preserved the shrine of Vesta, an important goddess who according to Ovid was not depicted in human form (*Fasti* VI, 295–8), as the *numen* of the hearth. Her holy fire was rekindled every year on 1 March by friction, using a piece of wood from a 'lucky"tree, and the small group of Vestal Virgins who tended it were held in the greatest esteem. They invoked the gods on behalf of the citizens of Rome, calling for instance on Apollo to cure diseases, and took part in many public rituals. Treasures such as an ancient statue of Athene, said to have been brought back from Troy, were stored in their temple, together with two figures of the Penates, household guardians of the foodstore, and only the Vestals were allowed access to the holiest inner chamber (Schilling 1985: 250ff.).

It was a great honour to become a Vestal, and the six girls who served in historic times came from patrician families; they could be admitted at the age of 7 and served for thirty years. It was said that the penalty for a lapse from chastity was to be buried alive, but after their time of service they were free to retire and marry, though apparently rarely did so. Every year they cleansed their temple with water from a sacred spring, and received grain from the new crop; one of their tasks was to prepare baked wheat flour sprinkled with salt to put on the heads of sacrificial victims, and they took part in many religious rituals. Mary Beard (1980) emphasizes the double character of the Vestals as matrons and virgins, and this is something characteristic of many goddesses. They probably originated in the hearth cult of the women of the royal household in the days of the early kings (Beard 1980: 13).

Between 7 and 15 June married women were allowed entry into the temple, walking barefoot and bringing gifts of simple food. Vesta's sacred animal was the ass, and this, together with the primitive method of kindling fire, the cleansing ceremony and the circular form of their temple, suggests that the cult was an ancient one (Dumézil 1966: 315ff.). The concept of the sacred hearth under the protection of a goddess is linked with the well-being of the state and the favour of the gods, as well as with the coming of harvest, storage of new grain and provision of food.

Women's sphere of influence in the house necessarily included the hearth, where water was heated and cooking done (see pp. 124–5). The day began with them lighting the fire, using wood which they had gathered (Segalen 1983: 85), though the men were responsible for chopping logs. The laying of wood on the fire might be linked with the successful birth of a child (see pp. 144–5). In houses where peat fires were kept in overnight, it would be the woman's task to kindle it afresh in the morning and cover it over at the end of the day; in some of the prayers collected by Alexander Carmichael in the Scottish Highlands and Islands, she called on Mary and Brigid to aid her:

> I will raise the hearth-fire
> As Mary would.
> The encirclement of Bride and of Mary
> On the fire, and on the floor,
> And on the household all.
>
> (Carmichael 1928: I, 233)

Again she appealed to Mary and Brigid when covering or 'smooring' the fire for the night to preserve it until morning. Ó Catháin (1995: 53ff.) notes the emphasis on the hearth as a centre in ceremonies connected with St Brigid.

When a new bride came into a prosperous household in Mortainais in France in the eighteenth century she was led round by her parents-in-law and visited the bakehouse, where she touched the kneading-trough and the bread-shovel and looked into the oven. On smaller farms she would touch distaff, broom and cooking-pot, the last associating her with both fire and water, and perhaps light a fire under it, 'symbolizing the hearth of which she was the guardian', or alternatively she might go round the pot-hook three times (Segalen 1983: 34–5). In rural France, Segalen points out, most of the women's cooking was done in the pot, by boiling and simmering, although men might grill meat for feast-days, just as nowadays it is they who organize the barbecue in the garden (Segalen 1983: 89).

The pot-hook and chain appears to have had symbolic importance in Anglo-Saxon England, judging from the magnificent workmanship of the suspension chain for the large bronze cauldron found in the Sutton Hoo ship-burial (Evans 1986: 79ff.). This was part of a treasure from a king's hall; on a much humbler level in later times it was on the pot-hook that the brownie who acted as a house-spirit used to swing: Mrs Leather heard from an old lady in Herefordshire in 1908 that a crook was often made on the 'sway', the iron bar over the fire from which pots and kettles hung, known as the 'Brownie sway', or a horse-shoe was put there for the brownie to swing on (Leather 1912: 48).

It was at the hearth and in the oven that the ritual baking was done, which played a considerable part from early times in religious rites associated with the goddess. In Ancient Greece pastry shapes in the form of genital organs were said to be made by the women and brought to the rituals of Demeter from which men were sternly excluded (see p. 54). It has been noted that loaves held in the laps of Mother Goddesses in Roman Britain may be of an oval shape with a central groove, perhaps suggesting the vulva (Henig 1993: 39). The Germanic goddess Nehalennia, shown on many carved stones recovered from the sand on the coast of Holland, has some of the attributes of the Mothers, and loaves carved on her altars are of a type known as *duivekatar*, oblong sacrificial loaves in the shape of a shin bone (Hondius-Crone 1955: 17, 107–8). Such a loaf might replace an animal sacrifice, and others might be in the shape of animal victims, like the loaf in the shape of a boar baked in Sweden at Yule (see p. 64). Within living memory in Varmland it was customary to bake the grain from the last sheaf into a loaf in the shape of a little girl, to be shared by all in the household (Grieg 1954: 171).

Special loaves were also baked for religious festivals, and large and elaborate Harvest Loaves, sometimes in the shape of sheaves of corn, may still be displayed in churches. In Anglo-Saxon England loaves might also be used as part of a ritual to bring fertility to the fields (see pp. 62–3). Milk or baked dishes were prepared to celebrate the first-fruits of harvest and Solheim (1956) pointed out resemblances between such customs in Norway and the Hebrides (see p. 63). Many examples can be found from Ireland in the rich records about Lughnasa recorded by Máire MacNeill (1962), while fruitcake might be left out as an offering to St Brigid on her Eve (see p. 37).

Special food was also prepared at certain key points in women's lives, and the wedding cake still remains an important symbol in England. Yvonne Verdier has studied the part played by *la Cuisinière*, the woman in rural France responsible for the organization of weddings, the food provided for the guests, and the meal brought to the wedded pair in the middle of their wedding night, a custom which can be traced back to medieval times and was continued into the twentieth century (Verdier 1979: 294ff.). This consisted of soup or spiced wine, evidently intended to aid fertility; it was pressed on the couple in spite of protests by a group of young people, organized by the *Cuisinière*. The phrase for this was 'to bring the pot', and in the nineteenth century a chamber-pot was used, but Verdier believed that the original symbol was that of the cooking-pot which represented the bride's entry into married life. The breaking of one or more pots might also form part of the wedding ceremonies (Verdier 1979: 309ff.). When her last child was married, the mother might scatter a bag of nuts as she danced, a symbol of her fertility passed on to others as she retired into the company of older women. Newly married couples offered special little cakes to the spirits of the local springs, while offerings of food might also be made there for girls hoping to find husbands (Verdier 1979: 316ff.). In Scandinavia a special porridge was made after a birth, to be eaten by the mother and the women attending her, and this was associated among the Saami with the goddess presiding over the birth (see pp. 145–6).

Like the cow-stall, the hearth needed special protection from evil forces. Some houses in Yorkshire had a post with a simple protective symbol set on one side of it, known as a witch post, an example of which can be seen in a house at the Ryedale Folk Museum in Yorkshire. A destructive supernatural figure in Russian fairy-tales who lies beside her hearth is the Baba Yaga; her possessions are a broom, a poker and a pestle and mortar, all to be found in the vicinity of the hearth (see pp. 180–1).

The close associations between St Brigid and the hearth, on the other hand, recall traditions of the benevolent goddess within the home. When Brigid had insufficient milk for churning, she prayed for divine help, ending with the words:

> My kitchen
> the kitchen of the White God,
> a kitchen which my King hath blessed,
> a kitchen which hath butter.
> Mary's Son, my friend, cometh
> to bless my kitchen
>
> (Stokes 1890: 186)

Brigid was said to work miracles with milk and butter (see p. 36) and with barley and malt in times of scarcity (see p. 139). She gave a hungry dog bacon, afterwards miraculously replaced in the larder, killed and cooked a calf for a poor woman who was starving, kindling a fire with the beam of her loom, ensuring that next day the calf was alive again and the beam back in its place. She turned stones into salt when the nuns were in need of some, salt being essential for the preservation of food, another important responsibility of the women of the household (Verdier 1976b). Brigid saved the contents of a water tub which rolled down a slope from spilling, and made a broken vessel whole. Once in a strange house she asked a dumb boy for the keys of the kitchen, in order to feed some unexpected guests, and he received the gift of speech in return for his help in dispensing hospitality (Stokes 1890: 191ff.). Here we have the saint ensuring plenty like a benevolent Mother Goddess, and taking a keen interest in every aspect of the housewife's work. Not only does her help extend to times of scarcity in the kitchen, so that the family can be fed and supplies kept up, but also she enables women to assist the hungry and to welcome both humans and animals in need. Her link with the hearth may account for the statement of Giraldus Cambrensis that she and her nuns tended a perpetual ashless fire, surrounded by a hedge which no man might penetrate, seemingly based on the tradition of the Vestal Virgins.

While the fire was essential for the preparation of both food and drink, another need was the constant provision of water, and this too was among women's responsibilities, and under the power of the goddess. It is significant that the Vestal Virgins were responsible for both the sacred fire and the sacred spring in their temple. It was women's work to fetch supplies of fresh water from spring or well, often held to be guarded by goddesses or local female spirits in Celtic areas (see p. 137). Water was essential to the household for cooking and brewing, for keeping children and the house clean, and for healing purposes. It was needed also for laundry-work, for which women were responsible; good laundrying was important for the reputation of the household, and it was linked with childbirth and marriage.

This is a side of women's skills and rituals to which comparatively little attention has been paid, but Yvonne Verdier (1976a) has brought out its importance in a study based on her fieldwork in the village of Minot, in the north of the Bourgogne (Burgundy). Here she discusses the figure of the Helper (*la femme-qui-aide*), the woman who came to assist at births and deaths, and who continued to do her much valued work, for which she received no payment, until officialdom suppressed her in the 1960s. She was not a midwife, and was careful not to act as such, although able to help in an emergency; her special contribution was to prepare for the birth and to care for the new-born infant, in particular, to bath and dress it. Similarly she came into a home where there had been a death, and took over the task of laying out and washing the body (see pp. 170–1). Thus her main duty was to wash, clothe and put in due order those newly entering the world and those who had just left it. These were dangerous tasks, and the use of water formed an essential part of this service. Such Helpers were always older women, and they received the title of 'Mother'.

The Helpers whom Verdier studied were also professional washer-women: laundering played a major part in women's lives and in the community. Clothes and linen were washed twice a year for those sufficiently prosperous to possess a six months' supply, and Verdier heard from the older women what a demanding and exhausting business it was when there were few laundries. In households in Minot there was a preliminary washing in the great tub with ashes and cinders (from the baker's oven) to provide potash, and next day the laundry-women arrived and took the wet laundry to the wash-house, where it was soaped, rinsed, beaten and left on stone tables till the water had run off and it could be spread out on hedges or on the grass to dry. As with the harvest, good weather was needed for this, and the 'great washes' were usually in the spring and autumn.

The labours of the washerwomen, which in earlier times would take place at a fountain or on the riverbank, had characteristics of a ritual. The women formed a formidable team, with their own hierarchy and camaraderie. As well as official washerwomen who were paid for doing the laundry, many housewives took their regular weekly washing to the washing place, and shared in the general chatter and gossip, usually described disapprovingly by male folklorists (Segalen 1983: 139). Men gave them a wide berth; much of the chatter included abuse of the menfolk, and those who passed might be met with rude gestures and remarks. Those who washed the linen of the neighbourhood knew a good deal about what went on in people's intimate lives; changes in a family's monthly washing, for instance, might tell them when a baby was on the way, and they were great scandalmongers.

As there were certain days in the year when spinning should not be done, or the goddess would be angry (see p. 104), so washing was forbidden at various times, especially between Christmas and the New Year or in Holy Week. To infringe this was said to wash away the life of someone in the house, to wash one's own winding-sheet, or to torment souls in Purgatory (Verdier 1976a: 116).

The 'great' washes in which many took part is something which goes back into the far past. We have the unforgettable picture of Nausicaa, her friend and her maids in Book VI of Homer's *Odyssey*, setting off to the river 'where there was enough clear water always bubbling up and swirling to wash the dirtiest clothes' (Rieu 1945) with a large wagon filled with the soiled clothes of the royal household. It may be noted that it is the goddess Athene herself who appears in the guise of a friend to prompt the daughter of the house to make sure her clothes are in good condition for a possible marriage: 'Let us go and do some washing together the first thing in the morning. I offer to go with you and help, so that you can get yourself ready as soon as possible, for you certainly won't remain unmarried long' (Rieu 1945). Homer's account bears out Verdier's description of the long, slow work of washing, followed by an active, joyous time once the clothes were put out to dry (Verdier 1976a: 113). After Nausicaa and the women had laid out the washing, they sang and played ball together, and are compared to Artemis and her Nymphs.

Of particular interest in Verdier's account (1976a: 121ff.) is the link between the washerwomen and the female spirits believed to haunt the springs and wells in the chalk country around Monat, where carvings of Mother Goddesses were set up in the Roman period. At one spring a brioche was dipped in the water as an offering to a rather dangerous supernatural female spirit called Greg, said to devour children until holy water was used to protect them. There are stories that local spirits could still be seen washing in some of the springs, pale women with lowered heads and downcast eyes, kneeling beside the water washing winding sheets. Sometimes there was a group of three, said to be lamenting over the past, present and future, and it was counted best to avoid the area on calm nights. The Helpers who bore the name of Mother resembled these spirits in that they were by no means wholly benevolent figures; *la mère Carré*, for instance, was a very dubious character, but the villagers accepted this and still sought her aid.

There is a link apparent between washing and destiny. Nausicaa's washing through the intervention of Athene was connected with the destiny of Odysseus, and also with that of the king's daughter, since it was associated with her coming marriage. The concept of the supernatural death messenger washing a shroud is found in Irish folklore, as Patricia Lysaght has shown in her study of the Banshee (Lysaght 1986: 130ff.). Such washing is attributed to the war goddess in early Irish sources, and foretells slaughter in battle, but there are also local recorded legends of supernatural washerwomen, not necessarily connected with death, which may have been more widespread in earlier times. There are tales from Brittany, Spain, and Lithuania of female beings washing and beating clothes with a beetle, and of 'White Ladies' similarly employed in German tradition (Lysaght 1986: 387, n. 48). MacPhail (1898: 91) records such figures from the Hebrides; one was seen washing the clothes of a boat's crew due to be drowned that year. They could, however, be rendered powerless if a man caught sight of one before she saw him, or seized her with his left hand, and in return for freedom when 'caught', such beings could grant the gift of wealth or of children. It appears that washing of clothes by supernatural female beings, like their spinning or weaving, might be seen as an omen of what was to come, or even as a means of bringing this about.

Yet another important use of water by the women was for brewing ale, the usual drink for all ages at a time when water was often suspect. Its association with a goddess may be seen in Ancient Egypt, where beer transformed the goddess Hathor from a wild lioness about to destroy humankind into a benevolent deity (Blecker 1973: 50). She is addressed in a hymn as 'Mistress of Both Lands, Mistress of Bread, who made beer with what her heart created and her hands prepared', and described as 'the Lady of Drunkenness, rich in feasts' (W. J. Darby *et al.* 1977: 529). The effects of fermented cereals may have been discovered accidentally by women baking bread, and it was women who did the brewing in Ancient Egypt, as may be seen from tomb paintings. The Egyptian method was to work the malt into a dough to convert the starch into maltose, and the women are shown kneading, sieving and brewing (W. J. Darby *et al.* 1977: 531). Although the rich drank wine, beer was the general drink in Egypt, and formed an essential part of offerings to the gods.

In medieval times in northern Europe, brewing was done mostly by women and, as with butter-making, often went wrong for no obvious reason. This was because the process depended on experience and judgement, with many different factors being involved. The grain most used was barley, which was stored for a time in the barn or oasthouse, then steeped in water and germinated until it began to sprout. It was dried in a current of warm air in the malting house, after which it would remain stable for some months. The malted corn was ground in early times by women using a quern and a sieve, and in later medieval times by men when mills came into use. It was not necessary to grind it finely, but each grain needed to be cracked so that the husk could float free in liquid. Once ground it was put into water and heated in a mash tun, so that the soluble starch was converted by enzymes in the malt to fermentable sugars. This solution, known as the wort, was drawn off, and further sugar washed out to get a dilute wort, until only the husks were left, to be used as animal feeding stuff.

It was at this point in the process that in England hops were added from about the fifteenth century onwards, giving the ale additional flavour and making it less perishable. Before this, mugwort or other herbs were used for flavouring, but the ale very soon turned sour. The wort was boiled for some time and cooled in large shallow trays of wood (causing a risk of infection) before being run into fermenting vessels where yeast was added. This was another hazardous part of the process as, while the temperature had to be kept low, excessive cold was injurious. Fermentation took several days, and went on after the beer was put into casks, sometimes with additional hops or sugar added. Some gas might be let out when the beer was finally put in the cellar, but if too much escaped it would go flat.

There was clearly much room for error here, with no exact means of testing the temperature or the length of time needed at various stages, while much depended on the original state of the barley and the weather. An example of the risks involved is Margery Kempe's account of her failure as a brewster in the fourteenth century, at a time when brewing was largely done by women outside the monasteries. She claimed that for three years she was the leading brewster in Lynne (King's Lynn in Norfolk), but suddenly things went wrong:

> For though she had ever such good servants, cunning in brewing, yet it would never succeed with them. For when the ale was as fair standing under barm as any might see, suddenly the barm would fall down, so that all the ale was lost, one brewing after another.
>
> (Butler-Bowdon 1936: 28)

A contrasting picture of successful brewing is that of St Brigid, for this was one of the many household skills at which she excelled, even when supplies were scarce. One Easter she was left with only one measure of malt in a sieve, and two troughs to hold the liquid. She used the first for steeping the malt in water, and then brewed the ale in the second; when this was distributed around seventeen churches at Easter, there was plenty for all (Stokes 1890: 188–9).

It was customary for women to brew their own ale at home up to about the seventeenth century. However, this involved much labour, and before hops were used beer was drinkable for only a few days, so that medieval women often preferred to buy from ale-wives and brewsters like Margery Kempe. Alternatively if they paid a 'fine' they could sell part of their own ale to their neighbours. There were official ale-tasters (mostly men) who judged the standard and price of the ale, and fixed the fine accordingly, and records of these payments have given information about the women (and occasionally men) who sold ale locally (J. M. Bennett 1986).

The brewing of ale depended on the use of both fire and water, and also on skill and luck; the association with a goddess as in Ancient Egypt might therefore be expected in the North. A detailed account of the brewing of ale for a wedding in section 20 of the *Kalevala* suggests the existence of an earlier myth concerning the origin of brewing. The mistress of Northland needed to brew a vast quantity of ale for her daughter's wedding, but declared that she did not know how brewing originated in the beginning; such knowledge was evidently held necessary for success. Then we are told how ale was first brewed by 'Osmo's daughter', 'the beer smith, the brewer woman', hinting at some possible mythological figure, though in Lönnrot's arrangement the discovery is made by the daughter of the house, who is to be the bride. Here we have a practical account of brewing after the wort has been produced together with some fantastic magical additions when the beer is fermented.

The girl first boiled up barley and hops, but did not know how to cause the mixture to ferment. She then created a squirrel from a splinter from the floor, by rubbing it between her palms and her thighs, and sent it off to fetch cones from the spruce and pine, but these had no effect. Then she created a gold-breasted pine marten in the same way from a wood shaving, and dispatched it to the den of the bear, to bring froth from the animal's jaws; but again the liquid failed to ferment. Finally from a pea pod she created a bee, which brought back honey, and this time the ale fermented and rose to the top of the cask and over:

> The young drink grew up
> in the grooved cask of new wood,
> inside the birch tub;
> it foamed high as the handles,
> roared up to the brims
> (Bosley 1989: XX, 384ff.)

When this occurred, the girl thought at first that she had ruined the drink, but the birds told her that all was going well, and so 'the beer got its good name, its famous honour'.

The mistress of Northland was then able to proceed with her brewing on an almost cosmic scale, using barley and hop catkins. She heated the mixture with hot stones and boiled it for months, so that the smoke from her fires could be seen for many miles; finally the ale was left to mature 'lying underground / in a stone cellar / in an oaken barrel / behind a bung of copper' (Bosley 1989: XX, 503ff.). Then it was necessary to find a singer if the results were to be fully successful, and Väinämöinen chanted a blessing over the ale, since no one else had the necessary knowledge.

Here honey was added as the final ingredient, as this possesses fermenting qualities; it could be added to ale, wine or fruit-juice to produce various types of mead, the intoxicating drink made with honey popular in many parts of the world (Simonsson 1956: 288). It is, however, apparently ale or beer (there seems no distinction at this stage between the two) which in the Viking Age was drunk at the annual religious feasts, and which was brewed by the women. A strange but vivid story in the late *Halfs saga ok Halfsrekka*, one of the Icelandic sagas full of legendary material, is of a competition between two queens in a kingdom in Norway as to which could brew the best ale for the feast, and on this their future depended. One of them, Alrek, appealed to Freyja to help her, suggesting a traditional link between brewing and the goddess, but Geirhild, her rival, put her trust in Odin, and turned to him. He dropped his spittle on the yeast, and the resulting brew was unsurpassed. As a reward for his help Geirhild had promised to give him what came between her and the cask; this proved to be her unborn child, the doomed King Vikar, who was forced to give up his life as a sacrifice to Odin when he grew to manhood.

Odin himself did no brewing, but the mead of inspiration, his gift to poets and orators, was continually associated with him in the myths and in early skaldic verse. According to Snorri (*Skáldskaparmál* 57) this wonderful drink was brewed by the two races of gods, the Æsir and the Vanir, when they finally made peace together. All spat into the vat to cause it to ferment, just as Odin did in the tale of the rival queens. Spittle has the effect of hydrolysing starch into fermentable sugar, and use has been made of this in various parts of the world (M. Barnard 1966: 12); it accounts for the attempt to use foam from the bear's jaws in the *Kalevala*. The mixture at first took the form of a giant called Kvasir, a word associated in several languages with alcoholic drink (J. de Vries 1957: II, 67). He was capable of answering all questions, but was killed by dwarves, who brewed mead from his blood. Possibly more than one myth has been used here, or perhaps Snorri was trying to account for the description of mead in early poems as 'Kvasir's blood'.

The mead of inspiration passed into the possession of a giant; one of the great achievements of Odin was to win it back for the gods (Davidson 1993: 72). The importance of this episode, thought by some to represent an early myth of the Indo-European peoples, may have pushed into the background the original link between brewing and a goddess in the poems and tales of Scandinavia and Iceland. But the important part which brewing played in women's lives for centuries, and the suggestion of powerful female figures associated with it, make it a relevant part of this study of the goddess as mistress of the household, the hearth and the spring.

THE BIRTH AND NURTURING OF CHILDREN

From the earliest time of which we have record, women have turned to the goddesses for help in bearing children. There were many rituals, spells and amulets known to women everywhere, for becoming pregnant, for a safe delivery in childbirth, and for the health and safety of the babies after birth. The birth of a child was fraught with mystery and danger for women just as hunting was for men, and good fortune and continued health for themselves and their children were of enormous importance to the family and to the community.

Archaeological evidence gives us some indication of how heavy a price women might pay in childbirth. Some Egyptian mummies, including those of royal wives, show evidence of horrible suffering as a result of pelvic abnormalties (Tyldesley 1994: 75). In the cemetery of Poundbury, Dorset, in Roman Britain, Margaret Cox estimated that as many as 51 out of 282 females of childbearing age died shortly after giving birth (Allason-Jones 1989: 36), while in her study of pregnancy and childbirth in Norway in comparatively recent times, Lily Weiser-All (1968) gives us appalling accounts of despairing attempts to help a woman in agony when the child could not be delivered.

The link between birth and the goddess is indicated by some of the earliest female figures from the Neolithic period, clearly depicted as pregnant (see p. 1). The figure of a goddess giving birth (Plate 1, p. 5) was found in a grain bin in one of the shrines at Çatal Hüyük in Turkey (see p. 53), while there were paintings in other shrines of a pregnant goddess. D. O. Cameron (1981: 22ff.) suggested that women may have come to give birth in what is known as the Red Shrine, which was strikingly different from the others. Here everything was painted red, and the burnished floor would have been easy to keep clean, while runnels were provided for taking away the water, and there were platforms on which the births could have taken place.

Cameron went on to suggest that the link between the heads of bulls in the shrines and the birth symbolism might be explained by the striking resemblance between the animal's horned head and the female organs of reproduction (D. O. Cameron 1981: 5). He claimed that those who developed the bull symbolism would have a considerable knowledge of anatomy because of the custom at Çatal Hüyük of allowing vultures to feast on dead bodies, shown in vivid paintings on the walls. It takes about twenty minutes for these birds to remove the flesh from a corpse, and those officiating at funeral ceremonies would have plenty of opportunity to learn about human anatomy. Cameron's theory of the symbolism of birth, death and rebirth in the art and ritual of the temple at Çatal Hüyük is hard to prove without more corroborating evidence, but certainly merits consideration.

Because childbirth was up to the nineteenth century something from which men were usually excluded, although they might assist in an emergency (Weiser-All 1968: 110), and the husband might be present (Biezais 1955: 181), there is little exact knowledge of methods used in early times, or how appeals to the goddesses were made. Joyce Tyldesley (1994: 73) quotes one tale from the Westcar Papyrus which describes the miraculous birth of triplets to the Lady Reddjedet in Egypt. Four goddesses arrived disguised as itinerant midwives, and the woman in labour sat on a birthing stool; Isis stood in front to deliver the babies, with Nephthys behind her, while Hekat hastened the birth, and Meskhenet declared the fortunes of the children. Here once more the goddesses are concerned with both birth and destiny.

In Ancient Egypt the woman giving birth either sat on a birthing stool or knelt or squatted on two low piles of bricks. These bricks were closely associated with Meskhenet, whose symbol was a brick with a woman's head on it, and were said to be used by Thoth to record the future of the new-born child. Another female protector before and at birth was the hippopotamus goddess Taweret (Great One), usually shown standing upright with her protruding belly which suggests pregnancy. Curved batons or wands carved from hippopotamus teeth were used during delivery, although it is not known how; some of them bear engraved images of the protective goddess and some the names of the baby and the mother (Tyldesley 1994: 259). Although Taweret was on the whole a beneficent goddess, Tyldesley reminds us that the hippopotamus is a dangerous animal and a potential killer.

The concept of a small group of female supernatural beings helping at a birth is one that continued into medieval times, probably reflecting the widespread custom of several women assembling to give assistance when a child was born. There were no official midwives in northern Europe until the eighteenth century, although women might be generally recognized as midwives by the community. In any case in the North it was often impossible because of weather conditions for midwife or doctor to reach the house in time to help with the birth (Weiser-All 1968: 109). Thus even women of high rank relied on help from women relatives and neighbours, some of whom might be 'wise women' or specially experienced in assisting at births.

In northern Europe in the nineteenth century there is evidence among village people not only for solidarity among the women when a child was born, but also of outbursts of active hostility towards men. Richard Wolfram (1933) in an article on 'Weiberbunde' (Alliances of Women) gives some striking examples of ocasions when no man dared to show himself. One of these was in Alsace when the local midwife was chosen, an important occasion for the married women of the community (Wolfram 1933: 142). An interesting comparison is found in an account quoted by Brumfield (1981: 124ff.) of a modern Greek festival held on 8 January, St Domnes' Day, in honour of the local midwife. It was attended by all women of childbearing age, while the men stayed indoors. The midwife sat on a throne, decorated with necklaces of figs, currants and carob beans, with an onion for a watch, and the women presented gifts to her, while kissing leeks or sausages produced by the older women. They then escorted her in a carriage like a bride and sprinkled her with water from the fountain, while dancing and singing lewd songs.

Some customs reported from Denmark in the nineteenth century by Evart Tang Kristiansen and others indicate even more aggressive behaviour when a birth took place. In some villages, about a dozen women would move into the house to help the new mother, so that the husband lost all his authority and was hardly permitted to enter without offering them gifts. Soon after the birth a wild celebration was held, attended by all the married women. They met in an upstairs room to drink beer, one of them going down to give good wishes to mother and child. On their way home they played various pranks, such as stopping up the chimney of a house, or running away with someone's wagon. They went round with what was called the *Barselpott* (birthing pot), collecting gifts to help the new mother; the custom was known as the *Konegild*.

If the women came across a man working out of doors, they might remove his trousers or take away his food; they might also harass childless couples. One informant told Kristiansen that his brother, a smith, got the women out of his smithy only by seizing a piece of red-hot iron in the tongs and threatening them with it. It was reported from North Schleswig that in the past women went crazy when a child was born, tearing off women's caps and perhaps destroying men's hats or filling them with excrement. They danced mad dances, even storming a school and making the teacher and children dance with them, and sometimes broke into houses 'like a Wild Hunt' (Wolfram 1933: 142ff.). It seems possible that in such wild, frenzied activity by women after a birth we have echoes of early practices associated with the wilder side of the northern goddesses, like those forming part of the cult of the goddess Demeter (Brumfield 1981: 18, 84, 107, 125). There are resemblances here to the aggressive behaviour of women in the harvest field when they encountered an unfortunate male stranger (see pp. 76–7).

Among the Saami (Lapps) of northern Norway, there were three goddesses of childbirth, Sar-akka, Juks-akka and Uks-akka, usually said to be the daughters of Madder-akka. *Akka* means Old Woman, or in Finland Great-grandmother or Ancestress (Lid 1946: 15), while *madder* means earth or ground (Ränk 1955: 17ff.). The goddesses of childbirth were said to live under the ground in a Saami hut or tent, but Ränk thinks Madder-akka's name refers to distant descent, and that she may have been the first ancestress. She as well as her daughters was sometimes said to help women in childbirth, or according to some informants she gave them permission to help when needed.

Sar-akka is said to have been a major helper of women in pregnancy and childbirth, and the early part of her name probably comes from *sarat/saret*, to split or divide, since she was the being who separated mother from child. The chopping of firewood in her honour during childbirth was supposed to facilitate delivery (Karsten 1955: 38). Weiser-All (1968: 21) records the belief that a pregnant woman had to lay wood on the fire in a certain way to avoid a breech birth, while she must not sit on a chopping block or step over it, lest the baby be born with a hare-lip. The special porridge given to the mother for her first meal after the birth was named after Sar-akka (Weiser-All 1968: 107) and three wooden matches might be put in this, one with a cloven end. It was eaten by other women of childbearing age at the same time, 'in Sar-akka's honour' (Karsten 1955: 44); offerings might be made to her, such as spinning wheels and reels, brandy poured on the ground, or a dog which was buried alive (Lid 1946: 16). Both Madder-akka and Sar-akka were said to help with menstruation, and to assist reindeer to calve. The Scandinavian Saami, for whom Sar-akka was very important, also invoked her to help children in illness.

The place of Sar-akka was in the middle of the house, by the hearth; that of Uks-akka, whose name means Old Woman of the Door, was by the threshold, and that of Juks-akka probably at the back of the house (Lid 1946: 16). There is some confusion as to the exact functions of these last two goddesses; Ränk (1955: 26ff.) believes that Uks-akka guarded the door and also protected the growing infant from accidents, the Virgin Mary later replacing her as door guardian. Juks-akka had a bow as her symbol, and her name means Old Woman of the Bow; a tiny crossbow might be hung near the child's cradle or put into the mother's porridge after the birth. Ränk thinks that she is the goddess who determined the sex of the child, and could cause a boy to be born, and that the bow was a male symbol. It may be noted that these three goddesses possess separate functions in their care and protection for mother and child, while the figure of Madder-akka, the grandmother, emphasizes the importance of the ancestress in the conception and birth of children. The group of four goddesses is found only among the Saami of Scandinavia; in Russia and Finland there was one main birth deity corresponding to Madder-akka, although a group may have existed earlier (Ränk 1955: 7).

The title of Earth-Mother is used for a professional midwife in Norway, and was previously in use in Denmark and parts of Sweden for the woman who delivered the child. It seems likely to have been derived from the earlier concept of the goddess of birth beneath the earthen floor, which survived up to the eighteenth century among the Saami, rather than from the custom of laying the new-born on the earth (Lid 1946: 11ff.). Another name given to the woman acting as midwife was Light-Mother, which Lid believes was based on the use of a special ritual candle to 'lighten' the new-born child and examine it after birth. The relationship between the Light-Mother and her 'Light-Child' was a close one; in some cases, particularly in Iceland, she looked after the child in her home for the first few days or for an even longer period, during which it was nourished either by a fostermother or with cow's milk.

The porridge generally known in Norway as *senge-graut* (childbed porridge) was called *none-graut* in certain areas, and *norna-greytur* in the

Faroes, meaning 'porridge of the Norns'. This suggests the possibility that, like the Saami goddesses, the Norns were originally a group of female beings associated with childbirth, determining the destiny of the new-born child (see pp. 119–20). It might also explain a reference to the Norns in the poem *Fáfnismál* (12) in the *Poetic Edda*, in which the hero Sigurd puts questions to the dying dragon Fafnir. He asks who are the Norns who come to help in time of need and make the choice between boy and maid (*kjósa moeðr frá mögum*). This line has puzzled editors and translators, who have assumed that it must mean delivering the child at birth. But the determining of the sex of the unborn child was the function of one of the Saami goddesses, and the mother would appeal to her if she were particularly anxious for a son. If similar powers were possessed by one of the Norns, this could explain the phrase in the poem.

Sigurd is also told in *Fáfnismál* that the Norns are 'of different origins, not of one race: some akin to the gods, some to the elves, and some daughters of Dvalin'. Those akin to the gods could be the great goddesses, Frigg and Freyja, mentioned as helping in childbirth in *Oddrúnargrátr*, a poem in the *Edda*, probably of eleventh-century date. Here Borgny is struggling to give birth, and her pain and increasing weakness are effectively conveyed. Oddrun, said to be the sister of King Atli, although we know nothing of her or Borgny from other sources, is summoned to help her; they knew each other in the past, although the poem later reveals that Oddrun blames Borgny for adding to her griefs. She has come, she declares, not out of friendship, but because she swore that she would always help in time of need, apparently meaning in cases of difficult childbirth; it would be interesting to know to whom these promises were made. Oddrun is evidently famed for her skill as a midwife, and her method is to use powerful spells, as she sits by the knees of Borgny in the traditional position of the midwife, either in front of the kneeling woman or behind her (Lid 1946: 13; Weiser-All 1968: 114). In *Sigrdrífumál* we are told that whoever helped at a birth would have runes inscribed on the palms of the hands, and would clasp the joints (*lidu*) of the mother, and call on the *dísir* (goddesses) for aid. In Borgny's case, Oddrun's spells were so powerful that twin children, a girl and a boy, were successfully delivered. Borgny was very weak, but her first words were those of formal thanks to her midwife: 'May the holy beings, Frigg and Freyja and other gods, help you even as you have saved me from danger.'

This appeal to several divinities is in keeping with the description of the Norns as being not only akin to the gods but also linked with elves and underearth beings. Frigg was evidently associated with childbirth; she bore the name Jord (Earth), which echoes the title of the Saami goddess Madder-akka, and she was said to know the fates of men (see p. 121). Her association with the birth of heroes is brought out in the strange tale at the beginning of *Völsunga Saga* of King Rerir and his wife, who had no children and prayed to the gods for a son; Frigg heard their prayer and appealed to Odin, who sent down the daughter of a giant in the form of a crow, bearing an apple which she dropped on to the knees of the king as he sat on a burial mound. He took it home and shared it with his queen, and she soon discovered that she was pregnant, but was unable to give birth to her child. In the meantime the king died of sickness, and after six years had passed with the child still unborn, the queen commanded that he should be cut out of her; and so the great hero Volsung came into the world and kissed his mother before she died.

According to this, Odin takes a hand in bringing about the birth of the hero, but he does not seem to make a particularly good job of it from the mother's point of view. This may be another example of the loss of independence by the goddess when the cult of the warrior god Odin was established, and hitherto powerful goddesses came to be represented as the wives of the gods. In the passage from *Oddrúnargrátr* referred to earlier, the gods as well as the two chief goddesses are said to grant help in childbirth. In the mythological tradition as presented in the *Edda* poems and by Snorri, Frigg is consistently portrayed as a Mother Goddess, protecting her son Balder (see p. 85), while Freyja is the goddess who promotes love affairs between men and women, although as a goddess of fertility it would be appropriate to appeal to her at a birth.

Another example of a Mother Goddess concerned with childbirth in northern Europe is Laima, remembered in Latvia and Lithuania, mainly in songs. Biezais considers her to have been an independent and powerful goddess of the Baltic peoples, although memories of her have been later influenced by Christian teaching about the Virgin Mary (Biezais 1955: 304). Her special day was Thursday, and her powers extended far beyond childbirth; in particular she was the goddess of luck and determined the destiny of individuals, while she brought about marriages for young girls and found them good husbands. She, rather than their mothers, gave them counsel and presided over marriages, which were not solemnized in church until the seventeenth century. It was said that when a girl died unmarried, Laima sat on the grave and wept (Biezais 1955: 207). This helps us to understand why both Freyja and Frigg are appealed to at a birth, since birth and destiny, and in the case of a daughter, marriage, are all closely linked.

Laima is very much a protective goddess of the home, said to be found in certain parts of the house, including the bath-house (see p. 127). Water must not be thrown out of the window on to her, so presumably she like the Saami goddesses was thought to be under the earth (Biezais 1955: 172ff.) Many of the songs about her are specially linked with birth, which in Baltic countries usually took place in the bath-house, or in rooms near it not in normal use; the bath-house, stated one early writer, was holier than the church. Men kept the path to it clear but, apart from the husband, would not go in when a birth was taking place. Again more than one goddess was there to help, for Laima is said to be accompanied by Mara, who was the special protectress of cows (Biezais 1955: 253ff.). There was a ceremonial meal after the birth, as in Scandinavia.

The woman helping at the birth was promised payment by the husband if all went well, and she began by unbinding the hair of the wife and unloosing her girdle. She carried keys like a housewife, for these could be a symbol of the release of the child (see p. 149). In a nineteenth-century account from Latvia, it is said that when a party took place in the bath-house after the birth, they stopped up cracks in the wall or window, and arranged branches of wood in pairs; there was an oak branch for a boy, a linden branch for a girl, and a rowan branch for protection for mother and child. Before the birth the expectant mother made a brush with twigs from a young birch, together with oak, linden and rowan, bound together with red thread; the new-born infant was struck with this on three successive Saturday evenings, after which the brush was taken to the sheepfold and the twigs scattered. The mother left a small gift, such as a garter, in the place where she washed, and a piece of gold when she and the child went back to the bath-house. She also gave gifts of gloves or stockings to women who helped with the birth. The bath-house ceremonies must be pre-Christian in origin, and there is a reference in a seventeenth-century text to the killing of a hen by the grandmother (Biezais 1955: 190). The symbolism of cutting wood may be compared with evidence from Scandinavia (see p. 144).

Laima is clearly associated with the destiny of the new-born child. She is called the Mother of Luck, and the same title was given to the Virgin Mary in the seventeenth century (Biezais 1955: 71). In songs she decides personal destiny, either good or bad, and determines the form and growth of maidens (Biezais 1955: 123); it seems that by sitting on two or three chairs she decrees how many marriages a woman will make, and the decisions are unalterable. The surviving songs about her show a feminine approach, and were evidently sung by women, although she also presided over the fates of men. Sometimes she was taken to represent good luck, while another figure, Nelaime, stood for bad luck (Biezais 1955: 139). Laima had extensive powers, and could be appealed to for bread, well-being of cattle, the growth of flax, and help in all times of trouble. Mara, the goddess associated with childbirth and the protection of cattle, was said to be specially concerned with the care of children after birth. There have been attempts to identify a trio of goddesses representing fate among the Latvians, but Biezais finds no justification for this.

As Christianity was established, the Virgin Mary, St Anne, and other female saints replaced the Norns and the Mother Goddesses as helpers and protectors of women in childbirth. There was a new fear for expectant mothers in medieval times: some parishes refused burial in holy ground to women who died in childbirth, in case this should desecrate the churchyard. At Long Melford in Suffolk a beautiful alabaster relief of the Virgin reclining in childbed, with the midwife beside her while the Magi bring gifts, was concealed under the floor to preserve it from the iconoclasts at the Reformation. It is not surprising that the people were determined to keep it, since this 'was the most urgent to pray before and to save' (Gibson 1990: 96).

Both the Virgin Mary and St Anne, revered as Mary's mother in medieval times, were powerful figures to whom wives and mothers turned for help. Both are found depicted on the magic drums of the Saami (Figure 24), apparently replacing Madder-akka and Sar-akka (Ränk 1955: 27). Mary was said to hold the keys which released the child from the womb, and a prayer recorded at a trial in Sweden in 1722 ran:

> Virgin Mary, gentle mother,
> loan your keys to me;
> to open my limbs
> and my members
> (Kvideland and Sehmsdorf 1988: 147)

In some parts of Sweden such prayers were forbidden after the Reformation. Silver keys were used as amulets, and a flower called Mary's Keys was placed in the bed of a pregnant woman (see p. 155).

A Latin charm cut in runes on a pin found at Bergen is an appeal for help in childbirth: 'Mary gave birth to Christ, Elizabeth gave birth to John the Baptist. In honour of them, be delivered! Come forth, child! The Lord calls you to the light' (Liestøl 1963: 19). This would probably be laid on

Figure 24   Figures of the Virgin Mary and St Anne depicted on Saami shaman's drum. Based on drawing given by Ränk (1955). Lelly Aldworth.

the stomach of the woman in labour, and there are examples of similar prayers to be said while laying hands on her body (Weiser-All 1968: 116). Mary herself acts as midwife in the Icelandic Saga of Bishop Gudmund (*Biskupa Sögur* II, 167ff.). A poor woman called Arnbjorg was well past her time for the birth of her child, but the labour pains did not begin. She prayed to God and Gudmund for help, and on a night of deep snow lay down to sleep in front of the altar in the chapel, with only one devout blind woman with her. Suddenly the chapel was filled with light, and she saw Gudmund and the Virgin Mary, and heard the Virgin tell the bishop to support her shoulders 'while I do my work'. The Virgin then stroked her stomach hard, and immediately the child was born.

Not only the Virgin but also her mother Anne was invoked by women in their need. Anne was said to have given birth to Mary after years of waiting for a child, and could therefore be appealed to by those desiring one. In the early fifteenth century Katherine Denston commissioned a poem by Oswald Bokenham, an Augustinian friar from Clare Priory, on the life of St Anne, which ends with a moving plea for the birth of a son and heir to John and Katherine, sadly never granted: 'Provide, lady ... if it please the grace of God above, through thy merits, a son of her body' (Gibson 1990: 107). St Anne was important not only as the mother of the Blessed Virgin but also as the grandmother of Christ, and she is represented in paintings of the fifteenth century as part of a trinity consisting of Mother, Daughter and divine Child, to which women might turn for help (see p. 84). She is shown teaching her little daughter to read and also to spin; she supports her divine grandson in her arms or on her lap. A German figure of St Anne in wood from the fifteenth century in the Burrell Collection at Glasgow shows her holding the hand of a young Mary at her side while she carries the infant Christ on her arm (Plate 8).

By the ninth century she was said to have married no fewer than three times, and by each marriage had a daughter named Mary. Mary Cleopas was declared to be the mother of James and Joses, while Mary Salome was the mother of James and John, Biblical figures who could thus be regarded as the cousins of Jesus. The theme of the Holy Kindred became a favourite subject in art: the three Marys with their offspring are depicted over the Lady Altar in the church at Ranworth in Norfolk, together with St Margaret, who broke out of the belly of the dragon and so was accepted as another saint who helped in childbirth. Women who came to be churched after giving birth would present themselves and their babies before this altar, and at Ranworth, in an area of great devotion to St Anne, there was clearly 'a sense of the sacred dimension of family life' (Duffy 1992: 181). In paintings of the Holy Kindred, the matron Anne presides over the three young mothers and their children, charming infants and lively toddlers occupied with their toys, while the husbands sometimes form a supportive group in the background (Sheingorn 1990).

Plate 8 Statue of St Anne in wood, holding the Christ Child, with the Virgin Mary at her side. Ht 115.5 cm. Courtesy Glasgow Museums: Burrell Collection.

The goddesses who helped with childbirth were also concerned with the protection and training of children. The influence of Artemis over girls in Ancient Greece extended from birth to puberty (see pp. 16–18). In her temples and those of Athene girls could learn the skills needed in later life and be prepared for marriage, while Artemis helped both animals and women through the process of giving birth. In a study of the *Kourotrophos* (Nursing Mother) in Greek religion, T. R. Price (1978) claims that this concept has developed out of pre-Greek, Indo-European and Oriental concepts of the goddesses. The protective Nursing Mother may be a Mother Goddess, like Demeter, or a nurturer of children, like the Earth-Goddess Ge, or a virgin who like Artemis rears children (Price 1978: 2). Price sees Ge, Mother of the Gods and Giver of Nourishment, as a figure of remote antiquity and a powerful deity of the Indo-Europeans, often represented as a Virgin Goddess and differing from the Great Mother of Asia Minor. He argues that the cults of the nurturing goddesses are not the same as fertility cults, although both are concerned with the birth and growth of healthy children.

Among the Saami of northern Scandinavia the concept of nurturing goddesses can be seen in a simple form. The pattern found there, that of a grandmother and her three daughters, is repeated in the medieval extended family of St Anne, although there can hardly be any direct connection here. In the Baltic countries the goddess Laima is the guardian of young girls as well as a helper in childbirth, controlling their destinies and helping them to make good marriages.

The nurturing aspect of the northern goddess has been largely ignored, but must have been of considerable importance. There is some indication of this in popular literature, in the figure of the fairy godmother. Her role is particularly memorable in two well-known fairy-tales which reached us through Charles Perrault, a French writer of the late seventeenth century, with unconventional views on children's education. He, or possibly his son, rewrote a number of tales in a witty, elegant and yet homely style, some of which introduce a supernatural helper of young girls in distress, who is called as fairy godmother.

In the tale of the 'Sleeping Beauty' (Opie and Opie 1974: 81ff.), the king asked all the fairies known to him to act as godmothers to his baby daughter, and each brought the child a gift. These were not material gifts, however, for the fairies were bestowing her destiny upon her and determining her appearance, disposition and abilities. Unfortunately one fairy omitted from the list of guests decreed in her anger that the princess should die in her youth when she pricked her finger on a spindle. This decree could not be wholly undone, but one of the other godmothers was able to change the sentence of death to a sleep of a hundred years, from which the princess should be awakened by a noble prince who was to become her husband.

In Perrault's seventeenth-century world, the Christian godmother is the figure which comes closest to the supernatural female Helper of earlier tradition. She was the donor of gifts and benefactor of the family; she appeared at or soon after the birth of a child, and took an active interest in the child's health and well-being. She was recognized by the Church and played a part in the baptismal ceremony, so that she was associated with the Otherworld. It is unlikely that Perrault invented the term godmother, since it was used in Brittany: Wentz (1911: 203) heard of a local fairy known as Margot ma Commère (my godmother), and people referred to 'our good mothers the fairies'.

The tale of Cinderella is widespread across the world; as long ago as 1893 Marion Cox collected 145 variants, and many more can now be added. She divided them into three main groups, which she called Cinderella, Catskin and Cap o'Rushes; the pattern throughout is that of a young girl ill-treated by a cruel stepmother or an unreasonable father, who is saved by a supernatural woman helper and finally makes a splendid marriage. Sometimes it is the dead mother of the girl who comes to her aid, or an animal helper given by the mother, but in many versions it is the fairy godmother. She appears in the kitchen when Cinderella is weeping because she is not to go with her stepsisters to the ball in the palace, and provides her with wonderful clothes and a coach so that she can arrive as a great lady and meet the prince. The idea of marvellous dresses provided by the supernatural helper so that the girl is transformed from her shabby and miserable state into a glorious figure is a recurring theme in the tales, but the prince has to find and recognize her in her humble surroundings before her final happiness can be achieved.

In the Grimms' tales, fairy godmothers are not mentioned, although in 'The Shuttle, the Spindle and the Needle' a human godmother brings up a motherless girl and leaves her a house and equipment for spinning when she dies, which results in the heroine marrying a prince. There are, however, wise women and supernatural helpers who assist girls in need. One of these is Frau Holle, who provides a link between godmother and goddess. Holle is one of the local goddess figures in German popular tradition who encouraged girls in their spinning and taught them how to run a household well, rewarding good workers and punishing the slovenly (see pp. 104–5). They helped new wives and assisted in childbirth, and it was said that new-born babies came from Holle's pool. In one of the tales Frau Holle helps a girl with a cruel stepmother and takes her into her service, so that she is assured of a successful future and a good marriage. Thus in stories which for hundreds of years have entertained children, we find memories of the ancient nurturing goddesses, figures to whom young girls might turn for counsel and support when their parents failed them.

CHAPTER V

MISTRESS OF LIFE
AND DEATH

——— ·◆· ———

THE HEALING GODDESSES

Women's responsibilities and skills in pre-Christian times included the provision of home medicine and nursing, which necessitated the growing and collecting of herbs. Part of a girl's education consisted in learning what herbs to gather, and Verdier in her work on women in rural France noted that when girls were forced to miss school in the summer to look after the cattle or sheep, along with their grandmothers, the older women would show them where the useful plants grew (Verdier 1979: 170). The herb garden formed an important part of the home, providing plants for cooking as well as for the treatment of illness and healing of wounds and injuries.

Mugwort (*Artemisia vulgaris*) for instance was used extensively in home medicine, and has been singled out as 'the female herb *par excellence*' (A. C. Cameron 1993: 177), wormwood being another useful member of the same family. Mugwort grows on waste land and hedge banks, and there is nothing spectacular about it, but it has long been valued over a great part of the world for its varied powers, and Armstrong (1943) suggested that it could have been one of the first herbs to be cultivated. The volatile oil, bitter substances and tannin in the flower shoots provided an excellent seasoning for meat and fish and also made fat easier to digest, while it was used to flavour beer before hops were available (Loewenfeld 1964: 156). On the medical side it was held to be effective for the treatment of diabetes, rheumatism, and various diseases connected with the womb and with menstruation; one early name for it was Motherwort. In Scotland the plant was thought to be a cure for tuberculosis, and a rhyme attributed to a mermaid urges young girls to eat mugwort:

> If they wad drink nettles in March
> And eat muggons in May
> Sae mony braw maidens
> Wad no gang to clay.
> (Chambers n.d.: 331)

It is worth noting that this advice was said to be given by a female supernatural being, and it becomes understandable why Laima, who wept when young girls died unmarried, was said to reside in wormwood and mugwort (see p. 127). Armstrong gives instances of its association with goddesses in the Far East and in Mexico, while in Ancient Greece it was said to grow on the mountain of Artemis (Armstrong 1943: 26).

Another possible indication of the link between healing plants and the goddess is the surprisingly large number of flowers called after the Virgin Mary in later times, such as Our Lady's Bedstraw and Our Lady's Mantle. Such names are applied to different flowers in various parts of the country, as Geoffrey Grigson (1955) has shown in his *Englishman's Flora*. Some, like 'Virgin's Bower' for the clematis, or 'Rosemary', appear not to have been originally associated with the Virgin Mary (Friend 1883: 80ff.), while others, like 'Marybud' for the marigold, gained their names because they were used to decorate churches for the Virgin's festivals (Friend 1883: 101). However, some flowers linked with the goddess in pre-Christian times may afterwards have been named after the Virgin.

Our Lady's Bedstraw (*Galium verum*), a plant used to curdle milk in cheesemaking in northern Europe, was said to have been used with bracken for the bed in which Christ was born, after which the flowers changed from white to gold (Grigson 1955: 343). In Germany the plant was put into the bed of a woman in childbirth, and also into her shoes for protection after the birth. Our Lady's Mantle (*Alchemilla*), which collects water drops in its leaf clusters, was also renowned for its special powers. In Scotland and Ireland it was held to cure elfshot in cattle, and generally thought to heal wounds, stop bleeding, and to help women to conceive (Grigson 1955: 138).

The names of both these plants appear to have come into England from Germany, where they were known as *Unser Frauen Bettstroh/Marien Bettstroh* and *Frauen* or *Marien Mantel*, while Mary's Mantle (*Marikaabe*) was a name used in Norway. In Scandinavia the early purple orchid (*Orchis maculata*) was called Mary's Keys, and this was placed in the bed of a pregnant woman to help in childbirth (see p. 149). In Germany the same name might be given to the cowslip or primrose.

The Lady's Thistle (*Silybum marianus*) has marks on its leaves resembling milk, said to be caused by the Virgin's milk dropping on it as she suckled the Christ Child. Evelyn in the seventeenth century had heard that this plant increased the flow of milk for nursing mothers (Grigson 1955: 388). Our Lady's Thistle is similarly named in France and Germany.

The Puritans felt sufficiently strongly about such flower names to substitute Venus for Our Lady, and it seems reasonable to suppose that the Virgin has sometimes replaced an earlier supernatural figure. Names of Frigg or Freyja were retained in some flower names in Scandinavia: Grimm (1883: I, 303) mentions the Icelandic name *Freyjuhar* (Freyja's hair) for the Lady's Hair Fern (*Adiantum capillus veneris*). The Bedstraw (*Galium verum*) was called *Freyjar gras* (Freyja's Weed) in Sweden, and later *Jungfru Marie Sanghalm* (Virgin Mary's Bedstraw) (Närrström 1995: 212). Alongside the extensive learned literature on herbs used in the medieval monasteries noted by Bonser (1963: 306ff.) and Meaney (1981: 38ff.), there must have been traditional women's lore concerning useful plants and flowers originally associated with the goddess.

However, the search for healing by divine help extended far beyond the practices in the home, and was something of major importance for men and women alike. In their helplessness in the face of sickness, accidents and death they turned to both gods and goddesses for reassurance and aid, and undoubtedly the goddesses were deemed to possess great healing powers.

In Celtic areas there is much evidence for such powers linked with the goddesses of streams and springs and the sources of great rivers. When the Romans established their rule in Gaul and Britain, they appear deliberately to have developed and commercialized some of the sites at thermal springs to which people went for healing, as clearly happened at Bath (Cunliffe 1986). Here a number of hot springs known to have natural therapeutic powers, especially effective for arthritis and gout, had already made the site a sacred place to which people came for healing. Soon after the Roman occupation an impressive temple with a bathing complex was built around it, attracting vast numbers of visitors who left rich gifts behind. About the end of the third century AD, the temple was enlarged and access to the springs restricted. The pool formed by the main spring of hot water was roofed over by a considerable feat of engineering, so that the only access for visitors was through a dim passage-way into a mysterious grotto, where the hot water surged out from a cavern in a cloud of mist and steam, adding greatly to the impressiveness of the sacred place.

The goddess who presided over this temple was called Sulis Minerva, a conflation of the local goddess, Sulis, with the Roman Minerva, goddess of wisdom and crafts, and therefore presumably of medicine (M. J. Green 1996: 33). Finds of Celtic coins suggest that offerings were being made to the goddess before the Romans developed the site (Cunliffe 1986: 1). In Roman times many women visited it, and models of breasts in bronze and ivory might be offerings from those suffering from cancer or mastitis (Allason-Jones 1989: 156–7), or possibly appeals for help in breast-feeding, or amulets presented to the goddess after a child was weaned (Henig 1988: 5). Evidently the goddess could act as avenger as well as benefactress, since curses scratched on lead were also thrown into the water, praying for a dire fate to overtake those who had stolen from the petitioners or done them harm (Tomlin 1988).

There are other examples of shrines in Roman Gaul to which many women came as pilgrims (Pelletier 1984: 110–11). One of these was the shrine of the goddess Sequana at the source of the river Seine, where it was customary for those seeking healing to present votive models of themselves in wood, sometimes full-length figures, sometimes busts or heads; there were also representations of babies in swaddling clothes, and rough models of single limbs, eyes or other parts of the body. A number of the figures

and heads clearly represent women, some delineated with considerable artis-
tic skill, although many damaged or worn figures wrapped in cloaks could
be of either sex. It cannot be claimed that women are in the majority (Deyts
1983: 74ff.). but again it was a goddess to whom the pilgrims came for
healing. Her name is given in inscriptions as Sequana, and a fine bronze
represention of her standing in her boat, with a duck's head on its prow,
is in the museum at Dijon (Figure 25). The springs at the source of the
Seine had no special healing qualities, but the wooden figures make it clear
that pilgrims hoped for all kinds of cures, including that of blindness, a
widespread affliction.

Thousands of wooden votive figures, many well-preserved, were also
found at Chalmalières in central France in 1968 (Deyts 1984: 192ff.), where
some standing upright were apparently placed round the spring. Pilgrims
are sometimes shown carrying a bird, just as some small stone figures found
at the Seine source have animals with them, or they may have baskets or
coffers. It is not known what divinity or pair of divinities was worshipped
at Chalmalières, but Miranda Green suggests that one impressive female
figure wearing a torc, dated to the first century AD, may conceivably be a
goddess (M. J. Green 1995: 17, 90).

As well as individual goddesses, like Sulis, other female divinities at the
healing shrines were partners of Apollo or Mars. An example of this is
Sirona, whose statue, with a snake twined round her right arm and holding three eggs in a bowl, was found at the thermal centre of Hochschied,
in the Moselle basin. A statue of Apollo was also found, and there had
been a wooden shrine here before some wealthy villa owner built a small
temple round the spring (Wightman 1970: 220–2). Sirona was popular at
thermal sanctuaries in the Rhineland (M. J. Green 1996: 29ff.); she was
worshipped with Apollo at Metz and elsewhere in the area inhabited by
the Treveri, although occasionally venerated alone.

Other goddesses to whom pilgrims went for healing were Damona, who
like Sirona is shown with a snake and had various male gods as partners,
and Ianuaria at Beire-le-Chatel in Burgundy, where an appealing little figure of a boy playing pan-pipes was dedicated to her in the healing shrine
(M. J. Green 1996: 32). There are also some female divinities who appear
to be Mother Goddesses (M. J. Green 1995: 104). Pelletier (1984: 110–11)
has pointed out that there are many instances of women acting as donors
at healing shrines in Gaul; they often made use of the hot baths, and were
frequent visitors at the sanctuaries at river sources.

An example in Britain of a small local place of healing, visited by members of the Roman army as well as those who lived in the district, is that
of the goddess Coventina, presiding over a spring at Carrawburgh on
Hadrian's Wall (Figure 26). Carved stones associated with this site show
her as a nymph or water-spirit, and in one case there are three such figures, although their exact relationship with Coventina remains doubtful

Figure 25 Goddess Sequana in boat from *Fontes Sequanae*, near Dijon. Ht 61.5 cm.
Musée Archéologique, Dijon. Eileen Aldworth.

(Allason-Jones 1996: 110). Many coins were offered here, as well as jewellery and small votive gifts. There is little direct evidence to connect
Coventina's cult with physical healing, but those who came to drink the
water, as in the case of springs associated with Christian saints, must have
included many hoping for healing and help in childbirth. As Allason-Jones
and McKay (1985: 10) put it: 'Coventina can scarcely have avoided acting
as a healer even if that was not her prime responsibility'.

Figure 26 Stele dedicated to the goddess Coventina from her well at Carrawburgh, Hadrian's Wall. Ht 74 cm. Chester Museum. Eileen Aldworth.

Inscriptions, occasional scenes on altars, and votive offerings found on sanctuary sites give some indication of how those who came to shrines in Gaul for healing approached a goddess (Pelletier 1984: 109–10). The suppliant might kneel in prayer, throw incense on to the flame on the altar, or offer an animal for sacrifice: this seems to be the reason why some of the pilgrim figures are shown carrying birds or small dogs (see p. 50). Those who worshipped Kybele in southern Europe might make the more expensive offering of a bull, and inscriptions suggest that this was often done by women; it seems to have been more than a thank-offering for a cure, however, and was perhaps part of an initiation ceremony.

Pelletier suggests that the wooden figures of pilgrims and the models of their afflicted parts, left at a shrine or thrown into water, should be seen as a form of sacrifice, a substitute for the person who brought them to the deity. It seems more reasonable, however, to suppose that many represent thank-offerings left as records of cures, like the crutches at St Winifrede's healing well at Holywell in north Wales (M. J. Green 1995: 193). A further possibility is that this was a means of leaving a likeness of oneself or the afflicted part of one's body under divine protection, in hope of a continued cure after leaving the sanctuary. The pilgrims might bathe in the water of the sacred spring, or drink it, and if they threw figures of themselves into the water or left them beside the spring, this could be viewed as a way of maintaining contact with the divine. Customs and rites clearly varied at different sanctuaries. At Sulis' temple at Bath anatomical models, apart from those of breasts, are rare, but gifts such as spindle whorls and hairpins were made, providing evidence for women pilgrims, as well as more valuable offerings of coins and jewellery.

Pilgrims at the larger sanctuaries like that of Sulis would probably be able to consult a doctor, for Roman physicians had no prejudice against divine healing, and the standard of medicine was relatively high in Roman Britain (Allason-Jones 1989: 156). Titus Janianus, for instance, may have been an oculist with a surgery at Bath, as his prescription for eye salve was found there. Some of these doctors may indeed have been women, since a woman described as *Medica* is shown on a funerary stone at Metz from the first century AD (Pelletier 1984: plate 40). Another means of seeking healing was to sleep at the sanctuary, in hope of receiving a dream from the presiding divinity. There was a dormitory at the temple of Sequana and possibly also at Bath (M. J. Green 1995: 91, 96), while worshippers of Damona appear to have practised healing sleep, on the evidence of one inscription (M. J. Green 1996: 32).

In southern Europe there were many healing sanctuaries of male divinities such as Asklepios and Apollo, but as Miranda Green (1995: 90) points out, the sanctuaries at sacred springs in northern Celtic areas were usually dedicated to goddesses. We know nothing definite as to the nature of Sulis, who may have been a solar goddess; she could injure as well as heal, since curses were left at her shrine. This method of seeking revenge continued into modern times, for in the nineteenth century various 'cursing wells' were known in Wales (Bord and Bord 1986: 84).

In Christian times shrines of women saints were often sited at a spring or well. At the visitations during the reforming years of the sixteenth century, there were indignant reports about holy relics used not only for ostentation but also in hopes of practical results; Eamon Duffy shows how people flocked to the monastic shrines as places of healing and help (Duffy 1992: 384ff.). At Bruton in Somerset, St Mary Magdalene's girdle was sent to women in childbirth, while the staff of St Moodwyn at Burton-on-Trent, a saint with a red cow as her companion, was used by pregnant women 'to leane upon, and to walk with yt, and have greate confidence in the same staff'. At the shrine of St Anne at Buxton by the hot springs, there were extensive offerings of crutches, shirts and sheets as well as wax images; Cromwell's agent had to seal the entrance to the baths and wells to keep out the crowds who came to wash in them. Another agent at the shrine of Our Lady of Caversham reported that even after his arrival about a dozen pilgrims arrived with images of wax. Traces of black oil in the water from St Katherine's Balm Well at Liberton near Edinburgh, caused by a coal seam at the source, were attributed to a drop of oil brought from the tomb of St Catherine on Mount Sinai, and believed to have given the water healing properties (Bord and Bord 1986: 105). The shrine of St Winifrede at Holywell in North Wales has been a place of pilgrimage since medieval times and continues to be so; the stone building which has housed it since the end of the fifteenth century was provided by Margaret Beaufort, the mother of Henry VII, and pilgrimages and cures there continued in spite of the Reformation.

Evidence of the part played by women doctors in the Middle Ages is scanty and difficult to assess, as Monica Green (1989) has shown in her study of women's medical practice and health care in medieval Europe. It is clear that some women doctors existed, but in surviving lists of names, official titles, such as leech, barber or apothecary, seem to be confined to men. As Hanawalt (1986: xiii) pointed out in a different context, women were probably able to practise their skills in various ways and have considerable influence in the community, but rarely held official positions. Moreover once medical training was given in the universities, doctors were naturally eager to protect their qualifications and resented interlopers such as women and Jews, who were not admitted to the medical schools.

There are, however, indications in early literature that women played a major part in healing in pre-Christian and early Christian times. In the sagas of the kings of Norway, there are references to women specially skilled in the healing of wounds. Such a woman is mentioned after the battle of Stiklastad in 1030, where St Olaf fell (*Heimskringla, Óláfs Saga helga* 234). After the battle, Thormod Bersason, wounded in the fighting, joined a group of injured men, and found

> there was a woman there binding up men's wounds; a fire was burning on the floor, and she was heating water to cleanse the men's wounds.

This healing woman is called a doctor (*læknir*). Some men were assisting her, and one of them told Thormod to ask her for treatment; she noticed how pale Thormod was and offered to attend to his wound. Her method was to give wounded men leeks and other herbs in water to drink, since if she could smell the leeks she knew the wound to be deep. She could see that there was an arrow in Thormod's side and tried to get it out with tongs; he told her to cut down to the iron, and gave her a gold ring as payment for her help; however, when he himself finally pulled out the arrow, which had gone close to his heart, he fell back dead.

Another woman doctor (*læknir*) is mentioned in *Droplaugarsonar Saga* (11). When Helgi, one of the famous brothers in the saga, was killed in battle along with his brother Thorkell and several other men, his brother Grim was severely wounded and thought to be dead. Their aunt Groa came out to meet those bringing back the dead and wounded, and thought Grim might be still alive. She announced that she and her son would watch over the bodies that night, and while people slept she went to find Alfgerd the doctor, and brought her back with her. The bodies of Helgi and Thorkell were prepared for burial next morning, and it was thought that Grim was laid in the mound with them, but he was taken away secretly by Alfgerd after she had attended to his wounds, to prevent news of his survival reaching his enemies. He spent the winter recovering and then stayed some years with a kinsman in another part of the country, finally returning to slay the man who had killed his brother Helgi.

Grim's own death came about when another woman claiming to be a doctor came to tend a wound in his foot which had turned septic. She bound it up and went away, but it became worse and finally caused his death. It was later discovered that this was a woman skilled in magic, the concubine of an evil Viking whom Grim had killed in a duel.

From this and other incidents in the Sagas of the Bishops (*Biskupa Sögur*) quoted by Jónsson (1912: 8ff.) it seems that both men and women skilled in healing were called in to treat wounds, a service which must have been in frequent demand in the Viking Age. St Olaf, Magnus the Good, and Snorri Goði in *Eyrbyggja Saga* are three examples of famous men who had the gift of healing. The term *læknir* (leech, doctor), however, appears to be specifically given to women called upon to treat the wounded after battle or visit sick and injured people in their homes. Saxo Grammaticus, writing in the last part of the twelfth and the early thirteenth centuries, has a tale in Book III of Odin disguised as a woman and claiming to be skilled as a doctor in order to gain access to the bedroom of a princess. Perhaps this should be seen as another example of Odin trespassing on the preserves of a goddess.

Little information concerning healing ritual has survived in mythological literature of the North. In the *Edda* poem *Sigdrifumál* the valkyrie who encounters the hero Sigurd drinks to both gods and goddesses, and asks for 'healing hands' to be given him along with the gifts of wisdom and eloquence. Snorri in *Gylfaginning* (35) includes Eir in his list of goddesses, calling her the best doctor among the Æsir, but we know virtually nothing about her; she is mentioned also in *Skáldskaparmál* (75) along with valkyries, but is singled out as one of the Norns who shape the lives of children. No satisfactory conclusions have been drawn from her name (J. de Vries 1957: II, 316). She is also mentioned in the poem *Fjölsvinnsmál*, surviving in a late paper manuscript, thought to contain some earlier mythological material. Here she is included among the maids of the goddess-like figure of Menglod ('necklace-glad'), whose names suggest that they are guardian spirits, and who are said to 'shelter and save' those who make offerings to them. They could be akin to the protective spirits of the house, guarding both men and women.

In the same poem we have the most imaginative passage in the *Edda* collection concerning a goddess of healing. The questing hero Svipdag asks Much-Wise the name of the hill on which Menglod is reclining, and is told:

> It is called Lyfjaberg, and has long brought
> joy to sick and suffering.
> She will become whole, though gravely ill,
> every woman who climbs it.

Lyfjaberg means Hill of Healing, and this is where the goddess sits surrounded by the helpful spirits. Although healing by a goddess – or indeed by a god either – has left little mark on the Norse myths as they have come down to us, there is no doubt that the healing power of goddesses was of enormous importance in daily life in the pre-Christian period, as was that of many women saints in Christian times. The goddess who presided over childbirth was held to possess power over life and death, and was revered as a lifegiver, both in the family home and in the courts of kings, though she might also pass sentence of death.

FUNERAL RITES

The part which women played at funerals is worth considering, since it may help us as to understand the association between death and the goddess. Details of pre-Christian funeral ritual in the early literature are sadly lacking, but there are two rich sources of information concerning the funerals of the Scandinavian ruling class in the Viking Age. The first is a detailed account by an Arab observer of the elaborate cremation funeral in 921 or 922 of a Scandinavian leader in Russia, and the second is the information gained from the contents of the Oseberg ship grave in Norway, dated to the first half of the ninth century, in which two women were buried.

The funeral on the Volga was very much a male-oriented affair, and much of the symbolism recorded could be associated with the cult of Odin. The dead man was a chief of the Rus, generally recognized to have been Scandinavian merchant adventurers who visited Russia for trade, bringing furs and slaves to sell in the markets. He died at Bulghar, the Bulgar capital on the Volga which was an important market centre. By good fortune an Arab expert in religious law, Ibn Fadlan, was making an official visit there at the time, in order to instruct the king of the northern Bulgars in the Islamic faith (Smyser 1965). He took great interest in strange customs, and was known as the Truthteller, because of his reputation as a reliable recorder. He was delighted to be able to witness the Rus funeral rites, since he had heard that these people held elaborate and unusual ceremonies when their leaders died.

This was the period of great ship graves in Norway and Sweden, and the long account gives us a unique opportunity to learn the impression made by such a funeral on an interested and impartial observer (Smyser 1965: 97ff.). While allowing for his ignorance of the language and the possibility that he may sometimes have been misled, there seems no doubt that he carefully recorded the rites which he himself witnessed, and did his best to find out what was going on behind the scenes.

The dead man was first buried for ten days while the necessary preparations were made for the funeral. This would correspond to the 'nine days and nights' mentioned elsewhere in connection with death, as when Odin hung on the World Tree as a sacrifice (*Hávamál* 139), or Hermod journeyed along the road to Hel (*Gylfaginning* 49). During this time they brewed a large quantity of *nabid*, the local drink, since there was much drinking at the funeral ('sometimes one of them dies cup in hand'), and a third part of the dead man's wealth was spent on this. It is to be presumed that women did the brewing, and they also are said to have made new clothes for the dead man, and prepared the couch on which he would lie. This was covered with Greek brocade (Byzantine silk), and the clothes were evidently most elaborate: the account mentions trousers and boots, a tunic and silk robe with gold buttons, and a hat of silk and fur. We are told that the person responsible for all these preparations was a sinister old woman, 'fat and louring', whom they called the Angel of Death: 'it is she who had charge of the clothes making and arranging of all things'. She had two younger women to assist her, called her daughters.

The identity of these women is a problem which Ibn Fadlan does not solve for us. The funeral took place far from home, and the Swedes, as the Rus are presumed to be, would be unlikely to bring their womenfolk with them. Therefore the immediate family and the widow of the dead man could not be present at the funeral to play their part. It is possible that they used a Slav woman to organize the ritual, and even conceivable that they had an established shrine there with a woman priestess brought from home, in order to officiate at funerals and other ceremonies; this might be necessary if the Rus traders came to Bulghar regularly every year. We know that there were also a number of women slaves, possibly Slavs, but these might also include Scandinavians (Davidson 1976: 101ff.). It was these who were asked if anyone would volunteer to act as the wife of the chieftain and to die at his funeral, and one girl agreed to this. Henceforward she was escorted everywhere by the 'daughters' of the Angel of Death, who treated her with great respect, even washing her feet; she spent her time drinking and singing as if she were a princess.

When the nine days were over, and the dead man was dug up, Ibn Fadlan was there to watch, and was able to report that although the body was now dark in colour, there was no objectionable smell. The dead man was dressed in his new outfit and laid on the couch, on a ship specially built for the cremation ceremony; this had been drawn on to the shore, and a wooden structure like a house erected over it, covered with fabric. The dead man was propped up with cushions and surrounded with fruit and fragrant plants, while food and drink were provided for him. Next came the killing of the animals: a dog, two horses, two cows, a cock and a hen. These were placed in the ship, as was done at the great Scandinavian ship-burials. Ibn Fadlan was told that before she died the girl had sexual intercourse with the kinsmen of the dead man 'for love and friendship', but there are differing versions as to where this took place.

What he did observe for himself was an impressive ceremony where she was lifted up before a structure resembling a doorway, and uttered words which described how she saw her dead parents and kinsfolk in the next world, and her master awaiting her in a fair green Paradise. Ibn Fadlan was told that she was asking to be taken to him. They gave her a hen, and like the woman who conducted Hading to the underworld in Saxo's tale (see p. 176), 'she cut off the head, which she threw away, and then they took the hen and put it in the ship'. The girl went on to sing a song of farewell to her female companions, like that sung by a bride before her wedding.

Finally she gave her arm-rings to the Angel of Death and rings to the two younger attendants, and drank cup after cup of ale until she became dazed. The old woman with some difficulty got her into the pavilion where the dead man lay, and the men then made a great noise striking their shields so that her cries would not be heard. Ibn Fadlan was told that the Angel of Death put a cord round her neck (or according to another version, her veil) and that two men strangled her while the woman plunged a dagger between her ribs. Sacrifice by strangling and stabbing is represented in the literature as associated with the cult of Odin (Davidson 1964: 52). After this the chief's nearest kinsman set fire to the scaffolding holding up the ship, while others threw in burning pieces of wood, till all was speedily engulfed in flames. A man told Ibn Fadlan that 'his lord, for love of him, has sent the wind to bring him away in an hour' and within that time the ship and its contents were reduced to ashes. A burial mound was built over the remains of the pyre, and a post erected with the names of the dead man and his king inscribed on it.

Evidently the Angel of Death and her helpers used the time before the funeral to teach the girl her part in the ceremony and the apparently elaborate lays which she sang before the crowd of spectators; she is said to have spent much of her time singing in the nine days before she died. Whether Slavonic or Scandinavian in origin, the ritual was clearly well established and fairly complex. There is evidence both from Russia and Scandinavia for the sacrifice of a young woman at a warrior's funeral (Davidson 1976: 307ff.), although this type of evidence is particularly difficult to assess when relying only on archaeological data (Davidson 1992).

It is significant that the funeral ritual, including the final sacrifice of the human victim, was organized by an aged woman, who was responsible for the preparation of the body, the laying out of the dead man on a bed, and the provision of a 'wife' to accompany him. The preparations for the cremation itself, the building of the ship, the house erected over it, and the making and lighting of the pyre, were in the hands of the men. Armed warriors supported the sacrificial rites by an organized clashing on shields to drown any cries from the victim, and two men assisted the Angel of Death by strangling the girl. In this case it seems likely that the dead man was of royal rank, perhaps a close kinsman of the king whose name was carved upon the memorial post on his mound. The allusion to kinsmen awaiting the girl in the Otherworld indicates that here the cult of ancestors and the presence of the dead chief in his mound were important factors remembered at funerals, though in this case those involved were far from their homeland. There is no indication that this particular chief was bound for Valhalla, in spite of links with Odin's cult, and unfortunately we have no information as to whether he died in battle.

The Oseberg ship-burial in Vestfold in southern Norway is dated about half a century earlier than the cremation on the Volga, and was excavated in 1903. It belonged to the greatest grave complex in Norway, used for about 250 years by the Yngling royal family (Ingstad *et al.* 1992: 19ff.); the suggestion that the queen buried there was Alfhild, wife of Gudrod the Magnificent, the Hunting King, and probably a priestess of the goddess Freyja, has been put forward by Anne Ingstad (see p. 112). Unfortunately the contents of the grave were much disturbed and damaged by those who broke into the mound a few years after the burial.

The ship had a house of wood built on it, like that described by Ibn Fadlan. This was of rough workmanship, but may have been covered by textiles to create a kind of tent (Ingstad *et al.* 1992: 211ff.) as was said to be done at Bulghar. Another parallel is the killing of animals to put into the ship; at Oseberg these were fifteen horses, two oxen, four dogs and a peacock. Two women had been buried in the ship, and must have been laid out on the fine beds provided for them; such beds would not be normal ship's furniture (Hoffmann 1964: 353), and it may be assumed that they formed an essential part of the funeral preparations, like the couch of the Rus chieftain. The presence of two beds suggests that the second burial on this occasion was that of a kinswoman or high-born priestess who died at the same time as the queen, rather than a slave used as a sacrificial victim (Ingstad *et al.* 1992: 81). The funeral procession depicted on the wall-hangings found in the ship (Figure 18, p. 109), which includes various supernatural beings, is valuable evidence for splendid ritual and for abundance of Otherworld symbolism (see pp. 108–9).

Many female characters, some from the Otherworld, are depicted on the hangings, indicating a strong link between the goddess and the realm of death. There is also much symbolism associated with the goddess Freyja in the contents of the grave, including the marked emphasis on spinning and weaving (see pp. 107–8). There were articles used for washing, which Ingstad explained as possibly symbolizing the power to bring rain (Ingstad *et al.* 1992: 252), but we know too that the washing of the body played an important part at a funeral (see pp. 170–1). A chest of corn was found as well as apples, berries and a grindstone, all appropriate symbols for Freyja as goddess of fertility. Unfortunately we have no knowledge of the lays which might have been chanted or sung at this funeral.

Undoubtedly dirges or laments formed an essential part of women's contribution to funeral rites; the practice has continued from very early times up to the nineteenth century in some areas of northern Europe, including Wales and Ireland. When lays were no longer formally composed and recited, the practice of women wailing and lamenting without words continued to be widespread.

An early reference to a dirge recited by a woman is found in the Anglo-Saxon poem *Beowulf* in the account of the funeral after the battle at Finnsburh. Queen Hildeburh, whose sons had been killed in a tragic struggle between her husband and her brother, gave orders that their bodies should be placed on the pyre along with that of their uncle, slain on the opposing side. She then mourned over her dead kindred, 'lamenting in mournful lays' (1117ff.). A second example of a woman mourning at a royal funeral comes when Beowulf himself is burned on a mighty funeral pyre. An aged woman with her hair bound up laments his death, predicting calamities and suffering for the Geats now that their great leader has been taken from them (3148ff.). Unfortunately the manuscript is damaged here, and it is uncertain if this Geatish woman is Beowulf's widow or a professional lamenter.

This lament differs from the song of praise in honour of Beowulf as king and hero, sung by his warriors as they ride round his mound after the funeral is over. The difference resembles that in our own day between the funeral service, where the bereaved family occupies the central position, and the memorial service for the distinguished dead, open to a much wider circle, usually held some time later. Elegies describing the entry of a dead king into Valhalla and his welcome by Odin, composed in Scandinavia by professional court poets, come into this second category. The poet Egil Skallagrímsson felt it important that he himself should be responsible for the lament for his dead son (see p. 176), and he composed the great poem *Sonartorrek*, intended to be recited at the funeral feast, some time after Bodvar had been buried (*Egils Saga* 78).

Accounts of dirges sung by women at funerals, some semi-professional lamenters wearing a special costume of coarse linen, have survived from Finland and the mid-Baltic countries (Honko 1974). More material comes from Russia, and from the people of the Caucasus. Rybnikov in the mid-nineteenth century stated that in remote areas of Russia every woman, even those of humble rank, would be capable of composing a lament; she might produce a new composition of her own or adapt an old one He refers to laments for dead children, for parents leaving orphans behind, and for dead husbands. One lament in an archaic form was recited by a woman from a poor background after her husband had been laid out. She bewails the fact that her poverty prevented her from being with him when he died, because she had to labour for her children, and laments her loss. A slightly different form of this lament is recorded for a more prosperous widow, and there are also laments by professional mourners (N. K. Chadwick 1936: 229ff.). The main theme is the sad future awaiting the bereaved, as in *Beowulf*.

Ralston (1872) recorded both marriage songs and laments for the dead from Russia, and tells us that in the nineteenth century there was a woman 'Wailer' (*Voplenitza*), who was responsible for seeing that the proper customs were observed at both marriages and funerals: she taught the bride how to mourn for the loss of her maiden freedom, and the widow and orphan to lament (Ralston 1872: 68, 342). It is noteworthy that something in the nature of a marriage farewell song was included in the tenth-century funeral on the Volga (see p. 165), when the girl to be sacrificed had just been chosen as the bride of the dead leader.

In Ireland the improvised lament by women over the dead is known to have taken place at funerals in the twelfth century, and has continued into the twentieth. There are references to the sad absence of a great funeral lamentation over the dead body of Christ in a poem of the eighth century composed by a monk named Blathmac, Son of Cú Brettan (Lysaght 1995: 165). This is dedicated to the Virgin Mary, with assurances that he would join with her now in lamenting over her son, while all the world would weep. While we have many descriptions from travellers who witnessed keening (*caoineadh*) over a dead body and sometimes give English translations of the songs, comparatively little has been recorded in Irish, but a few dirges from recent times survive. Patricia Lysaght (1995) has reviewed the existing material and discussed it in detail[†].

Both men and women might compose impromptu lamentations, some of which were remembered and handed down. Ó Súilleabháin (1967: 132) quotes one by the widow of a ploughman, bewailing her helpless state after the loss of her supporter:

[†]Some of this material is now available in a more recent article, '*Caoineadh os Cionn Coirp*: The Lament for the Dead in Ireland', in *Folklore* 108 (1997) 65–82.

Rise and stand up,
and tackle your ploughing-team!
Plough a five-inch furrow;
look at me, my treasure,
with nobody to help me
when I go reaping or cutting!
Who will do my business at the market?
Who will go the the Hill of the Mass,
as you lie stretched from now on? Och, ochon!

This was said to have been recited over her husband's body.

Croker (1844) in the first half of the nineteenth century described two professional keeners whom he had known. Mrs Harington from Cork led a wandering life, and was constantly given hospitality when a death took place because of her knowledge of Irish poetry. She could not read or write, but could translate 'elegantly' from Irish to English, and at funerals she seems to have adapted earlier laments rather than composed new ones. The second keener, Mrs Leary, was described as less cultured but very quick-witted. She would recite three or four verses and then improvise to finish the lament (Croker 1844: xxiv–xxvi). As time went on, impromptu laments were replaced by literary effusions, composed and printed after the funeral.

The custom of wailing for the dead was also carried out mainly by women, and was practised from antiquity up to the present time in various parts of the world. In Rome there is a link with the goddess Ceres in the custom of women to lament at cross-roads on certain days as part of her rites (Spaeth 1996: 107ff.). It appears to have been celebrated by all women, including maidens, in commemoration of the mourning of the goddess for her lost daughter Proserpina, and was held to be so important that after the terrible disaster at Cannae, when women were lamenting their dead relatives, the time of mourning was cut short in order to celebrate the *sacra Cereris anniversarium*.

In the Scandinavian north, mourning was thought of as one of the functions of the goddess, since both Frigg and Freyja are described as weeping. Frigg weeps first for Balder her son and then for Odin her husband, and it is she who organizes all creatures to weep for Balder, so that he may return from the realms of death. This concept of widespread lamentation, in which the whole of creation joins, is transferred to the death of Christ on the cross. In the Anglo-Saxon poem 'The Dream of the Rood', which may be as early as the seventh century, we are told that 'all creation wept, bewailing the fall of the King' when Christ died on the cross.

The goddess Freyja also sheds tears, and is said to be mourning for her husband Od (Oðr), who seems to be a doublet of Odin (Näsström 1995: 81–2). It is not clear in the Norse sources why Freyja is mourning; possibly here and in Snorri's vivid account in *Gylfaginning* of Frigg's attempt to bring Balder back from the underworld we have confused memories of an earlier fertility deity of the Vanir, whom the weeping goddess hopes to restore from death to bring new life into the world, like Isis and Kybele.

There is no doubt that in northern Europe formal laments and wailing at funerals were kept up by mourning women, long after other details of death rituals from earlier times were forgotten. In Wales, 'excessive grieving' at the funeral went on into the twentieth century, and many women were said to collapse with grief; certain old women might be paid to help with the weeping, although the Church and people in general disapproved, and attempted to stamp out such practices (Stevens 1976: 39). In Ireland no tears were shed openly until the dead had been laid out, after which all the relatives stood weeping around the bed. It was said that 'the women were much more demonstrative than the men and less restrained in their crying' (Ó Súilleabháin 1967: 130).

The custom of hiring practised keeners, recorded occasionally in Wales, was certainly well known in Ireland. Ó Súilleabháin (1967: 134) quotes an anonymous traveller's description of a Kildare wake in 1683, which refers to the hiring of experts 'if there be not enough to make out a good cry', adding that it is the women who are mostly observed to practise these things. O'Curry stated that there should be at least four such hired wailers, one at the head of the corpse, one at the feet, looking after the candles, and one more on each side (Ó Súilleabháin 1967: 136); these might be either men or women. Various Synods of Bishops in the seventeenth century attempted to put an end to the custom, and here specific references are made to female keeners in their prohibitions, such as the statement that 'no priest would attend a wake or funeral at which female keeners cried and screamed' (Ó Súilleabháin 1967: 138).

The people, however, were extremely reluctant to give up this ancient custom, which the Church described as pagan, and as late as the beginning of the twentieth century three women keeners were seen sitting on top of the coffin as it was taken to the churchyard, howling and wailing at intervals, and were finally driven off only by the priest with a whip (Ó Súilleabháin 1967: 143). Reasons for the increasing hostility of the Church have been discussed in detail by Patricia Lysaght (1995: 169ff.).

In Ireland there was a strict taboo on any member of the family 'laying out' the corpse. This duty was performed by a woman specialized in such work, known as the 'white woman' (*an bean bhan*), who washed the corpse and dressed it in grave-clothes (Ó Crullóich 1990: 152). This offers a close parallel to the work of the Helper (*la femme-qui-aide*) in rural France as described by Yvonne Verdier (p. 136), who gives a vivid picture of the essential part played by women before men took over as funeral directors. Verdier (1976a) points out the parallel between the washing of the new-born and that of the corpse, both being left to one particular older woman, who knew how such things should be done, and was greatly esteemed in the village. The dead had to be cleansed, and it was essential that the water used in the washing should be thrown outside the house, because the soul of the dead might be attracted to water. For the same reason no washing should be done in the house in which the corpse lay, lest it might plunge into the washtub, and no vessel of water should be left uncovered if someone was seriously ill. The old custom of covering mirrors, to which was later added that of covering the TV screen, might be linked with this, since they resemble water; it was thought that they might hold the reflection of the dead if the soul tried to escape into them. The Helper also shut windows and closed apertures, and stopped the clocks in the house until the burial was over. After washing the body, shaving it if necessary and arranging the hair, she dressed it in special garments, often left ready for this occasion long before death.

One of her duties was to prepare the bed on which the dead was to lie, covering it with a soft sheet which could be used in the coffin; clean white linen cloths were also put out in the room. Then the dead was laid out with the face covered, hands crossed, and a rosary and a sprig of box placed beside the body. Holy water was put on a table, and the family candle lighted; no fire or artifical light was allowed in the room.

It was customary to keep watch over the dead for three days, during which no housework was done, and a neighbour provided meals for the family. The Helper was also responsible for finding neighbours to help with the watch. The watching seems also to have been a responsibility of women from early times, although men might take part. In the tale of Groa's successful attempt to save the wounded Grim in *Droplaugarsona Saga* (see p. 162), she and her son kept the 'nightwatch' over the dead in an outhouse, and this gave her the opportunity to get her severely wounded nephew away to safety. Another reference to watching over the dead is found in *Laxdœla Saga* (49), when An the Black, one of those thought dead, suddenly revived, declaring that a woman whom he saw in a dream taking out his entrails and replacing them with brushwood had returned and restored the injured parts; his wounds were dressed, and he made a complete recovery. This episode incidentally suggests a memory of a healing goddess figure.

In Norway it seems that the custom of wakes was kept up until the eighteenth century, and perhaps later in some districts, but it gradually became a more solemnn occasion. The earlier idea that relatives and friends should show goodwill and kinship towards the dead until the body was taken from the house had meant that drinking and dancing were in order (Christiansen 1946: 31ff.). The watch for the dead was still kept in parts of Herefordshire when Mrs Leather was recording material in the opening years of the twentieth century (Leather 1912: 120). In some places they sat up all night, but not necessarily in the same room as the corpse. If it was 'somebody you cared about', they still watched over the body, on which they placed a candle on a plate of salt or a piece of green turf. In Wales a more lively wake was held, and people tramped up and down with the coffin while the mourners wailed; this was said to keep off evil spirits, and there are even accounts of the corpse being made to sit in its coffin, or pushed up the chimney (Stevens 1976: 29ff.). Such pranks were rigorously condemned by the Church, and gradually suppressed under the influence of Methodism.

In Ireland, however, they continued into the twentieth century, as Ó Súilleabháin (1967) has shown in *Irish Wake Amusements*. Much drinking, unruly behaviour and wild games as well as singing and telling of tales went on at the wake, and these, as Ó Súillheabháin's records show, were organized by the men present. The practice in more recent times was for a group of experienced women to lay out the corpse on a table, settle or bed, with a crucifix and a rosary, the preparations taking about two hours to complete. Then the keening began round the bed, and the next day preparations were made for the wake and stocks of food, drink and tobacco brought in, while the coffin, in earlier times made in the house, was ordered. During the day visitors came in to express sympathy and were offered refreshments. At nightfall people gathered in the house and stayed until about midnight, when the Rosary was said, but only close relatives and friends remained until morning.

It is clear that funeral ritual over a great part of northern Europe was divided between men and women. The men were responsible for the burial or cremation of the body, the making of the coffin, the digging of the grave or the building of the funeral pyre. They would also organize and take a lively part in the sports and games which went on before the final disposal of the body. If some kind of praise poem or speeches in honour of the illustrious male dead were composed, this would probably be done by men. The women, however, were responsible for the washing and clothing of the body and its laying-out, as well as for the lamenting and wailing for the loss they had suffered.

In this connection it is worth noting that Gearóid Ó Crullaóich sees the figure of the keening woman (*bean chaointe*) at a funeral as 'both a symbol and an agent of the transition of the individual deceased to an otherworld'. Thus she is opposed to the 'borekeen', the male figure who acts as master of ceremonies, organizing the rowdy wake-games; his responsibility is to assert the continuing vitality of the community so that it can re-estabish itself in the face of death (Ó Crullaóich 1990: 146–7). This is in keeping with the division of responsibility at the funeral, which may be seen 'as a kind of contest in liminal time and space for control or dominance of life'. It may be noted that in the lament *Sonartorrek* composed by the great Icelandic poet of the tenth century, Egil Skallagrímsson, for his son's funeral (see pp. 167–8), he alludes in verse 6 to the dangerous rent in the fence defending his father's family caused by the drowning of a young man of promise.

In pre-Christian times in northern Europe, animals might be sacrificed and a widow or a substitute put to death to accompany the corpse to the Otherworld, or to welcome him into his grave. In the account of the funeral of a Rus leader in the tenth century, we have a rare opportunity to recapture some of the wild and elaborate ritual which formed the background to such a sacrificial death. The indications are, however, that this practice was mainly limited to warrior leaders, and formed part of the rites of the warrior god Odin. Animal sacrifices appear to be associated with the goddess, as at Oseberg, and with the funerals of both men and women.

Since women prepared the dead for their last journey and composed funeral lays, they were in a position to keep up traditional beliefs regarding death and the after-life. There is always great reluctance to change and simplify funeral customs, as this is felt to deprive the dead of their due rights and honours. The idea of the dead in his burial mound, bringing prosperity to his people, lived on in Norse poetic tradition alongside the concept of the heroic dead journeying to join Odin in Valhalla, and it is this view of the Otherworld which seems most likely to be associated with the goddess. In the poem *Helgakviða Hundingsbana* II in the *Poetic Edda*, for instance, the hero rides back to his burial mound after his death in battle, to be welcomed by his supernatural bride, although compelled to return at sunrise to Odin's hall to join famous heroes fallen in battle (see pp. 176–7).

The lamentation by women at funerals, and their responsibility for the preparation of the dead for the last journey, is reflected in the idea of the mourning goddess. It is fitting that she should be seen as a liminal figure, the guardian of the gateway between life and death. Barbette Spaeth (1996) has pointed out this element in the concept of the Roman goddess Ceres, in her link with the *mundus*, a monument in Rome declared open on certain days of the year, so that the spirits of the dead could revisit the world they had left (Spaeth 1996: 63–5). Another goddess of the boundaries between the worlds was the Greek Artemis, who was associated with the deaths of women (see p. 18). The picture of the goddess mourning over the dead was transformed in Christian times into the portrayal of the Virgin Mary lamenting over the body of the dead Christ. The wooden sculpture by Fenwick Lawson in York Minster is an impressive proof of the continuing power of this familiar medieval image.

The evidence from Oseberg has revealed how magnificent a funeral might be given to a woman in the ninth century, carried to the grave with splendid ritual and extravagant generosity. Yet, in spite of the many pre-Christian graves excavated in northern Europe, our knowledge of funeral customs and their significance is all too limited. There is always hope here, however, that archaeology will provide new evidence, and help us to learn more concerning the part played by the goddess in the preparations for death and the concept of life in the Otherworld.

THE REALM OF DEATH

In northern Europe the link between the goddess and the realm of death has been traced back to very early times, and the menacing standing stones of Brittany from the fourth millennium BC have been claimed to represent female guardians of the grave (see p. 6). Indeed the association of the goddess who brought fertility and new life and growth into the world with the realm of death is a widespread and ancient concept.

A memorable account from the ancient world of the descent of the goddess into the underworld is found in poetry recorded on Sumerian clay tablets from the first half of the second millennium BC. Here the great goddess Inanna (Ishtar in a later Akkadian version) descends to the underworld, over which her sister Erishkigal rules, apparently with the intention of taking over her authority there. The result, however, in one of the most chilling description in mythological literature, is that Inanna was stripped of her divine powers one by one, represented by the jewels and adornments which she wore, until she was naked and helpless, and was transformed into a piece of rotting flesh hanging on the wall. Inanna was finally resurrected and brought back to the upper world, but had to find a substitute to die in her place.

One possible explanation of the journey of the goddess into death is that her descent took place at the time of year when the storehouses of grain and fruit were empty and food was coming to an end, while her return to new life was brought about by the god Enki when the rains transformed the desert into rich pasture land again (Jacobsen 1976: 62). Bernstein (1993: 41) claims that the two most important aspects of the underworld were 'its wealth as a storehouse of seed and its darkness as a repository of corpses'. This could account for Inanna's descent to the lower world and encounter with death by her power over the fruitful earth. Another female deity, her sister, is supreme in the underworld, and she may represent the shadow side of the radiant Inanna (Wolkstein and Kramer 1984: 158). The snatching away of Persephone and Demeter's search for her in Greek tradition is another example of the goddess threatened and bereaved by the power of death and yet surviving it, so that life may continue and spring return to the earth. The loss of a loved daughter is now a significant aspect of the myth, bound up with the changing phases in a woman's life and the move of energy and fertility to a new generation (see p. 53).

In Norse mythology the connection of the northern goddess with the land of the dead seems at first to have been obscured by the emphasis in the poetry on Odin's reception of dead kings and heroes in his hall in the Otherworld. The power of the goddess seems to be limited to her liminal aspect, expressed by the valkyries who escort the distinguished dead to the hall of Odin after they fall on the battlefield or die a sacrificial death. A dead hero is welcomed at the threshold of Valhalla by one of the maids of Odin, bearing a horn of mead.

However, it seems that this offering of a horn by a woman before the banquet was a symbol of major significance, as Michael Enright (1988) has shown; it was linked with the possession of sovereignty (see p. 183). Certainly it was of sufficient importance to be represented on a number of memorial stones from about the eighth century AD in Gotland, raised as memorials to the dead (Davidson 1976: 301ff.). At least twelve stones have survived where a woman holds up a horn to a warrior on horseback, while elsewhere the woman with her horn is depicted alone. These memorial stones often display a ship, possibly a symbol of death, as well as what appear to be representations of a hall, a dog and a flying valkyrie in a formalized scene in which the dead warrior arrives at the hall of Odin (Figure 27).

Such a reception is described in two Old Norse poems of the tenth century, *Hákonarmál* and *Eiríksmál*, celebrating the entry of dead kings into Valhalla, while the figure of the woman with the horn might be worn as an amulet, an example of which was found in the cemetery of Birka in Sweden (Figure 28). The welcome of a dead warrior by a supernatural female figure as a funeral motif may have been inspired by a similar scene depicted on memorial stones in the Balkans, in an area visited by Swedish vikings (Davidson 1976: 303ff.), but would not have been used so widely in the North to commemorate the distinguished dead had it not corresponded to a concept in their own world picture.

Figure 27 Top panel from memorial stone from Alskog, Gotland, showing woman with horn welcoming rider. Ht 174 cm. Statens Historika Museum, Stockholm. Eileen Aldworth.

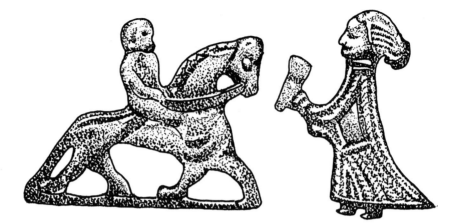

Figure 28 Silver amulet of rider, one of pair in grave at Birka, Sweden, ht 3.2 cm, with another of woman with horn from Klinta, Öland, ht 2.7 cm. Statens Historika Museum, Stockholm. Eileen Aldworth.

There is some indication indeed that the powerful goddess Freyja herself was represented as a welcomer of the slain. In the *Edda* poem *Grímnismál* she is said to have had half of those who died in battle while the other half belonged to Odin. Näsström (1995) suggests that Odin's expanding role as a warrior god and the concept of Valhalla may have reduced the earlier role of Freyja as the goddess receiving the warrior dead. There are hints that she also welcomed women; in *Egils Saga* (78) the hero's daughter Thorgerd, who wanted to convince her father that she would starve to death along with him when he was determined on suicide, declared that she would eat no supper 'till I come to be with Freyja'. Näsström (1995: 87) also suggests that the woman bearing stalks of hemlock, who rises out of the ground beside a brazier and conducts Hading to the underworld in the first book of Saxo Grammaticus' *History of the Danes*, might be based on the older tradition of the goddess leading mortals to the realm of death. The underworld to which Hading is taken includes not only warriors but also noble figures clad in purple; this is a very different tradition from that of the gloomy realm of Hel ruled over by a monstrous figure resembling a rotting corpse, given by Snorri in the *Prose Edda*.

Another example of a welcoming goddess is the valkyrie who in one of the Helgi poems of the *Poetic Edda* welcomes the hero into the burial mound as a loving bride (see p. 173). He joins her for one night before he rides through the air to Valhalla, and tells her not to lament for him, and it would seem that she offers him ale or mead when she welcomes him, according to his words in the poem:

> Well shall we drink a noble draught
> though lost to us now both love and lands.
> Sing shall no man a song of sorrow,
> though wide are the wounds upon my breast.
> Here shall our brides be shut in the howe,
> the heroes' *dísir*, with us, their husbands.

To which she replied:

> Here I have made a bed for you, Helgi,
> free from all care, kinsman of Ylfings,
> and in my arms I will lull you to rest.
> as when once I lay by the living king.

This heroic poem, full of obscurities, was written down in Iceland in the thirteenth century, and appears to preserve a different tradition from that of the warriors conducted to Valhalla after death. Helgi is indeed said to go back to Odin's hall after spending the night with Sigrun, but this idea of a valkyrie as a guardian spirit, who receives him on a bed within the gravemound, seems likely to belong to an earlier tradition of the king resting in the place of his ancestors (the Ylfings in the poem), received by the goddess (*dís*) who had been his guardian spirit in life. The fact that a plural form is used in this passage may simply be an example of the poetic plural, or may signify that Helgi and his companions after their deaths in battle are all welcomed by their *dísir*.

At the conclusion of the poem Sigrun laments that Helgi will not return a second time; he has presumably been held in Valhalla by the power of Odin. Sigrun is said in the prose commentary on the poem to be a valkyrie, but she is not one of Odin's maids. Similar valkyries who act as guardians of young warriors, are found in Saxo's history (Davidson 1980: 40ff.), while in the poem *Sigrdrífumál* such a being gives Sigurd the instruction necessary for a young warrior prince.

Another example of a guardian goddess is the 'wife' of Jarl Hakon of Halogaland, virtually king of Norway for some years and an opponent of the Christian Olaf Tryggvason. She is described as a richly adorned figure in a shrine, worshipped with great devotion by the Jarl, and called 'bride of Helgi'. She and her sister Irpa gave him active help in battle, calling down a fearsome hailstorm and shooting arrows 'which seemed to fly from every finger of the monstrous woman', each one finding its mark (*Flateyjarbók* I, 154–7). There is some confusion between her and Hakon's human wife, Thora. It seems likely that the name of the goddess was really Gerd, since this is the form found in an early skaldic verse, and Gerd is one of the names of the goddess Freyja. It seems that Hakon may have been turning to the same goddess when, defeated and hopeless, he is said to have been hidden in the earth under the swine (*Heimskringla, Ólafs Saga*

Tryggvasonar 48), since this could symbolize the mound of the goddess Freyja, one of whose titles was Sow. The fact that after Hakon's death Olaf Tryggvason had Thorgerd's image dragged out and burnt beside that of Freyr supports this view (Davidson 1993: 109ff.).

If Helgi were the mythical founder of Halogaland, this would explain Thorgerd's name 'Bride of Helgi', since she could become the wife of each ruler of the kingdom in turn. The idea of the guardian goddess welcoming the king in death was essentially an aristocratic concept, just as was that of kings and leaders granted entry to Valhalla, and this is one important aspect of the goddess in the Viking Age. Such a tradition could account for the noble figures of valkyries welcoming dead kings in poems like *Hákonarmál*, while Näsström (1995: 88) notes that some references to Hel in skaldic verse do not fit that gruesome figure as Snorri describes her, but might refer to Freyja.

Hel in the surviving literature is used as the name for the general abode of the dead, a shadowy realm which could serve as a term for the grave. The personification of this as a loathsome female figure symbolizing physical death, one of the children of the destructive power Loki, as found in *Gylfaginning* (33), hardly suggests a goddess. She is described here as 'half black and half flesh-coloured, somewhat drooping and grim to look upon', and is evidently a decaying corpse. Yet this is not the impression given in the account of Hermod's ride to Hel later in *Gylfaginning* (49). Hel, speaking with authority as ruler of the underworld, decrees that all things must weep for Balder before he can be released from her realm, and gifts are sent back to Frigg and Fulla by Balder's wife Nanna as from a friendly kingdom. Possibly Snorri earlier turned the goddess of death into an allegorical figure, just as he made Hel, the underworld of shades, a place 'where wicked men go', like the Christian Hell (*Gylfaginning* 3).

On the other hand, a goddess of death who represents the horrors of slaughter and decay is something well known elsewhere; the figure of Kali in India is an outstanding example. Like Snorri's Hel, she is terrifying in appearance, black or dark in colour, usually naked, adorned with severed heads or arms or the corpses of children, her lips smeared with blood. She haunts the battlefield or the cremation ground and squats on corpses. Yet for all this she is 'the recipient of ardent devotion from countless devotees who approach her as their mother' (Kinsley 1989: 116).

In northern Europe the memory of terrible goddesses of slaughter active on the battlefield is found in both Celtic and Germanic tradition (Davidson, 1988: 92ff.). There are indications that the dignified valkyries of tenth-century Norse literature were in earlier times fierce spirits of battle, devouring the slain; the word *waelcyrge*, 'chooser of the slain' in Anglo-Saxon glosses, is equated with the Latin word for Fury. The valkyries who were seen weaving on a ghastly loom composed of weapons, entrails and skulls (see pp. 117–18) belong to a similar tradition. Again we have references to

giantesses in skaldic verse who are huge and sinister beings, their appearance in dreams foretelling slaughter to come. They hold troughs for sacrificial meat, throw a series of human bodies into the jaws of a wolf, jerk off the heads of their victims with a bloodstained cloth, or sprinkle blood over the land (Davidson 1988: 95); they could be near relatives of Kali. These figures have survived in the literature recorded in Christian times because they have been relegated into the stuff of dreams and poetic imagery, not to be taken seriously.

Equally repulsive figures are found among the battle goddesses of early Irish literature (Davidson 1988: 97ff.). We have the Badb, described in 'The Destruction of da Choca's Hostel' as a swarthy woman with a big mouth, in a dusky mantle, with grey hair falling over her shoulders, or as a red figure on the edge of a ford, washing the chariot of a king doomed to die (Lysaght 1986: 199–200), There is again constant emphasis on the darkness of a corpse, on entrails, severed limbs and heads, and blood, and the figure of the supernatural washerwoman who foretells violent death (see pp. 137–8). It is said of the Mórrígan, another name for the battle-spirit: 'horrible are the huge entrails which the Mórrígan washes . . . many are the spoils she washes' (Lysaght 1986: 199). Here we have the fierce destructive side of death, with a strong emphasis on its physical horrors, so perhaps we should not assume that the gruesome figure of Hel is wholly Snorri's literary creation.

In the account of Hermod's ride to Hel in *Gylfaginning*, the source of which unfortunately is unknown, there is a female guardian on the road to the realm of death. This is the giantess Modgud, whose name ('fierce battle') could well be that of a valkyrie; she guards the bridge which Hermod must cross to reach Helgate and find Balder, and challenges all who pass over it. There is nothing particularly sinister recorded of her, and she waits under a roof of gold. Another female being present at a great funeral is the giantess called Hyrrokin ('Withered by fire'?), who launches the ship on which the dead Balder is burnt at his funeral. Yet another giantess, Hyndla (Little dog), in the poem *Hyndluljóð* named after her, is called by Freyja her 'sister in the cave'; she is in the underworld, and knows the secrets of ancestry. She is persuaded to recite the genealogy of Ottar, Freyja's lover, whom the goddess supports like a guardian valkyrie. Once more it seems that the power of the goddess over the realm of death is strongly linked with the cult of the dead ancestors whose enduring presence in their burial mounds benefits their people (Davidson 1988: 116).

Patricia Lysaght (1986: 216) in her study of the Banshee, the death-messenger in Ireland, distinguishes two separate early traditions, one of a 'red woman' associated primarily with death in battle, 'an aggressive and horrible figure', and another supernatural woman with a 'more benign, ancestral role' who is a type of guardian. She is associated with certain families considered of noble Irish descent, and with the ownership and fertility of land (Lysaght 1996: 154ff.). This guardian figure laments when one of the family dies, sharing the concern of relatives and friends. In southeast Ireland, however, she screams and shrieks in the manner of a hostile supernatural being. Here we seem to have once more the opposed characters of the goddess of death, represented as 'a beautiful woman or as a horrible loathsome hag' (Lysaght 1996: 160).

Undoubtedly there is a widespread link between female supernatural figures and the land of the dead, and it is they, rather than a male ruler like Pluto in Greek mythology, who are represented as possessing power over it, admitting mortals from the upper world, and conducting them along the lonely road, as well as possessing a store of wisdom concerning dead ancestors. The goddess of death appears in three different aspects: she foretells the coming of death so that she may be described as its messenger, like the Banshee. She helps to bring it about, as do the valkyries in Norse tradition, and the Mórrígan when she seeks the destruction of the hero Cú Chulainn. She acts as the conductor of the dead from this world to the next, another aspect of the valkyries and a possible role of Freyja as Great Goddess, while she welcomes the dead when they cross the threshold.

The associations between death and the goddess are by no means isolated from her other aspects in the world of the living. The goddess worshipped by the hunters over a vast stretch of time had her destructive, terrifying side, bringing death as well as bounty. This link with death lingered on in the figure of Artemis the Huntress, whose 'gentle arrows' could bring death to women (see p. 18). Another development of the hunting-goddess might be seen in the sinister Hekate, a goddess of the ancient world who was a powerful figure in popular belief among the women of eastern Asia Minor and classical Greece (Downing 1985). Offerings of dogs and selected foods such as eggs, garlic, cheese, mullet and a special cake surrounded by lighted torches were made to her (Flower Smith 1913), and she was regarded as a protectress against evil spirits because of her power over them. Hekate might be seen as queen of the underworld, linking her with Persephone (Paulys 1912: 2773), and she was a goddess of crops and of fishing as well as of death. She was held to roam the earth on moonlit nights accompanied by barking dogs and restless spirits who could not lie quiet in their graves; her influence may be seen in the widespread tradition of the Wild Hunt in north-western Europe, which might sometimes be led by a female huntress (see p. 49).

Yet another strange figure thought to be connected with the hunting-goddess is that of the Baba Yaga who plays an important part in Russian fairy-tales (Kravchenko 1987: 86ff.). She is depicted as a powerful old woman who devours living victims, including children, and her description recalls some of the earliest goddess figures, since she has huge breasts, posterior and thighs; she is also said to have a leg of bone, a long pointed nose and teeth of iron. She lies in a hut without doors or windows, which blocks the road by which the hero has to pass; it is supported on hen's or animal legs, and can be entered only by reciting a special formula to make it revolve. Inside the Baba Yaga squats or lies beside a fire, spinning or weaving. The hut, which sometimes seems to fit her tightly and may be fenced with human bones, has been compared to a coffin.

One of her functions seems to be that of a guardian of the road to the land of the dead, like Modgud; when the hero finds his way in, he demands food and a bath, and it has been suggested that this resembles the washing and funeral feast given to the dead (Kravchenko 1987: 124–5). The Baba Yaga also flies through the air in a mortar driven by a pestle, and this, together with her poker and broom point to a being connected with the hearth. However, she is also represented as the mistress of the forest, and can call on animals to help the hero if he wins her favour (Kravchenko 1987: 131).

Another figure linked with the world of the hunter from an earlier period in Anglo-Saxon England is the mother of Grendel in *Beowulf* (see p. 22). Here we have again a destructive being who blocks the way of the hero when he is descending to the lower world beneath the lake. She squats on his body and attempts to dispatch him with her knife, so that she too has something in common with the dangerous death-dealing aspect of the goddess of the forest and the wild creatures.

The goddess of death then is not confined to the underworld, nor separated from the goddess of the living. She is connected with the fruitful earth, with the spinning of destiny for each new life, and for weaving the fates of kings and warriors, and with the powers governing childbirth and healing. Thus the end of this book points back to the beginning. Far from representing one particular activity or aspect of human life, the goddesses of the north are figures bound up with the various aspects of women's lives. The northern goddess is undoubtedly a liminal figure, a goddess of thresholds, dominant at the various points of life which necessitate a change of direction and a break with the past, and death is the final rite of passage. She is by no means wholly a woman's deity; she possesses power over birth, healing and death, and in these provinces there is no division made between the sexes.

Studying the multiple roles of the northern goddesses brings a realization of their richness. Barbette Spaeth concludes her study on Ceres with a reference to the 'wonderful complexity and diversity that the entire pantheon of female divinities represented in antiquity' (Spaeth 1996: 151), and the same claim could undoubtedly be made for the goddesses of northern Europe.

CONCLUSION

———— •◆• ————

Every society nourishes itself through rituals and ceremonials, which
are all the more powerful when they are not articulated. These rituals recreate our past and speak to us about our future.
(Sister Frances Teresa, *This Living Mirror:
Reflections on Clare of Assisi,* p. 23)

This study of the roles of the northern goddess has been concerned with
many such rituals, particularly those which involved women and were
associated with their particular contributions to the life of the household
and community. In the case of the northern goddesses, we have no highly
developed cults and powerful temples, with priests or priestesses develop-
ing and maintaining myths and ceremonies. Nevertheless we know that
there were priestesses, and the evidence of the Oseberg ship grave gives
some indication of a vigorous cult associated with rulers and royal ancestors, so that the concept of the goddess was extended beyond the limits of
household and family. The implicit hostility of the Christian Church
towards this cult is a testimony to its power among the ruling class in pre-
Christian Scandinavia.

Here then is an aspect of the goddess which appears to be independent
of women's work and women's bonding. Traces of it can be seen in the
records of the early Scandinavian kings, and in the strangely moving though
confused and fantastic tales of the devotion of Jarl Hakon, the last pre-
Christian ruler to hold power in Norway, to Thorgerd, or more probably
Gerd, Bride of Helgi (see pp. 177–8). Again the poem *Ynglingatal,* composed by Thjodolf the Learned in the ninth century and used by Snorri in
Ynglinga Saga, lists the manner of death of a series of early kings of Sweden
ruling at Uppsala. It portrays strange and violent deaths coming to one
ruler after another through ruthless female figures, and Snorri interprets
these as queens or sorceresses. It seems more likely, however, that here we
have memories of the goddess herself, giving power and rule to kings, and
finally cutting short their lives and summoning them into the burial mound.
Indeed one of them falls from his horse to his death when he is riding
round the hall of the goddesses.

In such traditions, fragmentary and bewildering but lit up by sudden
vivid details that indicate memorable lost stories, there are hints of the
former political importance of the cult of the goddess, and her power to

determine the rise and fall of kings, later attributed to Odin. The importance of royal women in determining the choice of a ruler has been discussed by Michael Enright (1988) in his study of the woman with the mead-cup (see pp. 174–5). He shows how the formal offering of the cup of ale or mead by the queen to guests at a royal banquet had both religious and political significance among the Germanic and Scandinavian peoples, and that this ritual gesture was linked with both sovereignty and the relation of the king to his *comitatus*.

Again in Irish literature there is great emphasis on the connection between the good king and the fruitfulness of the land, so that, as Kim McCone expresses it, 'the king and the woman of sovereignty mate and interact as respective representatives of human society and the divine powers manifested in nature or the cosmos as a whole' (McCone 1990: 130); he points out also that the woman of sovereignty can serve as a harbinger of a royal death. Again, Maire Herbert traces back the concept of a marriage 'between the goddess of the land and its sovereign' to a myth of agriculturally based communities, where the female principle represents the natural forces of fertility and growth, and the male principle that of human intervention to ensure successful harvests (Herbert 1992: 264). We have seen also suggestions of a link between the horse goddess Epona or figures like Macha in Irish tradition and the power of the ruling king (see pp. 44–5), while in Scandinavia the guardian valkyries worked to establish the young prince destined to reign.

In both Norway and Ireland the king in whose reign the harvests failed was seen as a doomed figure. The failure of the sacred marriage, as we are reminded in the *Edda* poem *Skírnismál*, brought sterility and death to the land (see p. 86). This concept survived long into Christian times, and can be found in Shakespeare's treatment of the quarrel of the fairy king and queen in *A Midsummer Night's Dream* (II, 2). When Titania forswears 'the bed and company' of Oberon, the earth becomes sterile and the seasons disrupted. The rivers overflow so that the oxen cannot draw the plough, and the young wheat rots in the field, while frost blights the roses. Moreover the 'quaint mazes in the wanton green' remain untrodden; this is a point worth noting, since evidence from Scandinavia and Finland collected by John Kraft has shown that the walking of stone labyrinths was done by fishermen to control the weather and bring them good catches, and also by the Saami to help with the migration of the reindeer and bring protection against wild beasts for their herds (Kraft 1985: 11). Links with a goddess are suggested by the name *Jungfrudanser* (Virgin dances) given to stone labyrinths in parts of Finland, and also by the widespread children's game in which a girl stood in the centre of the maze and a boy had to find his way to her, or perhaps two boys raced to the centre from different entrances (Kraft 1985: 15ff.). Most records of this come from Scandinavia, but Kraft gives a reference to a similar game played in the turf maze at Saffron Walden in Essex in the eighteenth century, when boys competed to reach the girl in record time without stumbling, and there were 'wagers in gallons of beer' on the result.

Although the connection of the goddess with the power to rule and with politics has not received detailed treatment in this book, it must not be forgotten, since here we see her importance as a symbol in a man's world. There is a parallel from Ancient Rome in the strong link between the goddess Ceres, associated with the fertility of the earth, and the social class of the plebians, in opposition to that of the patricians in the Early Republic (Spaeth 1996: 81ff.). Here as with the northern kings the link was established through the fertility of the soil, since many of the plebs were farmers, but the result is very different from that in Scandinavia and Ireland. Spaeth sees a change in the political dimension of the goddess in the period of the Empire, however, when she became attached to the figure of the princeps and to his family (Spaeth 1996: 23). Another example of the political power of the goddess is seen in the introduction of Kybele's idol and cult into Rome at a critical moment in its history (see pp. 56–7). Even when Odin was established in Scandinavia as the deity who controlled battles between rulers, and allotted victory and defeat to great heroes, the female supernatural powers, the Norns and the valkyries, were still represented as determining the destinies of princes in both peace and war, and they remained potent symbols in art and literature. One basis for this was perhaps the close association of the goddess with birth and death, going back to very early times, but it is clear that her roles were by no means wholly confined to the activities and interests of women. We know that long before the development of agriculture there was a goddess who could aid or obstruct the hunters; she was clearly a central figure in a masculine world, and might be bitterly hostile to women.

It has to be recognized that the roles of the goddess continually overlap. Fertility of the land brings in an association with sovereignty and political power, while her close links with childbirth strengthen her role as arbiter of destiny. Her association with spinning and weaving is again joined to the fate of individuals, particularly those born to rule, and also with the birth, care and nurturing of young girls, while her link with hunting and the wild may extend that protection to boys and young men. The guardian of the wild creatures could take the domestic herds under her care, and become the patroness of kitchen and dairy. The goddesses associated with battle and destruction were also linked to the contours of the land, with cattle-rearing and the healing of a wounded hero, as Maire Herbert has shown in a study of their character in the Irish myths (Herbert 1996: 143ff.). Versatile goddesses like Hekate in the ancient world, and the many-sided female beings like Holda and Perht, whose memory survives in popular tradition in Germany, illustrate the wide range of powers which one goddess may possess.

It is in the areas where men and women are most vulnerable and seek most urgently for help, those of childbirth, illness, accident and death, that the favour the goddess was continually sought after, but again her activities in these realms were linked with her other roles and with her rule over the natural world. The northern goddesses are not specialists, and cannot be seen as individual divinities who concentrate on one particular side of life and activity, although, as with the Christian saints, one name might readily come to mind when seeking assistance in some special difficulty. There were local goddesses also, closely linked with one limited area of earth or water, to whom the farmer, the herder or the housewife might appeal on home ground, while there were special guardians of the women of the household, linked with their families over the generations.

In general the northern goddess may be viewed as the power watching over and sustaining life and growth in the natural world and in the human community, encouraging fertility, sexuality and marriage. She recognizes and laments the inevitable passing of each generation, and maintains a continuing link with the ancestors in their burial mounds. She may join in her activities with the male 'fertility' gods of the Vanir, such as Njord or Freyr in the Scandinavian north, but the gods on the whole are associated with organization and action in the community, and with such shared activities as warfare, work on the land, travel, herding, building and the establishment of law. While there were male deities as well as female ones who helped the hunters, the power of the goddess here appears to have been particularly associated with the preservation and fertility of the wild creatures. There are hints at times of a deep-seated hostility between the goddess and the semi-divine hero, such as Thomas O'Rahilly believed existed in Celtic myth (see p. 75), and which may perhaps be reflected in occasional suggestions of hostility between the Scandinavian goddesses and the heroes of Odin.

The goddess was not necessarily worshipped as a solitary being, since two or more female figures are frequently represented in company. This is evident in the cult of the Mothers, in rituals associated with the grain and the harvest, and in the goddesses of childbirth. The sacred hall at Uppsala was that of the *dísir*, goddesses in the plural. Jarl Hakon's Thorgerd appears along with her sister Irpa (see p. 177), while Saxo's heroes and young princes like Helgi in the *Edda* are likely to meet a band of three, seven or nine guardian valkyries, one of whom gives him a sword and foretells his destiny. One piece of evidence which has emerged from this study is that the group of goddesses is sometimes made up of women of different ages, so that we find the concept of the aged woman, hag or matriarch, alongside her daughter who has borne children, and perhaps her daughter in turn, the young virgin or bride. The goddess is linked with the successive turning-points in a woman's life: menstruation, marriage, childbirth and the menopause, all marked as significant events in the relationship of the goddess with the women of the household. They may be emphasized by the wearing of symbolic articles of clothing, by rites and ceremonies, by seclusion from the rest of the family, or by feasts and celebrations. These turning-points form the equivalent of the initiation rituals of the males which mark the transition from boyhood to adult manhood, or the official recognition of the youth as a warrior (Davidson 1989b). The goddess may contribute to these also in her role as guardian valkyrie, but the development of women is more complex, and there is more than one important crossing-point in their lives.

Even the last phase, the time when childbearing is over, had its demands and compensations; there were special responsibilities and rites associated with the goddess which might be restricted to older women, such as the instruction of young girls and the laying out of the dead. We are often told that it was the older women who organized and kept alive some of the more vigorous customs associated with the goddess cult, while their influence must have been of great importance in creating mythological scenes in weaving and embroidery for the recording of the old traditional tales. The importance of the cult of St Anne in later medieval times gives some indication of the significance of the older woman in the cult of the goddess.

It has been thought that this series of 'rites of passage' was represented by the waxing and waning of the moon (see p. 6). The suitability of the image makes the theory an attractive one, but direct evidence to support it from pre-Christian times in northern Europe in literature, art or popular traditions is singularly lacking. It may be noted that the gender of the moon is masculine among the Germanic peoples and the Scandinavians, as well as the Lithuanians and Slavs, while the sun is the feminine figure; again the sun is feminine in Irish and both masculine and feminine forms are found in Welsh (T. F. O'Rahilly 1976: 294). While the crescent moon may be found as an ornament worn by a goddess, there are no apparent indications of one special moon deity or of rites directly connected with the moon.

There are, however, definite links between the sun and the goddess in the North, as indeed might be expected because of the great dependence on the sun for raising crops, and the constant struggle against the winter dark. Miranda Green has found many examples of sun symbols on figures of female deities in pipe-clay, mainly from the first two centuries AD in Gaul and the Rhineland, and the goddess figures so copiously marked with these symbols appear to have formed part of a popular domestic cult among the poorer women (M. J. Green 1991: 127ff.). Such figures have been found in graves as well as in small shrines and house sites; the concept behind this could be the marriage between sun and earth goddesses, or perhaps simply 'to render them more powerful in their essentially domestic role' (M. J. Green 1991: 130).

One strong characteristic of the goddess is her function as a liminal figure, the guardian of the wild country and the boundary region, while presiding also over the series of boundaries to be passed in women's lives. It has been suggested that the close link between the dog and the goddess, which was established in the hunting tradition, might also depend on the fact that the dog can be viewed as a liminal creature; it is frequently encountered at boundaries and entrances, both as a protective and a hostile guardian. In Celtic tradition the goddess bridged the gap between the worlds of land and water. She was frequently invoked at funerals, and seen as a guide between the worlds, welcoming the dead into their new environment. Her link with the ancient cult of the ancestors seems to have been a powerful one in northern Europe, although the strong influence of the cult of Odin on the royal poets in Scandinavia has tended to obscure this in the early poems and tales.

The main characteristics of the goddess considered in this book are obviously not confined to northern Europe; they can be traced back to goddesses of the Mediterranean world and the Near East, and sometimes there are striking parallels even further afield. The goddess approached by the hunters was a potent deity across northern Europe and Asia for many thousands of years, and a similar goddess can be found in other parts of the world where hunting has been an essential way of life, such as Africa and North America. As in northern Europe, the goddess was worshipped in Ancient Greece and Rome as a force to help the seed to grow in the earth, playing her essential part towards a rich harvest. As a patroness of spinning and weaving, she dominated the world of queens and high-born women as well as those labouring in the spinning rooms of Ancient Egypt and Greece. Her influence was felt everywhere beside the hearth, in homes where women formed the established centre of the house, where children were eagerly awaited, but all too often lost at birth or in infancy, for motherhood, like the hunt, was an enterprise fraught with uncertainty and danger.

Although there may be signs of influence from the classical world on the North in the depicting of goddesses in art and literature in Christian times, there seems little evidence of direct influence in ritual. As Ralph Merrifield (1987) has shown, popular ritual may survive the religious beliefs which gave birth to it, 'reinterpreted in the light of current beliefs or adapted to relieve new fears' (see p. 78). The work of Solheim on the practices and rites connected with dairy-work and herding in the summer pastures in Norway provides many examples of appeals to the Virgin Mary which throw light on the probable relationship between women and the goddess in pre-Christian times. The character of the fairy godmother who has survived in children's fairy-tales and pantomimes is another tradition which reflects memories of the goddess as the nurturer and protectress of children, especially those ill treated and neglected by their families. The Christian concept of the guardian angel is a far less vivid conception.

Behind the influence of the goddess in the home and on the farm, as well as on women's crafts and skills, there is always the deeper link between the goddess and the natural world of mountains, forests, rivers and springs. She may appear as a bird, hind, mare, sow or heifer; Maire Herbert suggests that her power of changing shape is 'an expression of her affinity with the whole living universe of creatures, bird, animal and human' (Herbert 1996: 145). Gearóid Ó Crullaóich has stressed the many-sided nature of the Hag of Beare, and her association with wild nature, 'especially the storms of winter, the storm clouds and the boiling winter sea' (Ó Crullaóich 1988: 154); he suggests that this may have been partly a result of the influence of Norse cosmology and its personification of the forces of wild nature. On the Germanic side even the domestic figures of Holle and Perht have such links, when the thunder was regarded as the goddess reeling her flax (see pp. 104–5). Frigg's distaff could be seen in the starry heavens in Scandinavia, while Skaði in northern Norway was associated with wild nature and the icy mountains (Näsström 1995: 52). Such qualities, as Näsström points out, are contrasted with those of the Vanir, who bring warmth to the earth, help with the growth of young animals, and create the richness of harvest, or indeed of Thor, who battles against the frost-giants. There is a reflection of this wild aspect of the goddess in the riotous behaviour sometimes associated with her women worshippers.

The goddess therefore is more than a deity of the Vanir group, although she has close links with them, and Freyja and Freyr are represented as the children of Njord, the god of the Vanir associated with water and the sea. The many-sided nature of the goddess has led Emily Lyle in her study of the archaic cosmos to suggest that Dumézil's scheme for the division of Indo-European society into the three functions of the sacred, physical force, and fertility should be emended into a four-fold one. The fourth section would be ruled by the goddess, who, as Dumézil himself stated, symbolizes the three separate functions of the masculine gods, assuming and reconciling all three. Rather than being the deity of any one section of the community, she is 'the deity of the entire people' (Lyle 1990: 2). This seems to correct the over-emphasis on the goddess as a power hostile to and opposed by the gods of the Indo-Europeans, as presented by Marija Gimbutas. The view of the goddess as the fourth function can be partially reconciled with her position as supreme Mother Goddess or Great Goddess claimed by the Jungians, although there are examples of goddesses who do not fit into the maternal tradition. David Kinsley (1989) has pointed out that it is too often assumed or implied that a goddess must necessarily be associated with motherhood, fertility and the earth, for there are goddesses who have nothing to do with such things (Kinsley 1989: x). Examples of non-maternal goddesses in the north are Skaði and some of the hags, although they do have close links with the earth, and it would be hard to find a goddess figure in north-western Europe without at least one of the characteristics mentioned. But Kinsley is right in claiming that there are important aspects of the goddess which extend beyond these particular qualities.

It was to a goddess that women instinctively turned for help and support in their special needs and responsibilies, related to their life cycle, their work and their creative powers, their care of the home and children, and their skills in tending young plants and animals, together with healing and nursing and carrying out the last rites for the dead. But the representation of the goddess as a wholly benign figure, the champion and defender of women against men, is not supported by the evidence available from the pre-Christian past and from surviving traditions in north-western Europe. The goddess could also be a powerful, destructive figure, cruel and ruthless, associated not only with growth and healing but also with the untamed forces of nature and with the wilder aspects of human behaviour. We have to remember that Kali, goddess of death and destruction, and Pele, the goddess of the volcano in Hawaii, have their devoted worshippers. We belittle the goddess if we sentimentalize her, and see her as a being representing the ideal feminine nature, all sweetness and light. As Jung was careful to point out, beside the qualities of the mother archetype which can be summed up as 'all that is benign, all that cherishes and sustains, that fosters growth and fertility', there is also on the negative side of the same archetype: 'anything secret, hidden, dark; the abyss, the world of the dead, anything that devours, seduces and poisons, that is terrifying and inescapable like fate' (cited by Wulff 1982: 293). It must be stressed once more, however, that certain aspects of the goddess are not necessarily those of the archetypal mother, and Jung's other figure of the anima is certainly represented in the northern myths.

These problems as to the essential nature of the goddess confront us wherever she is worshipped, and apply to deities of northern Europe as well as to those of the classical world and countries round the Mediterranean and in the Near East in ancient times. The intention of this book has been to ascertain how much can be discovered about the goddesses of the North in spite of the limitations of the evidence available. I believe that by approaching the subject by way of the occupations and needs of women in the pre-Christian era, it is possible to find out a great deal about the part that the worship of the goddess in her various aspects played in their lives. However, we must never forget the strong influence of the hunting-goddess, a concept of enormous importance in northern Europe and Asia, which continued over many thousands of years, and influenced later beliefs and traditions. Another important influence could be that of the dark nights of winter and the intense cold of the northern countries. The goddess of palace and city culture had less opportunity to develop in the North, and the emphasis therefore has necessarily been on life in the home, on the farm or in the village, rather than in towns and cities.

The goddess does not appear as the champion of women as opposed to men, although certain elements of hostility between the sexes have been noted. Also as powerful male organizations developed in the cities, some of the skills in which women had taken a leading part, such as weaving, medicine and brewing, came increasingly under the control of men. What seems to emerge from the earlier period is rather the impression of a partnership between men and women in labour and exercise of skills, symbolized by the dividing up of the homestead. There are some indications in Scandinavia that in the Viking Age the figures of the goddesses lost something of their power through the creation by poets and story-tellers of the kingdom of Asgard dominated by the figure of Odin, and once-powerful goddesses were partially demoted into wives of the great gods.

Nevertheless the goddesses, in some way never made clear in the myths, escaped the universal destruction at Ragnarok in which Odin and his male colleagues went down fighting, together with the warriors of the human world. We are told that the earth was to emerge cleansed and purified from beneath the waves, and that a new young sun surpassing her mother in beauty would move across the heavens, while the sole descendants of man and womankind would come out from their shelter in the World Tree to re-people the land. We can be confident that in this new age the goddesses will be there once more, protective and threatening, with their special gifts and powers. Life could not continue on the earth without them.

BIBLIOGRAPHY

———— •✦• ————

Allason-Jones, L. (1989) *Women in Roman Britain*, London: British Museum.
—— (1996) 'Coventina's Well', in S. Billington and M. Green (eds) *The Concept of the Goddess*, London: Routledge.
Allason-Jones, L. and McKay, B. (1985) *Coventina's Well: A Shrine on Hadrian's Wall*, Hexham: Chester Museum.
Almgren, O. (1927) *Hällristningar och kultbruk*, Stockholm.
Armstrong, E. A. (1943) 'The ritual of the plough', *Folklore* 54: 250–7.
—— (1944) 'Mugwort lore', *Folklore* 55: 22–7.
Auerbach, L. (n.d.) Translation of *Laxdœla Saga*, awaiting publication.
Bannister, H. M. (1913) 'The introduction of the cult of St Anne into the West', *English Historical Review* 18: 107–12.
Barber, E. J. W. (1991) *Prehistoric Textiles*, Princeton, NJ: Princeton University Press.
—— (1992) 'The Peplos of Athena', in J. Neils (ed.) *Goddess and Polis: The Panathenaic Festival in Ancient Athens*, Hanover, NH: Dartmouth College.
—— (1994) *Women's Work: The First 20,000 Years*, New York and London: Norton.
Baring, A. and Cashford, J. (1991) *The Myth of the Goddess: Evolution of an Image*, London: Viking Arkana.
Barnard, M. (1966) *The Mythmakers*, Athens, OH: Ohio University Press.
Barnard, S. (1985) 'The *Matres* of Roman Britain', *Archaeological Journal* 142: 237–45.
Battaglia, F. (1990) 'The matrileny of the Picts', *Mankind Quarterly* 31: 17–43.
—— (1991) 'The Germanic earth goddess in *Beowulf*', *Mankind Quarterly* 31: 415–45.
Beard, M. (1980) 'The sexual stature of Vestal Virgins', *Journal of Roman Studies* 70: 12–27.
Bellows, H. A. (1923) Translation of *The Poetic Edda*, New York and London: American-Scandinavian Foundation.
Bennett, J. M. (1986) 'The village ale-wife: women and brewing in fourteenth century England', in B. A. Hanawalt (ed.) *Women and Work in Pre-Industrial Europe*, Bloomington, IN: Indiana University Press.
Bennett, J. A. W. and Smithers, G. V. (eds) (1966) *Early Middle English Verse and Prose*, Oxford: Oxford University Press.
Benoit, F. (1950) *Les Mythes de l'outre-tombe: le cavalier a l'anguipede et l'écuyère Epona*, Collection Latomus 3, Brussels.
—— (1954) *L'Héroïsation équestre*, Annales de la Faculté des Lettres, ns 7, Aix-en-Provence.
Berger, P. C. (1988) *The Goddess Obscured*, London: Hale.
Bernstein, A. E. (1993) *The Formation of Hell*, London: UCL Press.
Bertrand, S. (1966) *La Tapisserie de Bayeux et la manière de vivre au onzième siècle*, Rennes: Ouest-France.
Biezais, H. (1955) *Die Hauptgöttingen der alten Letten*, Uppsala.
Blacker, C. (1996) 'The Mistress of Animals in Japan: Yamanokami', in S. Billington and M. Green (eds) *The Concept of the Goddess*, London: Routledge.

Blecker, M. (1973) *Hathor and Thoth: Two Key Figures in Ancient Egyptian Religion*, Studies in the History of Religions (suppl. to *Numen* 26), Leiden.

Bonser, W. (1963) *The Medical Background of Anglo-Saxon England: A Study in History, Psychology and Folklore*, London: Wellcome Historical Medical Library.

Bord, J. and Bord, C. (1986) *Sacred Waters: Holy Wells and Water Lore in Britain and Ireland*, London: Paladin.

Borgeaud, P. (1988) *The Cult of Pan in Ancient Greece*, trans. K. Atlass and J. Redfield, Chicago: University of Chicago Press.

Bosley, K. (1989) Translation of *Kalevala*, Oxford: Oxford University Press.

Bray, F. (1984) 'Agriculture', in J. Needham (ed.) *Science and Civilisation 6*, Cambridge: Cambridge University Press.

Briffault, R. (1927) *The Mothers: A Study of the Origins of Sentiments and Institutions* (3 vols), London: Allen & Unwin.

Briggs, K. M. (1970) *A Dictionary of British Folktales* (4 vols), London: Routledge & Kegan Paul.

Brockbank, J. (1983) 'Plough Monday traditions around Cambridge: survival and revival', *Cambridge Review* 25 Oct: 184–7.

Brøgger, A. W. (1945) 'Oseberggraven Haugbrottet', *Viking* 8: 1–44.

Broholm, H. C. and Hald, M. (1940) *Costumes of the Bronze Age in Denmark*, Copenhagen: Nyt Nordisk Forlag.

Brookes, N., Gelling, M. and Johnson, D. (1984) 'A new charter of King Edgar', *Anglo-Saxon England* 13: 137–50.

Brown, J. (1970) 'A note on the division of labour by sex', *American Anthropologist* 72: 1073–8.

Brown, S. A. (1988) *The Bayeux Tapestry: History and Bibliography*, Woodbridge: Boydell.

Bruford, A. (1967) 'Scottish Gaelic witch stories: a provisional type list', *Scottish Studies* 11: 18–19.

Brumfield, A. C. (1981) *The Attic Festivals of Demeter and their Relation to the Agricultural Year*, New York: Salem Ayer.

Burkert, W. (1983) *Homo Necans: The Anthropology of Ancient Greek Ritual and Myth*, trans. P. Bing, London: University of California Press.

Burl, A. (1985) *Megalithic Brittany*, London: Thames & Hudson.

Burne, C. F. (1883) (with G. F. Jackson) *Shropshire Folklore*, London.

Butler-Bowdon, W. (1936) *The Book of Margery Kempe 1436* (a modern version), London: Jonathan Cape.

Cameron, A. C. (1993) *Anglo-Saxon Medicine*, Cambridge: Cambridge University Press.

Cameron, D. O. (1981) *Symbols of Birth and Death in the Neolithic Era*, London: Kenyon-Deane.

Campbell, J. G. (1900/1971) *Superstitions of the Highlands and Islands of Scotland*, Glasgow; New York: B. Blom.

Carmichael, A. (1928–71) *Carmina Gadelica* (6 vols), Edinburgh: Oliver & Boyd.

Chadwick, H. M. (1924) *The Origin of the English Nation*, Cambridge: Cambridge University Press.

Chadwick, N. K. (1936) 'Russian literature', in H. M. Chadwick and N. K. Chadwick (eds) *The Growth of Literature* II, Cambridge: Cambridge University Press.

—— (1959) 'The monsters and Beowulf', in P. Clemoes (ed.) *The Anglo-Saxons: Studies Presented to Bruce Dickins*, London.

Chadwick, S. E. (1958) 'The Anglo-Saxon cemetery at Finglesham, Kent: a reconsideration', *Medieval Archaeology* 2: 1–71.

Chambers, R. (n.d./1969) *Popular Rhymes*, London and Edinburgh; Detroit, MI: Singing Tree Press.

Charlton, L. (1779) *History of Whitby and of Whitby Abbey*, York.

Chaudhri, A. (1996) 'The Caucasian hunting divinity, male and female: traces of the Hunting-Goddess in Ossetic folklore', in S. Billington and M. Green (eds) *The Concept of the Goddess*, London: Routledge.

Christiansen, R. T. (1946) *The Dead and the Living*, Studia Norvegica 2, Oslo: Aschehoug.

Cox, M. (1893) *Cinderella: 145 Variants*, London: Folklore Society.

Crawford, O. G. S. (1957) *The Eye Goddess*, London: Phoenix House.

Croker, T. C. (1844) *The Keen of the South of Ireland*, London.

Cunliffe, B. (1986) 'The Sanctuary of Sulis Minerva at Bath: a brief review', in M. Henig and A. King (eds) *Pagan Gods and Shrines of the Roman Empire*, Oxford: Oxford University Committee for Archaeology.

Dahlstadt, T. (1991) *Kvinnors Moten med Vittra*, Umea Universite, Sweden.

Damsholt, N. (1984) 'The role of Icelandic women in the sagas and in the production of homespun cloth', *Scandinavian Journal of History* 9: 75–90.

Danaher, K. (1972) *The Year in Ireland: Irish Calendar Customs*, Dublin.

Darby, H. C. (1974) *The Medieval Fenland*, 2nd edn, Newton Abbot: David & Charles.

Darby, W. J., Ghalioungui, P. and Grivetti, L. (1977) *Food: The Gift of Osiris*, London: Academic Press.

Davidson, H. E. (1958) 'Weland the Smith', *Folklore* 69: 145–59.

—— (1964) *Gods and Myths of Northern Europe*, Harmondsworth: Penguin.

—— (1965) 'The man in the horned helmet', *Antiquity* 39: 23–7.

—— (1976) *The Viking Road to Byzantium*, London: Allen & Unwin.

—— (1980) *Saxo Grammaticus I–IX: Commentary*, Woodbridge: Boydell.

—— (1981) 'The restless dead: an Icelandic ghost story', in H. R. E. Davidson and W. M. S. Russell (eds) *The Folklore of Ghosts*, Mistletoe Series 15, London: Folklore Society.

—— (1988) *Myths and Symbols in Pagan Europe: Early Scandinavian and Celtic Religions*, Manchester: Manchester University Press.

—— (1989a) 'Hooded men in Celtic and Germanic tradition', in G. Davies (ed.) *Polytheistic Systems*, Cosmos 5: 105–24, Edinburgh.

—— (1989b) 'The training of warriors', in S. C. Hawkes (ed.) *Weapons and Warfare in Anglo-Saxon England*, Oxford: Oxford University Committee for Archaeology.

—— (1990) 'Religious practices of the Northern peoples in Scandinavian tradition', *Temonos* 26: 23–34.

—— (1992) 'Human sacrifice in the pagan period in north-western Europe', in M. Carver (ed.) *The Age of Sutton Hoo: The Seventh Century in North-Western Europe*, Woodbridge: Boydell.

—— (1993) *The Lost Beliefs of Northern Europe*, London: Routledge.

—— (1996) 'Milk and the Northern Goddess', in S. Billington and M. Green (eds) *The Concept of the Goddess*, London: Routledge.

—— (forthcoming) 'The Wild Hunt', in *Supernatural Enemies*, London: Routledge.

Davidson, H. E. and Chaudhri, A. (1993) 'The hair and the dog', *Folklore* 104: 151–63.

Dempster, C. (1888) 'The folk-lore of Sutherlandshire', *Folk-Lore Journal* 6: 145–89, 216–52.

Deyts, S. (1983) 'Les Bois sculptées des sources de la Seine', *Gallia*, suppl. 42, Paris.

Digby, G. W. (1965) 'Technique and production', in F. Stenton (gen. ed.) *The Bayeux Tapestry*, 2nd edn, London: Phaidon Press.

Downing, C. (1985) 'Hekate', in M. Eliade (ed.) *Encyclopedia of Religion*, London: Macmillan.

Dronke, U. (1969) *The Poetic Edda* I (Heroic Poems), Oxford: Clarendon Press.

Du Boulay, J. (1974) *Portrait of a Greek Mountain Village*, Oxford: Clarendon Press.

Duby, G. (1968) *Rural Economy and Country Life in the Medieval West*, trans. C. Postan, London: Edward Arnold.

Duffy, E. (1992) *The Stripping of the Altars; Traditional Religion in England 1400–1580*, New Haven, CT: Yale University Press.

Dumézil, G. (1966) *Archaic Roman Religion* (2 vols), trans. P. Knapp, Chicago: University of Chicago Press.

Duval, P. M. (1952) *La Vie quotidième en Gaule pendant la paix romaine*, Paris.

Ellinger, P. (1991) 'Artemis', in Y. Bonnefoy and W. Doniger (eds) *Mythologies*, trans. G. Honigsblum, Chicago: University of Chicago Press.

Ellmers, D. (1974) 'Eine byzantinische Mariendarstellung als Vorbild für Goldbrakteaten', *Jahrbuch der Römisch-Germanen Zentralmuseums Mainz* 18 (1971): 233–7.

Engelsman, J. C. (1979) *The Feminine Dimension of the Divine*, Philadelphia, PA: Westminster Press.

Enright, M. (1988) 'Lady with a mead-cup: ritual, group cohesion and hierarchy in the Germanic warband', *Frühmittelalterliche Studien* 22: 170–203, University of Munster, Berlin.

—— (1990) 'The goddess who weaves', *Frühmittelalterliche Studien* 24: 54–70, University of Munster, Berlin.

Erixon, S. (1961) 'Some examples of popular conceptions of sprites and other elementals in Sweden during the nineteenth century', in Å. Hultkrantz (ed.) *The Supernatural Owners of Nature*, Stockholm: Almqvist & Wiksell.

Evans, A. C. (1986) *The Sutton Hoo Ship Burial*, London: British Museum Press.

Farnell, L. R. (1896–1909) *The Cults of the Greek States* (5 vols), Oxford: Clarendon Press.

Faulkes, A. (ed.) (1967) *Two Icelandic Stories: Hreiðars þáttr and Orms þáttr*, London: Viking Society.

Feest, C. (1980) *The Art of War*, London: Thames & Hudson.

Ferro-Luzzi, G. E. (1987) *The Self-Milking Cow and the Bleeding Lingam*, Wiesbaden: Harrassowitz.

Flower Smith, K. (1913) 'Hekate's supper', in J. Hastings (ed.) *Encyclopaedia of Religion and Ethics*, vol. VI: 565, Edinburgh: T. & T. Clark.

Fontenrose, A. (1981) *Orion: The Myth of the Hunter and the Huntress*, Publications in Classical Studies 23, University of California.

Fowler, P. J. (1983) *The Farming of Prehistoric Britain*, Cambridge: Cambridge University Press

Frances Teresa, Sister (1995) *This Living Mirror: Reflections on Clare of Assisi*, Maryknoll, NY: Orbis Books.

Frazer, J. (1912) *The Golden Bough*, 3rd edn, V (Spirits of the Corn and of the Wild), London.

Friedrich, A. (1941) 'Die Forschung über das frühzeitliche Jagentum', *Paideuma* 2: 20–43.

Friend, H. (1883) *Flowers and Flower Lore*, London.

Fromm, M. (1967) *Kalevala Kommentar*, Munich.

Gamble, C. (1982) 'Interaction and alliance in palaeolithic society', *Man* ns 17: 92–107.

Ganz, T. (1993) *Early Greek Myth*, Baltimore, MD: Johns Hopkins University Press.

Gardanov, M. (1927) *Pamiatriki Narodnogo Tcvtvorehestva Osetin*, vol. 2, Vladikavkaz.

Geddes, A. (1951) 'Some Gaelic tales of herding deer or reindeer', *Folklore* 62: 296–311.

Geijer, A. (1979) *A History of Textile Art*, trans. R. Tanner, London: Philip Wilson.

Gelling, P. and Davidson, H. E. (1967) *The Chariot of the Sun and Other Rites and Symbols of Northern Bronze Age*, London: Dent.

Gelsinger, B. E. (1981) *Icelandic Enterprise, Commerce and Economy in the Middle Ages*, Columbia, SC: University of South Carolina Press.

Gibson, G. M. (1990) 'St Anne and the religion of childbed: some East Anglian texts and talismans', in K. Ashley and P. Sheingorn (eds) *Interpreting Cultural Symbols: St Anne in Late Medieval Society*, Athens, GA: Georgia University Press.

Gimbutas, M. (1982) *The Goddesses and Gods of Old Europe: Myths and Cult Images*, London: Thames & Hudson.

—— (1989) *The Language of the Goddess*, London: Thames & Hudson.

Glob, P. V. (1951) *Ard og Plov in Nordens Oldtid*, Jysk Arkaelogisk Selskabs Skrifter 1, Aarhus University Press.

—— (1974) *The Mound People: Danish Bronze Age Man Preserved*, trans. J. Bulman, London: Faber.

Graillot, M. (1912) *Le Culte de Cybele, mère des dieux à Rome dans l'empire romain*, Paris.

Grambø, R. (1964) 'The Lord of Forest and Mountain Game in the more recent folk traditions of Norway', *Fabula* 7: 32–52.

Granberg, G. (1935) *Skogsrået i yngre Nordisk Folktradition*, Skrifter Gustav Adolfs Akad. f. Folklivsforskning 3: 26, Uppsala.

Grant, A. M. (1811) *Superstitions of the Highlanders of Scotland*, London.

Graves, R. (1961) *The White Goddess*, London: Faber & Faber.

Gray, A. (1987) *Legends of the Cairngorms*, Edinburgh: Mainstream.

Green, M. (1989) 'Women's medical practice and health care in medieval Europe', in J. M. Bennett *et al.* (eds) *Sisters and Workers in the Middle Ages*, Chicago: University of Chicago Press.

Green, M. J. (1984) 'Mother and sun in Romano-Celtic religion', *Antiquaries Journal* 84(1): 251–8.

—— (1986) *The Gods of the Celts*, Gloucester: Sutton.

—— (1989) *Symbol and Image in Celtic Religious Art*, London: Routledge.

—— (1991) *The Sun Gods of Ancient Europe*, London: Batsford.

—— (1992) *Animals in Celtic Life and Myth*, London: Routledge.

—— (1995) *Celtic Goddesses: Warriors, Virgins and Mothers*, London: British Museum Press.

—— (1996) 'The Celtic goddess as healer', in S. Billington and M. Green (eds) *The Concept of the Goddess*, London: Routledge

Greene, W. C. (1944) *Moira, Fate Good and Evil in Greek Thought*, Cambridge, MA: Harvard University Press.

Grendan, F. (1909) 'The Anglo-Saxon charms', *Journal of American Folklore* 22: 105–237.

Grieg, S. (1928) Description of looms in A. Brøgger and H. Shetelig (eds) *Osebergfindet* (4 vols), I, 173ff., Oslo.

—— (1954) 'Amuletter og Guldbilder', *Viking* 18: 157–209.

Grigson, G. E. H. (1955) *The Englishman's Flora*, London: Phoenix House.

Grimm, J. (1883–8) *Teutonic Mythology* (4 vols), trans. J. S. Stallybrass, 1900, London: G. Bell.

Gruffydd, W. J. (1953) *Rhiannon: An Enquiry into the Origins of the First and Third Branches of the Mabinogion*, D. O. Evans Lectures 1951, Cardiff.

Grundy, S. (1996) 'Freyja and Frigg', in S. Billington and M. Green (eds) *The Concept of the Goddess*, London: Routledge.

Gunnell, T. (1994) *The Origins of Drama in Scandinavia*, Woodbridge: D. S. Brewer

Hanawalt, B. A. (ed.) (1986) *Women and Work in Pre-Industrial Europe*, Bloomington, IN: Indiana University Press.

Hauck, K. (1985) 'Motivanalyse eines Doppelbrakteaten ... (Zur Ikonologie der Goldbrakteaten 32)', *Frühmittelalterliche Studien* 19: 139–94.

Hedeager, L. (1992) *Iron Age Society*, trans. J. Hines, Oxford: Blackwell.

Henig, M. (1984) *Religion in Roman Britain*, London: Batsford.

—— (1988) 'Objects from the sacred spring', in B. W. Cunliffe (ed.) *The Temple of Sulis Minerva at Bath*, Monograph 16, Oxford: Oxford University Committee for Archaeology.

—— (1993) *Roman Sculpture from the Cotswold Region with Devon and Cornwall*, Corpus Signorum Imperii Romani I, Oxford: Oxford University Press.

Hennecke, E. (1963/1992) *New Testament Apocrypha*, ed. W. Schneemelcher, trans. R. M. Wilson, Cambridge: J. Clarke.

Henshall, A. S. (1950) 'Textiles and weaving appliances in prehistoric Britain', *Proceedings of Prehistoric Society* ns 16: 130–62.

Herbert, M. (1992) 'Goddess and king: the sacred marriage in early Ireland', in L. O. Fradenburg (ed.) *Women and Sovereignty*, Cosmos 7, Edinburgh: Edinburgh University Press.

—— (1996) 'Transmutations of an Irish goddess', in S. Billington and M. Green (eds) *The Concept of the Goddess*, London: Routledge.

Heyob, S. K. (1975) 'The cult of Isis among women in the Graeco-Roman world', in M. J. Vermaseren (ed.) *Etudes préliminaires aux religions orientales dans l'empire Romain* 51, Leiden.

Hirschon, R. (1981) 'Essential objects and the sacred interior and exterior space in an urban Greek locality', in S. Ardener (ed.) *Women and Space: Ground Rules and Social Maps*, London: Croom Helm.

Hoffman, M. (1964) *The Warp-Weighted Loom*, Studia Norvegica 14, Oslo.

—— (1983) 'Beds and bedclothes in medieval Norway', in N. B. Harte and K. G. Ponting (eds) *Essays in Memory of Professor E. M. Carus-Wilson*, Passold Studies in Textile History 2, London.

Hole, C. (1978) *A Dictionary of British Folk Customs*, London: Paladin.

Holtsmark, A. (1933) 'Vitazgjafi', *Maal og Minne*, 111–33.

—— (1939) 'Vefr Darraðar', *Maal og Minne*, 74–96.

—— (1944) 'Gevjons Plog', *Maal og Minne*, 169–79.

—— (1951) 'Skaro a Skiði', *Maal og Minne*, 81–9.

—— (1970) 'Skaði', *Kulturhistorisk Lexicon* 15: 382.

Hondius-Crone, A. (1955) *The Temple of Nehalennia at Domburg*, Amsterdam: J. M. Menlenhoff.

Honko, L. (1974) 'Balto-Finnic lament poetry', *Studia Fennica* 17: 9–61.

Hope, A. D. (1970) *A Midsummer Eve's Dream: Variations on a Theme by William Dunbar*, New York: Viking.

Hougen, B. (1940) 'Osebergfunnets Billedverk', *Viking* 4: 85–124.

Hull, E. (1927) 'Legends and traditions of the Cailleach Bhéarra or Old Woman (Hag) of Beare', *Folklore* 38: 225–54.

Hultkrantz, Å. (1961) 'The owner of the animals in the religion of the North American Indians', in Å. Hultkrantz (ed.) *The Supernatural Owners of Nature*, Stockholm: Almqvist & Wiksell.

Ingstad, A. S., Christensen, A. E. and Myhre, B. (eds) (1992) *Oseberg-dronningens Grav: vår arkeologiske nasjonalskatt i nytt lys*, Oslo: Schibsted.

Jacobsen, T. (1976) *The Treasures of Darkness: A History of Mesopotamian Religion*, New Haven, CT: Yale University Press.

Jamieson, J. (1879–92) *An Etymological Dictionary of the Scottish Language* (5 vols), Paisley: Alexander Gardner.

Jesch, J. (1991) *Women in the Viking Age*, Woodbridge: Boydell.

Johnson, B. (1988) *Lady of the Beasts: Ancient Images of the Goddess and her Sacred Animals*, San-Francisco: Harper.

Joliffe, N. (1941) 'Dea Brigantia', *Archaeological Journal* 98: 36–61.

Jones, C. W. (ed.) (1943) *Bedae Opera de Temporibus*, Cambridge, MA.

Jones, G. and Jones, T. (1949) Translation of *The Mabinogion*, London: Dent.

Jonson, B. (1603/1941–52) 'A particular entertainment of the Queen and Prince at Althorpe', in *Works* (2 vols), ed. C. H. Herbert and P. E. Simpson, Oxford.

Jónsson, F. (1912) *Lægekunsten i den Nordiske Oldtid*, Medicinsk-Historiske Smaaskrifter, Copenhagen.

—— (1932) *De gamle Eddadigte*, Copenhagen.

Kahil, L. (1977) 'L'Artemis de Brauron: rites et mystère', *Antike Kunst* 20: 86–98.

Karsten, R. (1955) *The Religion of the Samek; Ancient Beliefs and Cults of the Scandinavian and Finnish Lapps*, Leiden: E. J. Brill.

Keppie, L. J. F. and Arnold, B. J. (1984) *Corpus Signorum Imperii Romani*, Great Britain I, fasc. 4 (Scotland), British Academy, Oxford University Press.

Kershaw, N. (ed.) (1922) *Anglo-Saxon and Norse Poems*, Cambridge: Cambridge University Press.

Kiil, V. (1965) 'Gevjonmyten og Ragnarsdrapa', *Maal og Minne* 63–70.

Kinsley, D. (1989) *The Goddesses' Mirror: Visions of the Divine from East to West*, Albany, NY: State University of New York Press.

Knight, C. (1991) *Blood Relations: Menstruation and the Origins of Culture*, New Haven, CT: Yale University Press.

Krafft, S. (1956) *Pictorial Weavings from the Viking Age*, trans. R. I. Christophersen, Oslo: Dreyers Forlag.

Kraft, J. (1985) *The Goddess in the Labyrinth*, Religionsveten-skapliga Skrifter 11, Finland: Abo Akademi.

Kravchenko, M. (1987) *The World of the Russian Fairy Tale*, trans. P. Lang, European University Studies (Series 16), Slav Language and Literature 34, Berne and New York.

Kvideland, R. and Sehmsdorf, H. K. (1988) *Scandinavian Folk Belief and Legend*, Minneapolis, MN: Minnesota University Press.

Landnámabók (1968) (2 vols), ed. J. Benediktsson, Reykjavik: Hið Íslenzka Fornrit.

Leather, E. M. (1912/1991) *The Folklore of Herefordshire*, London: Sidgwick & Jackson.

Lichtheim, M. (1975) *Ancient Egyptian Literature*, vol. I, *The Old and Middle Kingdoms*, Berkeley, CA: University of California Press.

Lid, N. (1946) *Light-Mother and Earth-Mother*, Studia Norvegica I, Oslo.

Lidén, H. (1969) 'From pagan sanctuary to Christian church: the excavation of Maere Church, Trondelag', *Norwegian Archaeological Review* 2: 23–32.

Liestøl, A. (1963) 'Runer frå Bryggen', *Viking* 27: 5–53.

Lincoln, B. (1987) *Priests, Women and Cattle*, Berkeley, CA: University of California Press.

Lindow, J. (1978) *Swedish Legend and Folktales*, Berkeley, CA: University of California Press.

Linduff, K. M. (1979) 'Epona: a Celt among the Romans', *Latoma* 38(4): 817–37.

Lodrick, D. O. (1981) *Sacred Cows, Sacred Places: Origins and Survivals of Animal Homes in India*, Berkeley, CA: University of California Press.

Loewenfeld, C. (1964) *Herb Gardening*, London: Faber & Faber.

Long, J. B. (1985) 'Webs and nets', in M. Eliade (ed.) *Encyclopedia of Religion*, vol. XV, London: Macmillan.

Lot-Falck, E. (1953) *Les Rites de chasse chez les peuples sibériens*, Paris.

Lucas, A. T. (1960) 'Irish food before the potato', *Gwerin* 3: 8–40.

—— (1989) *Cattle in Ancient Ireland*, Rhine Lectures, Kilkenny.

Lyle, E. (1990) *Archaic Cosmos: Polarity, Space and Time*, Edinburgh: Polygon.

Lysaght, P. (1986) *The Banshee: The Irish Supernatural Death Messenger*, Dublin: Glendale.

—— (1994) 'Women, milk and magic at the boundary festival of May', in P. Lysaght (ed.) *Milk and Milk Products from Medieval to Modern Times*, Edinburgh: Canongate.

—— (1995) '*Caoineadh na Marbh*: Die Totenklage in Irland', *Rheinisch-westfalische Zeitschrift für Volkskunde* 40: 163–213.

—— (1996) 'Aspects of the Earth-Goddess in the traditions of the Banshee in Ireland', in S. Billington and M. Green (eds) *The Concept of the Goddess*, London: Routledge.

McCay, J. G. (1932) 'The deer-cult and deer-goddess cult of the ancient Caledonians', *Folklore* 43: 144–74.

McCone, K. (1990) *Pagan Past and Christian Present in Early Irish Literature*, An Sagart: Maynooth.

MacDougall, J. (1910/1978) *Folktales and Fairy Lore in Gaelic and English*, partly reprinted in A. Bruford (ed.) *Highland Fairy Lore*, London.

MacGregor, A. A. (1937) *The Peat-Fire Flame: Folk-Tales and Traditions of the Highlands and Islands* Edinburgh: Moray Press.

Mackeprang, M. B. (1952) *De nordiske Guldbrakteater*, Aarhus.

Maclagan, R. C. (1895) 'Notes on folklore objects collected in Argyleshire', *Folk-Lore* 6: 144–61.

—— (1914) 'The Keener in the Scottish Highlands and Islands', *Folklore* 25: 84–91.

MacNeill, M. (1962) *The Festival of Lughnasa*, London: Oxford University Press.

MacPhail, M. (1898–1900) 'Report of customs from the Highlands', *Folk-Lore* 9: 91ff.; 11: 437.

Magoun, E. P. (1969) Translation of *The Old Kalevala* Cambridge, MA: Harvard University Press.

Malone, C., Bonnano, A., Gouder, T., Stoddart, S. and Trump, D. (1993) 'The death cults of prehistoric Malta', *Scientific American* (Dec.): 76–83.

Mannhardt, W. (1868) *Die Korndämon: Beitrag zur Germanschen Sittenkunde*, Strassburg.

—— (1884) *Mythologische Forschungen*, Quellen und Forschungen 2: Sprach und Cult, Strassburg.

—— (1905) *Wald- und Feldkulte*, 2nd edn, vol. 2, ed. W. Heuschkel, Berlin: Gebrüder Borntrseger.

Manning, W. H. (1971) 'The Piercebridge plough group', *British Museum Quarterly* 35: 125–36.

Marshack, A. (1972) *The Roots of Civilization*, London: Weidenfeld & Nicolson.

Martin, M. (1703/1934) *Description of the Western Isles of Scotland*, ed. D. J. Macleod, Stirling.

Meaney, A. (1981) *Anglo-Saxon Amulets and Curing Stones*, BAR 96, Oxford: British Archaeological Reports.

Megaw, J. V. S. (1970) *Art of the European Iron Age*, Bath: Adams & Dart.

Mellaart, J. (1967) *Çatal Hüyük: A Neolithic Town in Anatolia*, London: Thames & Hudson.

Merrick, W. P. (1904) 'An old south Pembrokeshirre harvest custom', *Folklore* 15: 194–6.

Merrifield, R. (1987) *The Archaeology of Ritual and Magic*, London: Batsford

Molleson, T. (1994) 'The eloquent bones of Abu Huneyra', *Scientific American* 271(2): 60–5.

Näsström, B. M. (1995) *Freyja: The Great Goddess of the North*, Lund Studies in the History of Religions 5, Lund University.

Neils, J. (ed.) (1992) *Goddess and Polis: The Panathenaic Festival in Ancient Athens*, Hanover, NH: Dartmouth College.

Neumann, E. (1955) *The Great Mother*, trans. R. Mannheim, Billingen Series, Princeton, NJ: Princeton University Press.

Nilsson, M. P. (1938) *Nordisk Kultur*, vol. 22, Stockholm.

Nordal, S. (ed.) (1978) *Völuspá*, trans. B. S. Benedikz and J. McKinnell, Durham and St Andrews Medieval Texts 1, Durham: Department of English Language and Medieval Literature.

Oaks, L. S. (1986) 'The Goddess Epona: concepts of sovereignty in a changing landscape', in M. Henig and A. King (eds) *Pagan Gods and Shrines of the Roman Empire*, Oxford: Oxford University Committee for Archaeology.

Ó Catháin, S. (1995) *The Festival of Brigit: Celtic Goddess and Holy Woman*, Dublin: DBA Publications.

Ó Cathasaigh, D. (1982) 'Brigid', in J. Preston (ed.) *Mother Worship*, Chapel Hill, NC: North Carolina University Press.

Ó Crullaóich, G. (1988) 'Continuity and adaption in legends of the Cailleach Bhéarra', *Bealoideas* 153–78.

—— (1990) 'Contest in the Irish "Merry Wake"', in A. Duff-Cooper (ed.) *Contests*, Cosmos 6: 145–60.

O' Flaherty, W. D. (1980) *Women, Androgynes and other Mythical Beasts*, Chicago: University of Chicago Press.

Ó hÓgáin, D. (1990) *Myth, Legend and Romance: An Encyclopedia of the Irish Folk Tradition*, New York: Prentice-Hall.

Olrik, A. (1901) 'Odinsjægeren i Jylland', *Dania* 8: 139–73.

Olsen, M. (1909) 'Fra gammelnorsk myte og cultus', *Maal og Minne* 17–36.

Opie, I. and Opie, P. (1974) *The Classic Fairy Tales*, Oxford: Oxford University Press.

O' Rahilly, C. (ed.) (1967) *Táin Bó Cúalnge* (Book of Leinster), Dublin: Dublin Institute for Advanced Studies.

O' Rahilly, T. F. (1976) *Early Irish History and Mythology*, Dublin.

O Súilleabháin, S. (1967) *Irish Wake Amusements*, Cork: Mercier Press.

Owen, T. M. (1974) *Welsh Folk Customs*, 3rd edn, Cardiff: National Museum of Wales.

Paris, G. (1986) *Pagan Meditations on Aphrodite, Hestia, Artemis*, trans. G. Moore, Dallas, TX: Spring.

Paulsen, P. (1967) *Alamannische Adelsgraber von Nieder-Stotzingen*, Stuttgart.

Paulys (1912) *Real-Encyclopädie der classischen Altertumswissenschaft*, Stuttgart.

Peissel, M. (1984) *The Ants' Gold: The Discovery of the Greek El Dorado in the Himalayas*, London: Harvill.

Pelletier, A. (1984) *La Femme dans la société gallo-romaine*, Paris: Picard.

Phythian-Adams, C. (1983) 'Milk and soot', in D. Fraser and A. Sutcliffe (eds) *The Pursuit of Urban History*, London: Edward Arnold.

Price, T. H. (1978) *Kourotrophos*, Studies of the Dutch Archaeological and Historical Society, Leiden.

Ralston, W. R. S. (1872) *The Songs of the Russian People*, 2nd edn, London.

Ränk, G. (1949a) *Das System der Raumeinteilung in den Behausungen der nordeurasischen Volker*, Stockholm: Institut f. Folklivsforskning.

—— (1949b) *Die heilige Hinterecke im Hauskult der Volker Nord-Osteuropas und Nordasiens*, FF Communications 137, Helsinki.

—— (1955) *Lapp Female Deities of the Madder-Akka Group*, Studia Septentrionatia 6, Oslo.

Ranke, K. (1934) *Die zwei Bruder*, FF Communications 114, Helsinki.

Rees, S. E. (1979) *Agricultural Implements in Prehistoric and Roman Britain*, BAR 69, Oxford: British Archaeological Reports.

Reynolds, P. J. (1979) *Iron Age Farm: The Butser Experiment*, London: British Museum.

Rhys, Sir J. (1901/1980) *Celtic Folklore: Welsh and Manx* (2 vols), London: Wildwood.

Richardson, N. J. (1979) *The Homeric Hymn to Demeter*, Oxford: Clarendon Press.

Ridley, M. (1976) *The Megalithic Art of the Maltese Islands*, Poole: Dolphin Press.

Rieu, E. V. (1945) Translation of the *Odyssey*, Harmondsworth: Penguin.

—— (1950) Translation of the *Iliad*, Harmondsworth: Penguin.

Robertson, M. (1975) *The Parthenon Frieze*, London: British Museum.

Rockwell, J. (1982) *Evald Tang Kristensen*, Danish Folklore Society, Aalborg University Press.

Rooth, A. B. (1961) 'The conceptions of "Rulers" in the south of Sweden', in Å. Hultkrantz (ed.) *The Supernatural Owners of Nature*, Stockholm: Almqvist & Wiksell.

Rosenburg, A. T. (1929) 'Et Gudebillede fra Bronzealderan', *Danske Studier*, Copenhagen.

Ross, A. (1967) *Pagan Celtic Britain: Studies in Iconography and Tradition*, London: Routledge & Kegan Paul.

—— (1975) 'A wooden statuette from Venta Belgarium', *Antiquaries Journal* 55: 335–6.

Ross, M. C. (1978) 'The myth of Gefion and Gylfi and its functions in *Snorra Edda* and *Heimskringla*', *Arkiv f. nordisk Filologi* 93: 149–65.

Rundle Clark, R. T. (1959) *Myth and Symbol in Ancient Egypt*, London: Thames & Hudson.

Ruysbruck, W. (1928) 'Journal of Friar William Ruysbruck', in M. Konroff (ed.) *Contemporaries of Marco Polo*, London: Travellers' Library.

Sandars, N. (1968) *Prehistoric Art in Europe*, Pelican History of Art 1, Harmondsworth: Penguin.

Sax, W. S. (1991) *Mountain Goddess: Gender and Politics in a Himalayan Pilgrimage*, New York: Oxford University Press.

Schilling, R. (1985) 'Vesta', in M. Eliade (ed.) *Encyclopedia of Religion*, London: Macmillan.

Sebillot, P. Y. (1886) *Coutumes populaires de la Haute-Bretagne*, Paris.

Segalen, M. (1983) *Love and Power in the Peasant Family: Rural France in the Nineteenth Century*, trans. S. Matthews, Oxford: Blackwell.

Sheingorn, P. (1990) 'Appropriating the holy kinship: gender and family history', in K. Ashley and P. Sheingorn (eds) *Interpreting Cult Symbols: Saint Anne in Late Medieval Society*, Athens, GA: University of Georgia Press.

Simonsson, S. (1956) 'Om ölbryggens Uppkomst i Norden', *Nordisk Kultur* 13: 236–53.

Simpson, J. (1988) *Scandinavian Folktales*, Harmondsworth: Penguin.

Sjoedstedt, M. L. (1982/1994) *Gods and Heroes of the Celts*, trans. M. Dillon, Berkeley, CA: Turtle Island Foundation; Dublin and Portland, OR: Four Courts Press.

Smyser, H. M. (1965) 'Ibn Fadlan's account of the Rus', in J. B. Bessinger Jr and R. P. Creed (eds) *Medieval and Linguistic Studies in Honour of Francis Peabody Magoun, Jr*, London: Allen & Unwin.

Solheim, S. (1952) *Norsk Sætertradisjon*, Oslo: Instituttet for Sammenlignende. Kulturforskning.

—— (1956) *Horse-Fight and Horse Race in Norse Tradition*, Studia Norvegica 8, Oslo: Aschehoug.

Spaeth, B. (1996) *The Roman Goddess Ceres*, Austin, TX: Texas University Press.

Steensberg, A. (1986) *Man the Manipulator*, Copenhagen: National Museum of Denmark.

Stevens, C. (1976) 'The funeral wake in Wales', *Folk-Life* 14: 27–45.

Stokes, W. (ed.) (1890) 'Life of Brigit', in *Lives of Saints from the Book of Lismore*, Anecdota Oxoniensia I, 5, Oxford.

Struve, K. W. (1967) 'Die Moorleiche von Datgen', *Offa* 24, 33–76, Kiel.

Suhr, E. G. (1969) *The Spinning Aphrodite*, New York: Helios.

Sveinsson, E. O. (ed.) (1954) *Brennu-Njáls Saga*, Reykjavik: Hið Íslenzka Fornritafeleg.

Talbot, A. (1982) 'The withdrawal of the fertility god', *Folklore* 93: 31–46.

Thevenot, E. (1968) *Divinités et sanctuaires de la Gaule*, Paris.

Tillhagen, C. H. (1961) 'Die Berggeist Vorstellung in Sweden', in Å. Hultkrantz (ed.) *The Supernatural Owners of Nature*, Stockholm: Almqvist & Wiksell.

Timmer, B. (1940) 'Wyrd in Anglo-Saxon prose and poetry', *Neophilologus* 26: 24–33, 213–28.

Tolkien, J. R. R. (1936) 'Beowulf: the monsters and the critics', *Proceedings of the British Academy* 22: 245–90.

Tomlin, R. S. O. (1988) 'Curse tablets', in B. Cunliffe (ed.) *The Temple of Sulis Minerva at Bath*, vol. 2, *The Finds from the Sacred Spring*, Oxford: Oxford University Committee for Archaeology.

Toynbee, J. M. C. (1959) 'Daglingworth in Roman times', in O. M. Griffiths (ed.) *Daglingworth: The Story of a Cotswold Village*, London: Museum Press.

Turville-Petre, E. O. G. (1964) *Myth and Religion of the North: The Religion of Ancient Scandinavia*, London: Weidenfeld & Nicolson.

—— (1976) *Scaldic Poetry*, Oxford: Clarendon Press.

Tyldesley, J. A. (1994) *Daughter of Isis: Women of Ancient Egypt*, London: Viking.

Ucko, P. J. (1962) 'The interpretation of prehistoric anthropomorphic figurines', *Journal of the Royal Anthropological Institute* 92: 38–54.

Verdier, J. de (1976a) 'La femme-qui-aide et la laveuse', *L'Homme* 16: 103–28.

—— (1976b) 'Les femmes et le saloir', *Ethnologie française* ns 6: 349–62.

—— (1979) *Façons de dire, façons de faire*, Bibliothèque des sciences humaine, Paris: Gallimard.

Vermaseren, M. J. (1977) *Cybele and Attis: The Myth and the Cult*, trans. A. M. H. Lemmers, London: Thames & Hudson.

Vernant, J. P. (1987) 'Artemis', in M. Eliade (ed.) *The Encyclopedia of Religion* I, London: Macmillan.

Vigfusson, G. (1874) *An Icelandic–English Dictionary*, based on the collection of R. Cleasby, Oxford.

Vries, A. de (1974) *Dictionary of Symbols and Imagery*, Amsterdam: North-Holland.

Vries, J. de (1956–7) *Altgermanische Religionsgeschichte* (2 vols), Grundriss der Germanischen Philologie 12, Berlin.

Waschnitius, V. (1913) *Perht, Holda und verwandte Gestalten*, Sitzungen Kaiser Akademie d. Wisserschaften (Philos./Hist.) 174, Vienna.

Webster, G. (1986) *The British Celts and their Gods under Rome*, London: Batsford.

Weiser-All, L. (1947) 'Magiske Tegn pa Norske Frekar', *By og Bygd*, Årbok f. Norske folkemuseums, 117–44, Oslo.

—— (1968) *Svangerskap og fodsel i nyere norsk tradisjon*, Oslo: Norsk Folkemuseum.

Wentz, W. Y. E. (1911/1977) *The Fairy Faith in Celtic Countries*, Oxford: Oxford University Press; Gerrards Cross: Smythe.

Westwood, J. (1985) *Albion: A Guide to Legendary Britain*, London: Granada.

Whitehead, G. K. (1953) *The Ancient Wild Cattle of Britain and their Descendants*, London: Faber & Faber.

Wightman, E. M. (1970) *Roman Trier and the Treveri*, London: Rupert Hart-Davis.

Wikman, K. R. V. (1961) Introduction to Å. Hultkrantz (ed.) *The Supernatural Owners of Nature*, Stockholm: Almqvist & Wiksell.

Witt, R. E. (1971) *Isis in the Graeco-Roman World*, London: Thames & Hudson.

Wolfram, R. (1933) 'Weiberbunde', *Zeitschrift f. Volkskunde* 4: 137–46.

Wolkstein, D. and Kramer, S. N. (1984) *Inanna, Queen of Heaven and Earth: Her Stories and Hymns from Sumer*, London: Rider.

Wood, J. (1992) 'The fairy bride in Wales', *Folklore* 103: 56–72.

—— (1996) 'The concept of the goddess', in S. Billington and M. Green (eds) *The Concept of the Goddess*, London: Routledge.

Wright, J. (1896–1905) *The English Dialect Dictionary* (8 vols), London: Henry Frowde.

Wulff, D. M. (1982/1986) 'Prolegomenon to a psychology of the goddess', in J. S. Hawley and Donna M. Wulff (eds) *The Divine Consort: Radha and the Goddesses of India*, Berkeley Religious Studies Series, Berkeley, CA; Boston, MA: Beacon Press.

INDEX

—— .◆. ——